The British Economy in the Twentieth Century

British Studies Series

General Editor JEREMY BLACK

Published

Alan Booth **The British Economy in the Twentieth Century**
John Charmley **A History of Conservative Politics, 1900–1996**
David Childs **Britain since 1939**
John Davis **A History of Britain, 1885–1939**
David Eastwood **Government and Community in the English Provinces, 1700–1870**
Philip Edwards **The Making of the Modern English State, 1460–1660**
W. H. Fraser **A History of British Trade Unionism, 1700–1998**
Brian Hill **The Early Parties and Politics in Britain, 1688–1832**
Katrina Honeyman **Women, Gender and Industrialisation in England, 1700–1870**
Kevin Jefferys **Retreat from New Jerusalem: British Politics, 1951–1964**
T. A. Jenkins **The Liberal Ascendancy, 1830–1886**
David Loades **Power in Tudor England**
Ian Machin **The Rise of Democracy in Britain, 1830–1918**
Alexander Murdoch **British History, 1660–1832: National Identity and Local Culture**
Anthony Musson and W. M. Ormrod **The Evolution of English Justice: Law, Politics and Society in the Fourteenth Century**
Murray G. H. Pittock **Inventing and Resisting Britain: Cultural Identities in Britain and Ireland, 1685–1789**
Nick Smart **The National Government, 1931–40**
Andrew Thorpe **A History of the British Labour Party (2nd edn)**

British Studies Series
Series Standing Order
ISBN 0–333–71691–4 hardcover
ISBN 0–333–69332–9 paperback
(*outside North America only*)

You can receive future titles in this series as they are published by placing a standing order. Please contact your bookseller or, in case of difficulty, write to us at the address below with your name and address, the title of the series and the ISBN quoted above.

Customer Services Department, Macmillan Distribution Ltd
Houndmills, Basingstoke, Hampshire RG21 6XS, England

The British Economy in the Twentieth Century

Alan Booth

palgrave

First published 2001 by
PALGRAVE
Houndmills, Basingstoke, Hampshire RG21 6XS and
175 Fifth Avenue, New York, N.Y. 10010
Companies and representatives throughout the world

PALGRAVE is the new global academic imprint of
St. Martin's Press LLC Scholarly and Reference Division and
Palgrave Publishers Ltd (formerly Macmillan Press Ltd).

ISBN 0–333–69841–X hardback
ISBN 0–333–69842–8 paperback

This book is printed on paper suitable for recycling and made from fully managed and sustained forest sources.

A catalogue record for this book is available from the British Library.

Library of Congress Cataloging-in-Publication Data
Booth, Alan.
    The British economy in the twentieth century / Alan Booth.
        p. cm. — (British studies)
    Includes bibliographical references and index.
    ISBN 0–333–69841–X (cloth)
    1. Great Britain—Economic conditions—20th century.
    2. Great Britain—Economic policy—20th century. I. Title.
    II. Series.
    HC256 .B68 2001
    330.941'082—dc21
                                                      2001027370

10   9   8   7   6   5   4   3   2   1
10 09 08 07 06 05 04 03 02 01

Printed in China

Contents

List of Tables

List of Figures

Preface

This book was written in a mood of growing disenchantment with the level of debate on recent British economic performance. It begins from two convictions: that the comparative framework is a vitally important foundation for any assessment of national economic performance, and that the twentieth century as a whole is a far more useful perspective than the more commonly chosen period from 1945 onwards. There are too many special features in the 1940s, 1950s and early 1960s for which economists and historians seem disinclined to control or allow when making their assessments of growth and performance. Over the whole century, profound dissimilarities in economic structure and the differential impacts of international depression and war can be less easily swept under the carpet and must be addressed in the organisation of the inquiry, however imperfectly or imprecisely. The very uncritical and unsophisticated way in which the British, and especially the English, viewed their economy popularised a despairing view in which de-industrialisation, supply-side failure in manufacturing, institutional sclerosis and an anti-industrial culture figure prominently. The idea of a 'British disease' remains. The English appear to believe that only they can make the most egregious blunders in organising industrial production, whereas international best practice can only be found in the USA, Germany, France, Japan, the Netherlands and elsewhere. It is not yet clear whether this is part of a national inferiority complex (as we drive our French cars, listen to Italian opera on our Swedish hi-fis, watch US programmes on our Japanese TVs and rely on German or Italian kitchen equipment to prepare 'continental' food) or a deep hope that, once the obvious faults have been rectified, Britain will become Great again. It is most likely a contradictory mixture of the two, with overlays of many other aspects of the national psyche.

The following chapters make a rather different case, using both recently published work and that which has been part of the common currency for years. Over the long run and in a properly comparative context, the frailties of British manufacturing made only a minor contribution to Britain's relatively slow growth, and even the seemingly persuasive catalogue of supply-side industrial weaknesses is less compelling when put to even the most rudimentary comparative test. On the other hand, the standard tool kit with which economists and historians disassemble British economic performance has few levers to prise open 'comparative failure in services', 'limited structural potential' or 'limited catch-up potential', which were underemphasised themes throughout the postwar years. These inadequately researched propositions undoubtedly made a much larger contribution to Britain's relative economic retardation in the twentieth century than did failures on the supply side of manufacturing, and this book makes the first faltering steps to redress the analytical balance.

The research for this book was begun during an enlightening and extremely enjoyable year spent as visiting professor in the Institute of Economic Research at Hitotsubashi University in Tokyo. I am particularly grateful to my Japanese colleagues for the inspiration and fresh perspectives that they gave me and to the Institute's librarian (whose stock of books and journals on the UK economy is hugely impressive) for consistent help and good humour. As I began my work, news of Sidney Pollard's death reached Japan. I have owed much to Sidney throughout my academic career. As an undergraduate I read his books on twentieth-century Britain with relish and care. My undergraduate essay citations to Sidney Pollard almost certainly exceeded those to all other British economic historians combined. He was the external examiner for my doctoral thesis, gave me my first university teaching job, and commented very constructively on the typescript of a textbook which was a competitor to his own best-seller. Unfortunately, I have not had the benefits of his wisdom, thoroughness and good sense in completing this project. It would have been infinitely better if it had been exposed to Sidney's sharp eye. There is very much with which he would have profoundly disagreed but this book, however inadequate, is dedicated to the memory of Sidney Pollard. He will be sorely missed.

1 Introduction

From being the world's dominant nation at the turn of the twentieth century, Britain entered the new millennium as a moderately successful, medium-sized, post-imperial power, unable to decide whether its best interests lay with Europe or North America. Britain's strength in 1900 rested upon military and strategic conditions that we now believe to have been transient. Britain's international position also rested upon the comparative power of its economy, but there has been no real agreement about how the British economy should or could have performed in the twentieth century. The vast majority (but not all) believes that the economy should have been stronger, but no-one has ventured to estimate Britain's feasible growth rate. Economists, historians, political scientists and other social theorists have contributed to these debates. Until comparatively recently, reliable assessments of this diverse and specialised literature were few. Since 1990, however, the number of textbook treatments has multiplied and readers now have an extensive choice. This volume does not pretend to be a comprehensive analysis of Britain's twentieth-century economy. In the space available only the main themes can be identified and the barest outlines given. It is, however, distinctive in making the theme of Britain's relative decline its central concern and investigating at least some of the economic, institutional and cultural dimensions of that process. The aim is to reach a balanced assessment of Britain's economic performance since 1900 in a manner appropriate for first-year undergraduates and college students without a substantial background knowledge of the subject. It is also written in the hope that the educated adults of the twenty-first century might make more rational judgements about national economic performance than their counterparts in the last quarter of the twentieth.

1

The Extent and Ideology of Decline

In 1900 the age of high imperialism was drawing to a close, but fresh challenges to British economic, political and military power were opening. European nations had scrambled throughout the last decades of the nineteenth century to divide up the wider world and bring new lands within their systems of economic and political control. Britain's was the largest and most economically, if not politically, integrated empire the world had ever seen, but there were worrying signs that all was not well. Militarily, imperial tensions had emphasised the extent to which defence had been neglected and shown the need for sharp rises in spending, especially on the Royal Navy (Cain and Hopkins 1993a, 202–3). The ability of heavily outnumbered and outgunned Transvaal farmers to frustrate and defeat the British army during the Boer War (1899–1902) pointed to more general military deficiencies. At the same time, parts of British industry were in obvious difficulty from foreign competition. The balance of trade was heavily dependent upon cotton textile exports to India, where signs of vulnerability were beginning to accumulate. At home, the most obvious challenge was to find some accommodation with the working class. As a result of earlier reform acts, increasing numbers of working-class male electors were becoming enfranchised, but the mood of manual workers, especially the unskilled, was uncertain. Social and economic conditions for the bottom third in the income distribution were precarious, as the social survey movement would soon reveal. The unskilled had demonstrated some ability to organise into general unions and there were political parties with a socialist tinge waiting in the wings. Britain may have been the richest country in the world in 1900 (as will be seen in Chapter 2, comparative statistics of economic performance are difficult to construct and controversial) but it was clearly under challenge. One of the central themes of twentieth-century historiography is that Britain failed the test of these challenges and endured a process of continuous decline.

There is not much doubt about Britain's loss of international prestige and power. The British empire managed to survive the crises of both the early 1900s and the enormous disruption of the First World War that brought down the Ottoman, Russian and Austro-Hungarian empires. But the USA had already superseded the UK as the world's leading economic and financial power, surging far ahead of the UK in terms of manufacturing power and rivalling British living standards even before the outbreak of war (Table 1.1). The US economy moved even further ahead in the 1920s, producing approximately 40 per cent of the world's manufactures and creating a substantial lead in productivity and income per head. Although it was obvious that Britain's international position was in secular decline, the country continued to 'punch above its weight' in two areas. Though under increasing internal pressure, the empire remained intact and found a new sense of purpose (in British eyes, at least) in the 1930s, and, secondly, Britain retained a big share of world manufactured trade, albeit in difficult international conditions. In short, Britain's response to the challenges posed at the start of the century was mixed. There were some areas of surprising resilience, but the steady relative decline in Britain's international wealth had begun (Table 1.2). Criticism of British economic performance was intermittent, and targeted mainly at the older, export industries. There were, however, less sanguine souls, Winston Churchill in particular, who attempted to stir up a wider debate about Britain's political and economic organisation, but without any real success (Cannadine 1997).

After the Second World War, new challenges had to be faced. Britain had emerged from the war effectively bankrupt, with an overstretched economy and massive popular expectations of economic and social improvement. For a decade and a half economic progress appeared satisfactory and the British began to come to terms with the idea of affluence, but in the later 1950s British mass opinion suddenly awoke to the realisation that other countries were growing much faster and overtaking our living standards. Areas of strength were increasingly difficult to find. Britain's share of world trade now contracted alarmingly. Its role in the world became much less certain as the empire disintegrated and the long-standing ambiguities about Britain's relationship with continental Europe were inadequately resolved. The performance of the economy became politicised to a frightening degree. Governments came to believe that their hold on office depended upon their ability to manage the economy effectively, or at least to persuade enough people that the opposition

Table 1.1   *Indicators of the UK's position in the world economy, 1900–92*

	Index of GDP per head (UK=100)	Index of GDP per worker hour (UK=100)	Share of world exports (%)	Share of world manufactured exports (%)	Share of world manufactured output (%)
1900					
UK	100	100	15.0	35.5	18.5
France	62	59	8.4	15.4	6.8
Germany	68	73	11.6	23.9	13.2
USA	89	105	15.0	12.5	23.6
1913					
UK	100	100	13.9	32.0	13.6
France	69	67	7.2	12.8	6.1
Germany	76	82	13.1	28.1	14.8
USA	105	120	12.9	13.8	32.0
1928**–9*					
UK	100	100	10.8	23.6	9.9*
France	89	75	6.0	11.5	6.0*
Germany	83	79	9.8	21.6	11.6*
USA	132	136	15.7	21.5	39.3*
1950–3*					
UK	100	100	10.3	26.5	8.4*
France	76	72	5.0	10.3	3.2*
Germany	63	56	3.2	7.5	5.9*
USA	140	161	16.8	28.7	44.7*
1973					
UK	100	100	5.1	9.4	4.9
France	108	112	6.3	9.9	3.5
Germany	110	105	11.7	22.9	5.9
USA	138	147	12.3	16.6	33.0
1979–80*					
UK	100	100	5.5*	9.4	4.0*
France	113	118	5.8*	10.9	3.3*
Germany	117	116	9.7*	21.5	5.3*
USA	141	142	11.1*	16.8	31.5*
1990**–2*					
UK	100	100	5.1	8.8*	
France	114	124	6.3	10.1*	
Germany	123	115	11.3	21.0*	
USA	137	121	12	17.0*	

Note: asterisked figures in columns 3,4 and 5 are for asterisked dates in left-hand column.
Sources: Column 1: calculated from Maddison 1995, Table D.1a
         Column 2: calculated from Maddison 1995, Tables J5, C-16a; idem 1982, Table C.10 with adjustments.
         Column 3: calculated from Maddison 1995, Tables I1, I3; idem 1989, Tables D1, D5.
         Column 4: see Table 3.1 below and the notes thereto, which define 'world' in a different way from that in col. 3.
         Column 5: Bairoch 1982, Tables 10, 13.

Table 1.2 Levels of real GDP per capita, selected countries, 1900–98 (1990 international $)

1900	1913	1950	1973	1994
1. UK 4 593	1. Australia 5 505	1. USA 9 573	1. Switzerland 17 953	1. USA 22 569
2. New Zealand 4 320	2. USA 5 307	2. Switzerland 8 939	2. USA 16 607	2. Switzerland 20 830
3. Australia 4 299	3. New Zealand 5 115	3. New Zealand 8 495	3. Canada 13 644	3. Hong Kong 19 592
4. USA 4 096	4. UK 5 032	4. Australia 7 218	4. Sweden 13 494	4. Japan 19 505
5. Belgium 3 652	5. Canada 4 213	5. Canada 7 047	5. Denmark 13 416	5. Denmark 19 305
6. Netherlands 3 533	6. Switzerland 4 207	6. UK 6 847	6. Germany 13 152	6. Germany 19 097
7. Switzerland 3 531	7. Belgium 4 130	7. Sweden 6 738	7. France 12 940	7. Singapore 18 797
8. Germany 3 134	8. Netherlands 3 950	8. Denmark 6 683	8. Netherlands 12 763	8. Norway 18 372
9. Denmark 2 902	9. Germany 3 833	9. Netherlands 5 850	9. New Zealand 12 575	9. Canada 18 350
10. Austria 2 901	10. Denmark 3 764	10. Belgium 5 346	10. Australia 12 485	10. France 17 968
11. France 2 849	11. Austria 3 488	11. France 5 221	11. UK 11 992	11. Austria 17 285
12. Canada 2 758	12. France 3 452	12. Norway 4 969	12. Belgium 11 905	12. Belgium 17 225
13. Sweden 2 561	13. Sweden 3 096	13. Germany 4 281	13. Austria 11 308	13. Netherlands 17 132
14. Ireland 2 495	14. Ireland 2 733	14. Finland 4 131	14. Japan 11 017	14. Australia 17 107
15. Spain 2 040	15. Italy 2 507	15. Austria 3 731	15. Finland 10 768	15. Sweden 16 710
16. Norway 1 762	16. Norway 2 275	16. Ireland 3 518	16. Italy 10 409	16. Italy 16 404
17. Italy 1 746	17. Spain 2 255	17. Italy 3 425	17. Norway 10 229	17. UK 16 371
18. Finland 1 620	18. Finland 2 050	18. Spain 2 397	18. Spain 8 739	18. New Zealand 15 085
19. Portugal 1 408	19. Greece 1 621	19. Portugal 2 132	19. Greece 7 779	19. Finland 14 779
20. Japan 1 135	20. Portugal 1 354	20. Singapore 2 038	20. Portugal 7 568	20. Taiwan 12 985
21. South Korea 850	21. Japan 1 334	21. Hong Kong 1 962	21. Ireland 7 023	21. Ireland 12 624
22. Taiwan 759	22. South Korea 948	22. Greece 1 951	22. Hong Kong 6 768	22. Spain 12 544
	23. Taiwan 794	23. Japan 1 873	23. Singapore 5 412	23. South Korea 11 235
		24. Taiwan 922	24. Taiwan 3 669	24. Portugal 11 083
		25. South Korea 876	25. South Korea 2 840	21. Greece 10 165

Sources: for 1900: Maddison 1995, Tables D-1a, D-1b, D-1e; for remainder, Crafts 1997, Table 1.

was even less competent. The bearpit of party politics is scarcely the best backdrop to incisive investigation of economic strengths and weaknesses. The usual suspects were well and truly rounded up and condemned. What passed for examination was often little more than unthinking prejudice, and the growing economic difficulties of the later 1960s merely brought out the worst in academic analysis. Some of what was written in the 1970s about a 'British disease' is now positively embarrassing to read. The idea, frequently advanced, that Britain's culture and institutions were *uniquely* ill suited to modern industrialism now looks extreme. The 'British disease' was always an absurd idea, part of what Tomlinson (1996) termed 'the ideology of declinism'. Nevertheless, the idea that the national economic arteries had hardened and narrowed as a result of two centuries of industrialism took root. The notions of deep national failure and of being imprisoned by the past had immense popular resonance. The diagnoses of eminent economists and political scientists were bleak enough (Britain had become 'ungovernable' and its economy had begun to 'de-industrialise'), but at a more popular level the British disease appeared to be terminal. A leading tabloid newspaper famously asked if the last person to leave the UK would kindly switch off the lights.

Economic historians have (almost) always insisted that 'decline' should be prefaced by the word 'relative': the British economy registered positive rates of economic growth throughout the century, except perhaps for the turbulent years of the First World War and the postwar slump. There are now historians prepared to argue that the weakness of the later twentieth-century British economy was grossly exaggerated. Many of the trends that caused so much concern in the 1970s – the deceleration in the growth rate, the fall in manufacturing's share of total output and the rise of that of services, the dramatic increase in unemployment rates – were evident in many developed economies (Supple 1994a; 1994b). From the 1970s Britain continued to grow more slowly than the average for all developed countries and its slide down the league tables proceeded at roughly the same pace (Table 1.2), but it is not yet ready for the knacker's yard. Perceptive commentators, usually from abroad, quite failed to understand the British obsession with its precise position in the rankings by income per head or output per worker; the real gulf is that which separates the developed from the developing nations (McCloskey 1990, 48). It is evident that Britain's income per head fell relative to its European neighbours (Table 1.2) but scarcely at all relative to incomes in the developing world (Figure 1.1). On average, incomes in Africa remained only one-tenth of those in the UK and Asian incomes roughly one-fifth of British levels (Maddison 1995, 212). In crude material terms, the average Briton was approximately four times better off at the end of the century than at the beginning. There were also enormous improvements in life expectancy, health, individual security, housing standards and opportunities for occupational and social mobility for the great mass of the population, which were at least as substantial as the crude material gains. The improvements in life chances and welfare, however these terms are defined, progressed at a comfortably faster rate than in any previous century.

This 'ideology of declinism' is, however, only part of the story of Britain's misperception of its own economic performance. There were also brief periods of enormous optimism that the British economy would regain its 'rightful' place among the richest of the rich nations. In the mid-1980s, for example, a British 'economic miracle' was proclaimed to the world on the basis of a sustained upswing from the slump of 1979–82. It mattered little that the pace of economic growth was slower in the 1980s than in the 1960s, that unemployment and inflation were higher and that the current balance of payments deficit had grown enormously: there was no shortage of academic, media, financial and industrial commentators ready to claim that the economy was better positioned than it had been for many years. At the level of popular discourse, even this limited sense of balance and perspective was missing. The 'feel-good factor' encouraged ordinary British citizens to run down their savings and borrow heavily to invest in assets whose rapidly inflating prices they could not in many cases afford. In the early 1930s J. M. Keynes complained of the herd mentality of the stock market. Half a century later, excessive 'bullishness' had spread to the mass population. Ironically, US economists developed the rational expectations hypothesis, the central precept of which was that individual citizens did not persistently misinterpret economic trends, just before British firms and families were crippled

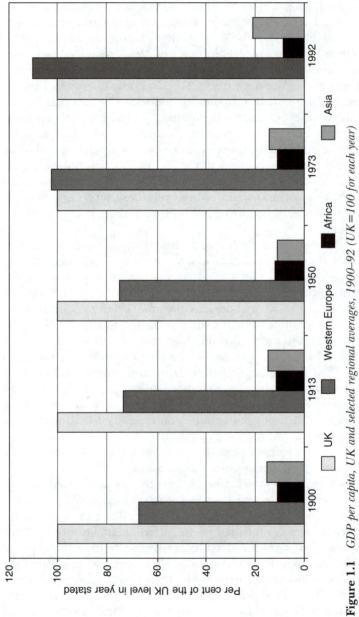

Figure 1.1 *GDP per capita, UK and selected regional averages, 1900–92 (UK=100 for each year)*
Sources: Maddison 1995, Tables D-1a, E3.

by debt because of their inability to distinguish the 'feel-good factor' from economic fact. Despite optimistic accounts from the late 1980s on, it seems highly improbable that the British economy experienced a miraculous rejuvenation at the end of the twentieth century. A similar wave of euphoria was manufactured in the 1950s and a sense of confident anticipation was fashioned in the mid-1960s. Both bubbles were intense but quickly burst.

These abrupt changes of tone suggest that the British have neither fully come to terms with their loss of international position nor been able to distinguish between absolute political and relative economic decline. In his entertaining and intelligent study of what it means to be English at the end of the twentieth century, Jeremy Paxman (1999) argues that the English cannot resist believing in two mutually inconsistent propositions: that Britain has become enfeebled but is at the same time incomparable. The idea lingers that Britain could and should become a major force in the world, but it has been equally easy to convince us that the 'British disease' has tightened its grip. The British (but especially the English) have almost completely lost the ability to make rational, considered judgements about the state of the nation.

Methodological Considerations

The interpretation of economic performance in the recent past clearly requires the skills of both historical and economic analysis. Since the early 1970s, there have been periodic skirmishes between 'historical economists' (those who test economic models, usually by means of quantitative historical data) and 'economic historians' (who tend to believe that each historical episode is in some way unique and needs to be studied in its specific context) over precedence in the analysis of twentieth-century British economic performance. This friction is unfortunate, since both approaches are necessary for an understanding of Britain's position. The influx of model-building and model-testing expertise into historical analysis has provided new insights into key areas of performance, such as understanding Britain's growth trajectory, its productivity record and key aspects of its foreign trade performance. Thanks to the historical economists, the quantitative base from which to study British economic performance has broadened and deepened. The impact has been substantial and fundamental.

Although it is obviously essential to use economic theory to understand economic change, and no-one would deny the major contribution of applied economic analysis to our understanding of twentieth-century economic development, there are limitations to what economists can tell us. Economic theory is concerned with the intermediate levels of explanation, with proximate rather than fundamental causes of economic outcomes (Alford 1996, 2–3). Rates of investment, the structure of markets and the pace of technical change are the stuff of modern economic analysis. But economic theory offers little to explain why structures and rates are as they are, still less to account for the underlying causes of economic change and development. The dominant neo-classical orthodoxy in contemporary economics views the world as a smoothly running machine, operating in a controlled, harmonious, unchanging environment to allow detailed investigation of how individual parts react to controlled changes in local conditions. In addition to these strong assumptions about space and environment, neo-classical theory traces change by comparative static analysis, so that change occurs in 'rational' rather than 'real' time. Abstract theories can, potentially, be applicable to all societies at all times, but there are obvious dangers on the reverse side of this particular coin. By excluding influences that face real economic agents in real time, neo-classical theory runs the risk of cutting itself off from the defining characteristics that shape actual decisions and actual economic performance. Rather than operating in a controlled, harmonious world of equilibrium, individuals and organisations are forced to make decisions in a dynamic and uncertain environment. Instead of viewing the economy as a machine, it might be better to see it as an organism, in which complex interactions take place and can feed back on one another. The discussion above of 'bullishness' and the 'feel-good factor' suggests that people react to the reactions of others. Their perceptions might be profoundly shaped by institutional forces, uncertainty, ignorance or any number of factors that neo-classical analysis excludes from the analytical system.

Institutions, uncertainty and dynamic disruptions are, however, the central concerns of macroeconomics. The neo-classical assumption of an unchanging economic environment, the *ceteris paribus* rule, cannot apply when the whole economy as a complete functioning system is the focus of analysis. Macroeconomic theorising tends to be more open and, in the hands of great analysts like J. M. Keynes, can be intuitive and free-wheeling. As a result, macroeconomic theory tends to generate doctrinal disputes among professional economists whereas the equilibrium model of neo-classical microeconomics does not. It is not unknown for macroeconomists to overstep the boundaries of intuitive analysis into undisciplined value judgement. Some of the more egregious contributions to the literature of both the 'British disease' and the '1980s economic miracle' were perpetrated by professional economists playing to the gallery. Even without such unwelcome complications, it is extremely difficult to predict with confidence in such an indeterminate, open system. In general, macroeconomic forecasting has an unenviable reputation for error (Ormerod 1994). To note these limitations is certainly not to call for economic analysis to be ignored or discarded. The contribution of economists to our understanding of the proximate causes of Britain's economic performance has been immense. Key relationships have been identified and explored. But economic analysis can be only 'part of the hybrid nature of historical analysis and explanation' (Alford 1996, 3). In understanding motive and behaviour it is necessary to place economic analysis in its social, political, ideological, institutional or cultural context. There is ample space and an undoubted need for both historical economists and economic historians in understanding the recent economic past. Indeed, the breadth of the writing on British economic performance since 1900 indicates that economic analysis must be set within the widest framework of historiography.

These disputes over the respective roles of inductive economic and deductive historical methods of analysis have diverted attention from other important methodological issues. Much of the discussion about Britain's economic performance is implicitly comparative, but little attention has been paid to either the need for or the basic principles of comparative analysis. It is easy to demonstrate why comparison should form at least some part of any study of the twentieth-century British economy. A gathering of leading economists in the late 1970s became highly concerned at the medium-term implications of Britain's rising import penetration and contracting manufacturing sector (Blackaby 1978). A more comparative perspective would have shown, however, that the issue of most concern at the time, the rise of import penetration, was, by itself, a red herring: Germany 'suffered' from much higher levels than the UK. The real issues concerned the complex interrelations between market growth, export sales and import penetration (see Table 1.3). This is far from being an isolated example: a comparative dimension can provide an extremely useful reference point for any hypothesis. However, comparisons require national statistics compiled on common principles and standards. For the period since 1960 the OECD *Historical Statistics* are invaluable, and for earlier years Angus Maddison's (1982; 1989; 1991; 1995) growth accounts provide a massive and reliable database for an ever-expanding list of countries. There are, however, gaps, especially for the period before 1945, and individual scholars have been left very much to their own devices. The results can range from the hugely impressive, such as Broadberry's (1993; 1997; 1998)

Table 1.3   *Manufacturing output and trade, selected countries, 1970–87*

	1970	1978	1981	1987
Growth in real manufacturing markets (1970 = 100)				
West Germany	100.0	103.3	109.2	109.1
UK	100.0	108.9	87.1	90.0
Italy	100.0	108.1	119.1	133.7
France	100.0	127.8	132.5	133.7
Manufacturing exports as a percentage of domestic production				
West Germany	26.1	36.9	40.8	47.6
UK	15.8	24.1	24.8	29.7
Italy	18.9	35.8	36.1	35.8
France	17.4	23.9	25.6	28.8
Percentage share of the domestic market for manufactures taken by imports*				
West Germany	19.5	28.4	32.6	38.7
UK	14.2	19.0	24.7	33.2
Italy	16.3	26.9	29.7	31.3
France	16.2	21.1	23.6	27.4

* Figures in the last column of this panel relate to 1985.
Source: Cutler et al. 1989, Tables 1.5, 1.16, 1.17.

investigation of comparative productivity performance since 1870, to the frankly disappointing.

Against which economies is British performance to be compared? The most obvious requirement is that comparator nations should have roughly similar initial levels of output and productivity to the UK (Feinstein 1990a). Countries that begin with a high level of productivity will necessarily grow more slowly over the long run than those with low initial levels and with the capacity for catching up. Unfortunately, over a century this is a very restrictive condition and would limit comparisons from 1900 to the USA and Australia. Much can be gained by comparing British development and performance with those of the USA; Australia, on the other hand, faced rather different economic problems. But there are also limits to the value of a comparison between a continent and a small island whose main claim to fame lay in its ability to develop the world market for low-cost manufactures in the nineteenth century. There are very good reasons for adding to the list European countries with approximately the same population and resource endowment as the UK. France and Germany are the obvious choices, but neither is perfect. The frequent adjustments of Germany's territorial boundaries during the century create measurement difficulties, and France suffered the costs and then reaped the benefits of its very large, very conservative agriculture, which was run down very rapidly after 1950. The rough similarities of the three major European economies in terms of the size of their populations and national incomes, and the broad equivalence in manufacturing efficiency, make it useful to pursue comparisons with France, Germany and the USA. To cast the net any further would bring in still more countries with low initial levels of output and productivity.

If it is important to use a rational and consistent basis for explicit comparisons, it is equally necessary to recognise when inappropriate analogies are 'smuggled' into an argument. Much was written in the 1980s about Britain's failure to create a developmental state, in which a strong and centralised administrative system plays a leading role in resource allocation for the private sector, with Japan as the most celebrated example (Marquand 1988). However, developmentalism implies a very specific economic, political and institutional context, which did not apply to twentieth-century Britain. The developmental state was almost certainly an inappropriate model for the UK and any other developed economy – even Japan after 1973 (see Katz 1998). Just as good comparisons can inform, so poor choices can positively mislead. For this reason, the cursory attention paid to comparative methodology in the literature on Britain's economic performance is disappointing.

Structure and Organisation

There are six further chapters in this book, each of which examines one aspect of Britain's twentieth-century economic performance. The initial focus of Chapter 2 is to assess the scale and dynamics of relative decline in a comparative framework. This survey leaves no doubt that relative decline did occur, but suggests that the case for especially poor performance in the first two decades of the century and during the 'golden age' from 1950 to 1973 is less compelling than is usually assumed. The chapter has two further goals. First, it offers a preliminary survey of some of the main explanations of Britain's apparent economic failure and establishes an agenda for more detailed discussion in subsequent chapters. The last section then examines the vexed question of the distribution of the fruits and burdens of economic growth. Britain's changing role in the world economy is the focal point of Chapter 3, which begins with the major changes in the patterns of trade and payments. Of central concern is the extent to which Britain's world role damaged its competitive performance and vice versa.

Chapters 4 (on industry and entrepreneurs), 5 (on the labour market) and 6 (on economic policy) are similar in scope and organisation. Each attempts to survey the principal developments of the twentieth century and to use this outline as a foundation for assessing the issues and arguments raised in Chapter 2. Ideally, these surveys should be arranged on a thematic rather than a chronological basis, though it is almost impossible to avoid chronology and the conventional periodisation entirely. The point of departure for Chapter 4 is a survey of the changing economic structure at both the sectoral (primary, manufacturing, services) and sub-sectoral levels. The focus switches to one of the most strongly held arguments about British economic weakness: that British entrepreneurs and managers consistently failed to understand and harness advanced technical change. Constraints on space make it possible to illustrate the discussion with only a limited number of case studies, but examples are drawn from motor vehicles, chemicals, metals and textiles. The changing patterns of employment, unemployment and labour relations are surveyed in Chapter 5. After outlining the main trends, the discussion picks up another theme raised in Chapter 2: the extent to which economic performance may have been damaged by distinctive features of Britain's system of industrial relations and the structure of its labour market institutions. The main goals of Chapter 6 are to outline the pattern of government growth throughout the century, explain the main changes in the strategic objectives of economic policy and assess the controversies surrounding state intervention in two areas: the steady growth of welfare spending and the 'postwar settlement' after 1945. Once again, the main goal is to consider a theme raised in Chapter 2, that inappropriate economic policies may have damaged economic performance.

The final chapter is organised somewhat differently. By far the most controversial argument to have been raised in the later twentieth century was the claim by Wiener (1981) and Barnett (1986) that British culture was in some way antipathetic to modern manufacturing industry. These two works were commended for the freshness and provocative nature of their approach, but they are not difficult to locate in a broader historiographical tradition. Much has been written on the power of cultural forces, inculcated in the public schools, to shape the decisions of policymakers, within both government and leading financial institutions, away from the immediate needs of manufacturing industry. This 'cultural critique' forms the subject matter of Chapter 7 and launches a brief survey of the distinctive patterns of British schooling.

Most chapters are illustrated by simple descriptive statistics. Where possible this material is presented in charts and figures rather than in tables. There are two main reasons for this. The first is simply that charts are more visually attractive and therefore more likely to be examined and to convey information. The second is to avoid the illusion of hardness, exactness and precision that numbers customarily impart. For the most part, the charts and tables attempt to present a picture that covers the entire century rather than sub-periods, but there are some exceptions to this rule. As a result, the base statistics are almost invariably drawn from more than one source and have required a greater or lesser degree of reconciliation. Many of the charts and tables that illustrate Chapter 5, for example, have required a substantial degree of adjustment to the data in the original sources to provide plausibly consistent series. More commonly, material from official statistical sources for the years since 1947 have been matched with material drawn from Feinstein's (1972) economic accounts for the British economy since 1855. It is usually safe to assume that the reliability of historical statistics diminishes as one moves back from the present and down from aggregate measures into components of national income. Wars and major economic disruptions create particular problems, however, especially in measuring the capital stock, so the margins of error during the 'trans-war' periods (1913–24 and 1937–51) rise considerably (Feinstein 1972, 20–2; Matthews et al. 1982, 612–13). Feinstein's estimates have been the most valuable resource for economists' and historians' attempts to understand British economic development since the mid-nineteenth century. However, the advent of cheap and powerful computers in the 1990s encouraged the development of new ways of assembling estimates of national income from Feinstein's estimates of the component parts and methods of analysing the available data (see Chapter 2). The range of uncertainty about Britain's economic performance since 1900 seems to be increasing rather than diminishing.

2 Economic Growth and Welfare

This chapter examines Britain's growth record and suggests that the notion of relative decline needs to be handled with more care and sophistication than hitherto. More and more countries did indeed surpass British living standards during the twentieth century, but they did not power ahead as the 'declinist' literature has assumed. At the end of the century living standards in France, Germany, the UK and the USA stood in almost exactly the same relative position as at the end of the 'golden age' in 1973, and the relative gap between British and US living standards had changed little since 1950. Much of the analysis of Britain's relative decline has been predicated upon more or less abject performance by manufacturing industry and, although there were obvious signs of relative deterioration against European countries between 1950 and 1973, in the longer term the main problems in fact resided elsewhere. The standard analytical tools of convergence, institutional failure and supply-side weaknesses in manufacturing are not well designed to understand British economic performance in the longer run. Despite the problems, the British economy delivered substantial improvements in material welfare for the vast majority during the twentieth century, but there were very clear and disturbing signs that a substantial minority had been excluded from the benefits of economic growth after 1967.

Defining and Measuring Growth

Economists define economic growth as the rate of change of productive potential over time. 'Productive potential' is what the economy can produce when all factors of production (land

17

and raw materials, labour, capital and, more controversially, entrepreneurship) are fully employed, but this is a conventional definition. There is always some margin of unused or under-utilised labour or capital equipment, and in practice growth is measured as the rate of change in national income between peaks of the trade cycle that have reasonably comparable levels of economic activity. 'National income' itself is usually defined as the *'net value'* of all *'economic goods and services' 'produced'* within the *'nation state'* in a specified period, usually a year, but all the italicised terms are potentially controversial (see Kuznets 1966, 20–6). The most frequently employed measures of national income are gross domestic product (GDP: the total production of goods and services in the economy in a year) and gross national product (GNP: GDP plus net income from abroad). They can be expressed in terms of current prices or, after allow-ing for price changes, in constant prices (real GDP). In theory, national income may be measured by three separate routes (total income, total expenditure and total output), which in an ideal world should produce identical results. In practice, these esti-mates are rarely entirely independent, always diverge and have a disturbing tendency to be furthest apart in periods of most severe economic difficulty or change. Over a long span of years, as used in this chapter, profound difficulties arise in allowing for changes in both the quality of products and the composition of output. Those with particular concerns (in environmental, distributional or quality of life issues, for example) have drawn up alternative series, but most economists and historians continue to use the conventional measures, despite the difficulties, because they remain the best available indicators of economic progress and the pace of economic change. There is a long tradition of interest in 'political arithmetic' in Britain, going back to Sir William Petty in the seventeenth century, but systematic work on defining and measuring the British national income began only in the twen-tieth century with the work of Colin Clark (1937). His efforts were extended and developed within Whitehall during the Sec-ond World War. British national income statistics since 1945 are generally regarded as highly reliable, but the divergence between the income, expenditure and output measures is recognised as a weakness. The normal method of reconciling the inconsistencies has been by averaging (and producing 'compromise' estimates), as used in British official statistics and the work of the most eminent and authoritative researchers on Britain's growth record (Feinstein 1972, 8–22; Matthews et al. 1982, App. A). An alternative method has, however, been developed and utilises the relative reliability of the component parts of national income to reconcile the inconsistencies and produce 'balanced' estimates of national income. These are available for the periods 1870–1913 and 1920–90 and give a subtly – but only subtly – different picture, as will become evident. British official statistics and internationally standardised data sets invariably employ the 'compromise' method and hence will be used throughout, but, on occasion, it will be illuminating to note the different results obtained by using the 'balanced' estimates.

The definition of growth at the beginning of this section implied that its central concern was the change over time in the long-run trend of productive potential. Actual output may change as a result of new production facilities, new machines or the adoption of new methods, all of which will raise productive potential, or from the shorter-run impact of changes in output arising from random economic movements or the working of the business cycle. The measurement of trend and cycle used to be a question of judgement, with researchers seeking to identify cyclical peaks and troughs in especially sensitive data series, and then measuring trends across cyclical peaks with approximately equal levels of unemployment. There are now commonly accepted terminal years from which measurements are taken: 1899–1913, 1913–51 (1924–37 for within the inter-war years), 1951–73, 1973–9 and 1979–90. The most suitable end year for the century as a whole is not yet clear. At the time of writing, confirmed GDP figures for 1998 were the latest available and were used as the terminal date for the study. However, the identification of trend, cycle and random disturbance has now been revolutionised by the use of powerful econometric programmes. These techniques are still at the developmental stage, with disagreements about the most appropriate methods, but they are transforming our understanding of economic progress and performance, as will become evident in the discussion of the Edwardian climacteric.

Real GDP may be divided by population to give real GDP per capita, or living standards. This is the measure most often used when commentators are interested in the welfare supplied by economic growth to the nation's citizens. When the focus is turned to the efficiency of the productive side of the national economy, there are a number of measures of productivity from which to select. The simplest is to divide real GDP by the nation's workforce, making conventional allowances for part-time and other non-standard patterns of work. This is GDP per worker, or labour productivity. There are, however, substantial differences in the national conventions of hours worked in the 'normal working week', and still wider variations in the hours worked in the 'normal working year'. To allow for such variations, economists have developed a second measure of labour productivity, GDP per hour worked, reasoning that statistics should be sensitive to the preference of some societies to take the rewards of high efficiency in the form of greater leisure. Although there have been some notable investigations into working hours, this is another area in which the reliability of the statistics is uncertain and diminishes in earlier parts of the century.

Thus far, the focus has been entirely upon British statistics. The previous chapter made it clear, however, that we can make some sense of British economic performance in the twentieth century only in a comparative context. It is essential to have some method of comparing levels of output, welfare and efficiency in Britain with those elsewhere. This clearly involves the conversion of national values into international units. The simplest method is to use the exchange rate, and convert into sterling, dollars, euros or whatever. But economists have always known that the exchange rate is of limited value in comparing price levels, since it tends to apply only to 'traded' goods and services, and excludes those for which there is no competition from imports. Since the 1970s, economists have made increasing use of purchasing power parities (PPPs), comparing directly the cost of a selected, representative basket of goods and services. PPPs are continually updated and improved, but their application to historical data raises problems. Improvements to PPPs since 1970, when applied to per capita national income estimates for 1913, have been enough to raise Britain's living standards from only 80 per cent of the US level to near parity, in successive editions of Maddison's survey of comparative economic performance since 1700 (Table 2.1). Measures of output per hour worked are even more volatile, as they are subject to changing information not only on PPPs but also on hours worked (see Table 2.1). Maddison's efforts to supply the quantitative-historical building bricks to understand international economic performance have been absolutely heroic, but experience has taught the dangers of reaching strong conclusions from his standardised estimates covering the years before 1920.

Table 2.1   *The comparative dimension: changing measures of Britain's living standards and efficiency, 1913 and 1870–1992*

(a) Living standards: Britain's per capita GDP in 1913 relative to that of the USA:

Year of Maddison's study	Location	Price standard	UK relative levels
1982	Tables A2, B2	1970 US $	79.1
1989	Table 1.3	1980 US $	81.3
1991	Table 1.1	1985 US $	82.9
1995	Table D-1a	1990 International $	94.8

(b) Relative efficiency: Output per hour worked relative to that in the USA, 1870–1992

	1870	1913	1950	1973	1979	1987	1992
In Maddison 1982, 98:							
France	60	54	44	76	86		
Germany	61	57	33	71	84		
UK	114	81	56	64	66		
USA	100	100	100	100	100		
In Maddison 1991, 53:							
France	56	48	40	70		94	
Germany	50	50	30	64		80	
UK	104	78	57	67		80	
USA	100	100	100	100		100	
In Maddison 1995, 249:							
France	60	56	40	76			101
Germany	70	68	35	71			95
UK	115	86	62	68			82
USA	100	100	100	100			100

The Growth Record: Falling Behind the USA and Europe

The standard picture of Britain's growth rate since the mid-nineteenth century is given in Table 2.2, columns 2–4. There appears to be a slowdown in the half-century after 1870, only for growth rates to accelerate again in the twentieth century, especially after 1951. The pattern is evident in the output, living standards and productivity measures. Growth rates in the last quarter of the twentieth century were less rapid than during the 'golden age', as the period 1951–73 has become known, but compare favourably with the rates achieved before 1951. Perhaps the most remarkable feature of this pattern is its steadiness: the changes in the rhythm of growth were remarkably small, apart from the deceleration around the First World War. The contrast with the extreme volatility of domestic opinion about economic performance is very stark. On the face of it, the most difficult periods to interpret are those which embrace the two world wars, since both involve obvious measurement problems. The economy in 1913 was at the top of a heated boom, whereas the peak of the business

Table 2.2 *UK rates of growth of output, living standards and productivity since 1856 (annual percentage growth rates)*

Period	Balanced Real GDP	Compromise Real GDP	GDP per capita	GDP per worker
1856–73		2.2	1.4	1.3
1873–1913	1.7*	1.8	0.9	0.9
1913–24		−0.1	−0.6	0.3
1924–37	2.0*	2.2	1.8	1.0
1937–51	1.9*	1.8	1.3	1.0
1951–73	2.9*	2.8	2.3	2.4
1973–9	1.4*	1.5	1.5	1.3
1979–90	2.1*	2.2	2.0	1.5
1990–8		2.0	1.7	

Note: * Balanced estimates give a different pattern of cyclical peaks.
The measurements in this column are 1874–1913, 1925–37 and otherwise as indicated.
Sources: Column 1: Solomou and Weale 1991, Table 3 (for 1874–1913); Sefton and Weale 1995, Table A3.
   Column 2: Matthews et al. 1982, Table 2.1; ONS 2000, Table 1.3.
   Column 3: Matthews et al. 1982, Table 16.1; ONS 2000, Table 1.5.
   Column 4: Matthews et al. 1982, Table 21; ONS 2000, Table 1.3; OECD 1995.

cycle in 1924 was a comparatively weak affair. In the second 'trans-war' period, the situation was reversed. The pre-war business cycle was muted (with still at least one million unemployed in 1937), whereas in 1951 the capitalist world economy reached another inflationary business cycle peak. The estimates of economic growth in these two very important periods are therefore rather problematic, but they have caused fewer waves in the literature than has the suggestion of a slowdown after 1870, and particularly after 1899.

There has long been a debate in British economic history about performance during the period 1870–1914 (see McCloskey 1970; Pollard 1989; Alford 1996). To anticipate the discussion of Chapter 4, the essence of the story is that Britain's industrialisation had been comparatively narrow, based on the old staple industries of cotton, iron and steel, coal, shipbuilding and railways, which had long passed their phase of rapid growth of output and productivity. After 1870, competition from the USA and Germany intensified and Britain's competitors embarked upon a rather different industrial path, with higher investment in machinery and more systematic attempts to apply science to industry. Discussion of the microeconomic level is essentially for subsequent chapters. At the macroeconomic level the central issue is the evidence for and timing of a 'climacteric', or deceleration, in Britain's output and productivity growth trends. The question of the timing of a slowdown in the pace of British economic growth in the second half of the nineteenth century goes back at least to the 1950s (see the literature surveyed in Aldcroft and Richardson 1969), but a key moment in the debate came with the publication of the seminal study by Matthews and colleagues (1982). They firmly identified a slowdown, concentrated in the years after 1899 and most manifest in a considerable deceleration in productivity growth as measured by output per worker. But the evidence is patchy (Table 2.3). Productivity figures that derive from the income measure of GDP show virtual stagnation in productivity growth after 1899 whereas those from the output measure show no real slowdown. This inconclusive picture stimulated new econometric work on the period. 'Balanced estimates' of GDP have been produced for the period 1870–1913 and show no slowdown in the rate of growth within the period (Solomou and Weale 1991, Table 4)

Table 2.3   Rates of growth of real GDP per worker, UK, 1856–1913 (annual percentage growth rates)

	Income measure	Expenditure measure	Output measure	Compromise estimates
Whole period				
1856–1913	1.0	1.0	1.0	1.7
Two long swings				
1856–82	1.2	1.3	1.2	1.2
1882–1913	0.9	0.8	0.8	0.8
Four phases				
1856–73	1.3	1.4	1.1	1.3
1873–82	0.9	1.0	1.2	1.3
1882–99	1.5	1.3	0.9	1.1
1899–1913	0.1	0.3	0.7	0.5

Sources: Feinstein 1990c, Table 3; Feinstein et al. 1982, Table 8.3.

but little difference from compromise estimates for the period 1874–1913 as a whole (Table 2.2). Others have applied econometric tests to identify breaks in trend in the GDP statistics and have found either that no such breaks occurred between 1873 and 1913 or only weak evidence for slower growth after 1899 (Greasley and Oxley 1995; Crafts et al. 1989). This remains a highly controversial debate, but the case for an Edwardian 'climacteric' is receding. Greasley and Oxley (1999, 73) recently examined the whole period from 1856 to 1938 and found no break in trend rates of output *or* productivity growth before 1913: 'It was the impact of the First World War, rather than late Victorian frailties, that caused a break in long-established industrial growth trends'. In fact, this interpretation sits easily with a careful appraisal of much wider-ranging evidence of the period by Pollard (1989), who concluded that the challenges faced by the British economy at the turn of the century stimulated a major reappraisal at many levels of economic activity. For Pollard, as for Greasley and Oxley, the First World War provided the real turning point, but there remain substantial differences of view on the ultimate cause of the break in trends.

To take the discussion further it is necessary to put British growth performance into a comparative context. Maddison's (1995) figures have been used for Table 2.4, which compares

Table 2.4 *Rates of growth of GDP, GDP per capita and GDP per hour worked, 1899–1997 (annual percentage growth rates)*

	1899–1913	1913–50	1950–73	1973–9	1979–92	1899–1992
Growth rates of real GDP						
France	1.5	1.1	5.0	2.8	2.0	2.4
Germany	3.1	1.1	6.0	2.3	2.3	2.8
UK	1.3	1.3	3.0	1.5	1.7	1.8
USA	3.9	2.8	3.9	2.8	2.2	3.2
Growth rates of GDP per capita						
France	1.3	1.1	4.0	2.3	1.5	2.0
Germany	1.6	0.3	5.0	2.5	1.8	2.0
UK	0.5	0.8	2.5	1.5	1.4	1.3
USA	1.9	1.6	2.4	1.8	1.2	1.8
Growth rates of GDP per hour worked						
France	1.6*	1.9	5.1	3.2	2.5	2.8*
Germany	1.5*	0.6	6.0	4.1	2.0	2.5*
UK	0.9*	1.6	3.1	2.3	2.1	2.0*
USA	1.6*	2.5	2.7	1.7	0.9	2.1*

Note: In calculations of GDP per hour worked, the start year is 1900, not 1899.
Sources: Maddison 1995, Tables B-10a, D-1a, J-5; idem 1989, Tables C7, C8; idem 1991, Tables C8–C10.

British growth rates since 1899 with those of France, Germany and the USA. The most outstanding feature of the first half of the twentieth century is the huge relative advance of the US economy, as measured in its rate of growth of output and productivity (Table 2.4) and its increasing domination of world manufacturing production (see Table 1.1 above, final column). This surge forward by the US economy was particularly powerful during both 'trans-war' periods. The British and continental European economies, by contrast, were badly handicapped by destruction and the severe disruption of costs and competitiveness associated with the First World War. For Britain there was additional frailty because of the damage to world trade and payments from the war and the Versailles peace settlement at a time when the British economy was still massively geared to international exchange. Cost and competitiveness problems can, in theory, be overcome by an appropriate rate of exchange, but there were difficulties for Britain on this score (see Chapter 3). By the mid-1920s, Britain had apparently adjusted to many aspects of the new order, but unemployment became a constant reminder of the inadequate pace and scale of change (see Chapter 5).

There is no doubt, however, that, as Britain was making its painful transition to the new international conditions, the US economy powered ahead. This story is usually told solely in terms of the productive power of US manufacturing as giant, vertically integrated US corporations exploited mass production methods to a much fuller extent than their European rivals did. It is evident from Table 1.1 above that the US shares of world manufacturing output and trade rose consistently from 1900 to 1950. These figures and this argument are grist to the 'declinist' mill since it is easy to suggest that British firms could and should have followed the US lead. The traditional story of US manufacturing success and UK failure to match it is, however, simplistic. There were substantial US relative productivity advances in many other sectors which cannot be explained in terms of British failure and US superiority. US firms established a huge productivity lead in mineral extraction (reflecting US exploitation of much more favourable resource endowments) and the utilities (again reflecting US resource endowments and superior scale economies) and very important relative gains in agricultural productivity as labour was transferred from farming into higher productivity sectors (Broadberry 1998). Productivity leadership in manufacturing will explain only part of the US lead in GDP per hour worked (column 2 of Table 1.1). Nor should we overlook the changing rhythms of comparative economic performance. The world slump of 1929–32 hit Britain less hard than its rivals, and recovery came earlier and stronger than in most other countries. Thus, in terms of living standards (growth of per capita GDP) relative decline was reversed during the 1930s, and productivity (GDP per hour worked) grew at approximately the same pace as in Germany but more slowly than in France and the USA. All the European countries fell further behind the USA during the 'trans-war' years, 1937–50, but more as a result of wartime dislocation than from any destruction of productive capacity (Armstrong et al. 1991, 7–11).

Britain's living standards were also overtaken by European economies during the long postwar boom (Table 1.2 above). The French and German growth rates accelerated rapidly between 1950 and 1973, whether measured by output, living standards or productivity (Table 2.4). Britain's failure to experience an economic miracle during the golden age has been at the core of the 'declinist' literature. Almost every other European nation enjoyed a vigorous spurt of growth at some stage during this period. The world economy boomed after 1951, and European countries were in the vanguard. Many European economies had been severely dislocated by war, but were capable of very rapid spurts of growth once order was restored. The most obvious threat to the realisation of this enhanced potential for growth lay in balance of payments weakness and a recurrence of the protectionist and restrictive policies that followed the First World War. On this occasion, however, there was a profound determination not to repeat past mistakes. The US government provided substantial quantities of aid to Europe in both 1945–6 (reconstruction finance) and 1947–52 (Marshall Aid) (Milward 1984). The problems of scarcity and over-reliance on North American sources of supply were addressed by liberalisation, first at regional and then at global levels. Faster growth of trade and output helped to foster producer and consumer confidence. In most countries there was a postwar settlement committing governments to prioritise internal over external needs. In turn, many governments used these new commitments to press employers and unions to act in ways that enhanced national economic growth potential as much as sectional interest (Eichengreen 1996). Finally, there were new agreements on the management of currencies to prevent the beggar-my-neighbour policies of the inter-war years. Taken as a whole, this is an impressively coherent set of policies for the longer term. However, it was assembled piecemeal on a decentralised basis by those responding to short-run pressures and clearly worked better for some countries than others. Nonetheless it worked.

The British economic acceleration was not of the same order, but post-1945 comparisons need great care. Figures 2.1 and 2.2 show the growth trajectories of Britain and other economies in the twentieth century. For France, Germany (Figure 2.1), Italy and Japan (Figure 2.2), some part of the strength of postwar growth, especially during the golden age, was clearly related to the fall of output in the late 1930s and 1940s relative to the trends established in the inter-war years. German scholars, in particular, have explored the idea of a long-run 'normal rate of growth',

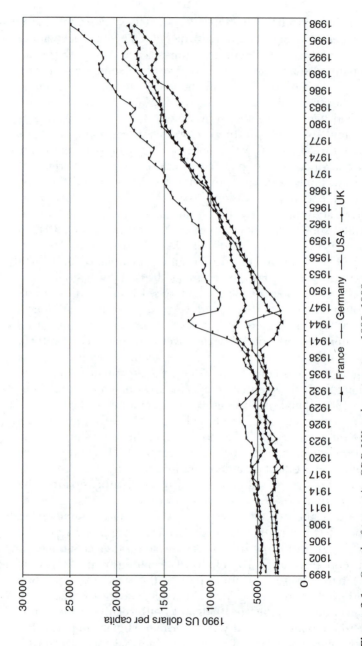

Figure 2.1 *Growth of per capita GDP, UK and comparators, 1899–1998*
Source: Maddison 1995, Table D-1a; OECD, *Main Economic Indicators*, various issues.

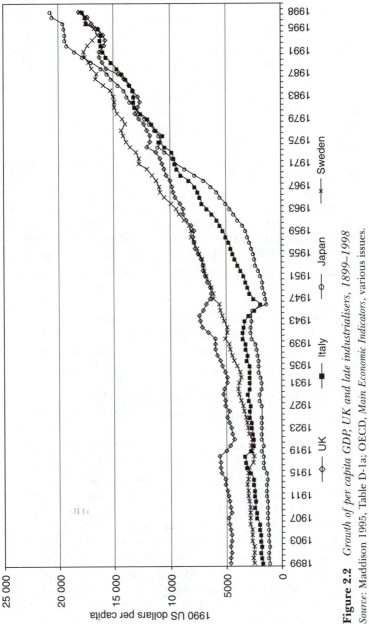

Figure 2.2 *Growth of per capita GDP, UK and late industrialisers, 1899–1998*
Source: Maddison 1995, Table D-1a; OECD, *Main Economic Indicators*, various issues.

with the economy reacting to any displacement from this path by subsequent acceleration until the economy returns to its 'normal' trend path (see the literature cited by Dumke 1990). This, too, is highly controversial, not least because twentieth-century experience in both France and Germany cautions against the assumption of any stable, underlying normal or natural growth rate. But the core idea is gaining broader support (see van de Klundert and van Schaik 1996). Clearly, some of the angst about Britain's relatively poor growth rate during the golden age has been misplaced. There were two good reasons why France, Germany (from our immediate comparators), Italy and Japan (as representative 'late industrialisers') should have grown faster than the UK during the long boom. They enjoyed much greater scope for 'reconstruction growth' than did the UK, as Figures 2.1 and 2.2 clearly show; and all four had a much bigger reservoir than the UK of low-productivity workers in agriculture and self-employment to redeploy into modern industry. The first category is a nightmare to define and estimate, but Dumke (1990) suggested that the size of the 'war shock' is a powerful predictor of national growth rates during the period 1950–80. The gains from structural change are equally difficult to define and measure, but one estimate for the first half of the golden age suggested that France and Germany had advantages that may explain approximately 30 per cent of their faster growth (Denison 1967, Tables 21–23), and Broadberry (1998) argued that in the longer term both Germany and the USA 'overtook' Britain largely by shifting resources out of agriculture. Britain's level of manufacturing productivity certainly deteriorated by comparison with that of Germany between 1950 and 1973 and the relative size of the British manufacturing sector contracted, but problems in manufacturing are but one part of a much more complex story.

These observations help explain why the growth rates of France and Germany were closer to those of Britain after the 1970s, in terms of both GDP per capita and GDP per hour worked (Table 2.4). By 1973 France and Germany had exhausted most of the structural gains from switching resources out of agriculture. There were compensating gains for the UK, notably the discovery of North Sea oil and gas, which boosted productivity in Britain's utilities and the extractive industries. These changes occurred against the background of deceleration in the world economy as the uniquely favourable conditions of the 1940s and 1950s slowly evaporated (Maddison 1991). Britain's growth rates slowed in the 1970s, but by rather less than its main European competitors, and from 1979 on the rates of growth of living standards and productivity were roughly similar in Britain, France and Germany (Table 2.4). This convergence of European growth rates can be interpreted as a British economic renaissance, but there are good grounds for scepticism. Britain's growth rate since 1979, however it is measured, was no faster than the British average for the century as a whole and well below the rates achieved by the country during the golden age. Britain maintained its position relative to France and Germany since 1973, but late industrialisers, among both European and Asian nations, continued to overtake the UK. In this sense, relative decline continued throughout the century. However, apart from the very small states (Iceland, Luxembourg, Switzerland) and the special cases (Norway, Denmark), European living standards clustered close together. According to the OECD (1999, Appendix), in 1997 British living standards were 90–95 per cent of those in France and Germany, as they were in 1973. There is nothing here to justify the diagnosis of a continuing, possibly intensifying, 'British disease'.

Analyses of the Problems

Until comparatively recently, economists relied upon neo-classical models to investigate economic growth. The most basic neo-classical model sees growth of output as dependent upon the growth of inputs of capital (machinery, buildings, and the like) and labour. Beyond a certain point, however, there will be diminishing returns to each factor of production. An increase in the stock of capital, given the amount of labour employed, will produce a less than proportionate increase in output. This process is progressive, so that new investment may ultimately cease because of low and declining profitability. Technical change, however, by making labour and capital more productive, can offset the effects of diminishing returns, but technical change has been treated as almost a gift from heaven. The neo-classical framework has no independent way of explaining the rate of technical progress, which is assumed to expand at a regular, if unobserved, rate. Although its implications seem distinctly at odds with the experience of real twentieth-century economies, neo-classical analysis has produced the most widely used technique to analyse growth, growth accounting. Despite the reservations of some economists, growth accounting became the standard method of thinking about the sources of growth.

At its simplest, growth accounting divides the increase in total output into two parts, that which is caused by growth of the inputs of factors of production and that which is the result of changes in the efficiency of these inputs. If the economy satisfies specific, stringent requirements, it is possible to weight capital and labour inputs by the share of profits and wages in total income, to form Total Factor Inputs (TFI). The 'efficiency' element noted above (Total Factor Productivity – TFP) is the residual after the rate of growth of TFI is subtracted from the rate of growth of GDP. Movements in TFP arise from a wide range of influences (economies of scale, technical progress, changes in economic structure, the impact of institutions). The best practitioners of growth accounting break this measure down still further to try to identify the separate impact of as many components as possible, but the technique still cannot explain the pace of technical change. However, the method will decompose the source of growth accurately between TFI and TFP only if the economy under investigation meets the tough requirements noted above (for a discussion, see Alford 1988, 16–18). Growth accounting has provoked some very strong opinions for and against but the technique has now become a routine part of any treatment of growth in the modern capitalist economy and is central to the standard works. Table 2.5 reproduces Maddison's growth accounts for the USA, UK, France and Germany since 1913. As noted above, the growth of output is the sum of the growth rates of weighted capital input, weighted labour input and TFP, though there are minor errors due to rounding. The most obvious points to emerge from Table 2.5 are that the USA was favoured by a consistently faster rate of growth of labour input and, in the period 1913–50, by a significantly higher rate of TFP growth. The highest rates of TFP growth were, however, recorded by France and Germany during the golden age. This should not be unexpected. British TFP performance was no

Table 2.5 *Growth accounts for selected countries, 1913–87 (annual average percentage contribution to the growth of output)*

	Contribution to GDP growth from:			
	Weighted labour input	*Weighted capital input*	*TFP*	*Rate of growth of GDP*
1913–50				
France	−0.2	0.7	0.7	1.2
Germany	0.5	0.5	0.3	1.3
UK	0.2	0.7	0.4	1.3
USA	0.9	0.6	1.3	2.8
1950–73				
France	0.3	1.7	3	5
Germany	0.2	2.2	3.5	5.9
UK	0	1.8	1.3	3
USA	1.7	0.8	1.1	3.7
1973–87				
France	−0.4	1.6	1	2.2
Germany	−0.7	1.5	1	1.8
UK	−0.3	1.2	0.8	1.8
USA	1.9	0.7	−0.1	2.5

Source: Maddison 1991, Tables 5.10, 5.19.

worse than moderate: better than US rates apart from 1913–50 and close to those of France and Germany, apart from 1950–73. Yet, the British economy is widely believed to have failed. To understand why, it is necessary to look at the interrelated discussions of convergence, supply-side weaknesses and institutions.

One of the more interesting implications of neo-classical growth theory is that growth rates of rich and poor countries should converge. The heavy investment in richer countries should lead to diminishing returns to capital and encourage investors to seek out opportunities in poorer countries where higher returns are available. Thus growth rates in the rich countries should sag, and those in the developing world should rise. In the 1950s, evidence for such convergence was scarce (Kaldor 1961). The publication of Maddison's (1982) data on the long-run growth performance of the developed economies stimulated new work on 'convergence', but among the rich countries, and in particular on the different rates of technical progress in 'leader' and 'follower' countries. Abramovitz (1986, 390) argued that the 'follower' countries need to acquire the 'social capability' to adapt the technology of the 'leader' to their specific circumstances to reap the full advantages of convergence and catch up. There are a number of distinctive elements in social capability but all are in some way concerned with facilitating technology transfer in the widest interpretation of the term. Convergence theorists see the spread of US manufacturing methods, often given the shorthand term 'Fordism', to other developed economies as the engine of convergence and accelerated growth during the golden age (Abramovitz 1994; Baumol 1994). The convergence hypothesis provided a convenient framework for a lengthening list of studies that identified problems on the supply side of British manu-facturing. These weaknesses (which are discussed in detail in Chapter 4) include poor managers, inadequate research and development (R&D), badly organised firms, a weak competitive environment and obstructive unions (see Crafts 1991a; 1991b) and could be presented as limiting Britain's 'social capability' to adopt and adapt US technology. Thus, an important strand of the literature argues that the British economy grew slowly because of barriers to change in manufacturing industry throughout much of the twentieth century and portrays relative decline as a very protracted process.

It is one thing to point to a long list of recurrent supply-side weaknesses, but quite another to account for this stubborn per-sistence over time. The market mechanism should reward those firms able to overcome supply-side constraints and penalise those that cannot. If domestic firms cannot cope, then foreign multi-nationals have a powerful incentive to move in (for a discussion of multinational activity in the UK during the century, see Jeremy 1998, ch. 7, and the literature cited therein). Social scientists have turned to *institutional* explanations to account for the failure of the market to work its tricks, and institutional failings have become a staple of analyses of the twentieth-century British economy. Researchers disagree about how institutions should be defined and investigated but, simplifying heroically, there are two basic approaches. The first sees institutions as rules of behaviour that establish the incentive structures for economic activity. The second interprets institutions as organised interest groups that battle over the allocation of resources. The former can conveniently be considered with convergence analysis. The latter is better treated separately.

The former derives much of its force from the work by North (1990) on property rights and transactions costs. These ideas underpin Chandler's (1977; 1990) explanation of the creation of the giant, vertically integrated corporation in the USA. Chandler argued that large-scale US firms found managerial decisions more effective than market co-ordination as the scale of production increased. Lazonick and collaborators suggested that British business could not follow the US lead because 'the very market-co-ordinated structures of industrial organisation that had previously allowed [the British] economy to become the international industrial leader undermined the incentives and constrained the abilities of British enterprises and industries to make the transition to [US-style] managerial co-ordination' (Lazonick 1994, 165; Elbaum and Lazonick 1986). British firms of the later nineteenth century relied heavily on skilled labour not only in production but also in the management of labour and work processes. They enjoyed low managerial costs and developed plentiful supplies of relatively cheap skilled workers. But major economies of scale in large-volume production ensured that long-run competitive advantage lay with the evolving US system, despite its high fixed managerial costs. British manufacturing found it very difficult to adopt US methods. The culture of competition among firms, the shortage of managerial talent and the obstruction of craft workers created insuperable institutional barriers to change. This is a subtle, yet relatively simple, argument. It is backed by an impressive range of case studies (see Chapter 4) and is consistent with major studies of the evolution of British management structures (Gospel 1992) and of the resistance of British managers to new ideas (Coleman and MacLeod 1986; Keeble 1992). Its greatest strength, however, is its ability to knit together the convergence and supply-side explanations of a British 'economic failure'. This institutional argument tries to explain how practices that were the foundation of competitive strength became outmoded and resistant to change. Many examples of institutional failure have been identified. But British market structures were different from those of the USA, and it is not clear that the Elbaum–Lazonick hypothesis paid sufficient attention to fundamental economic differences between the UK and the USA that might have affected the viability of US systems in the UK (Kirby 1992). Interestingly, the US multinationals operating in Britain in the early twentieth century (and the small number of British firms that adopted US corporate structures) performed uncertainly; there was no guarantee that US methods would bring success in the UK (Coleman 1987; Jones 1988).

The major weakness of accounts based on convergence, institutions and supply-side weaknesses is their preoccupation with manufacturing. Reference has already been made to Broadberry's sectoral productivity estimates for the UK, the USA and Germany back to roughly 1870, and this is the appropriate place to examine in more detail his conclusions and their implications for British economic performance. The central plank of Broadberry's account is that US manufacturing labour productivity levels were already about twice the British levels in 1870, and were at approximately the same relative position in the 1930s and at the end of the 1970s, despite some substantial swings in the intervening period. Similarly, German and British labour productivity levels were very similar in both 1870–1937 and in the 1980s. In the intervening period, again Britain's relative position deteriorated and then improved. These patterns are consistent with a form of catching-up – since a period when one country opens a labour productivity gap is followed by a period of narrowing – but show no tendency for Germany, the USA and the UK to converge on the same level of labour productivity in manufacturing (Broadberry 1993, 773). The broad outlines are given in Figure 2.3, which also shows van Ark's postwar figures for comparison.

There are clear indications that other European nations either had similar levels of manufacturing productivity to Germany and the UK throughout the twentieth century (Norway, Sweden, Denmark, the Netherlands) or converged on these levels during the golden age (France and Italy) (Broadberry 1997, 51–7). Of course, these estimates may be unduly flattering to the UK, and they have been criticised, but they are not radically out of line with other postwar estimates, as Figure 2.3 indicates. The implications for the discussion of twentieth-century British economic performance are substantial. The picture described in Figure 2.3 offers no real support to the idea of a persistent and serious

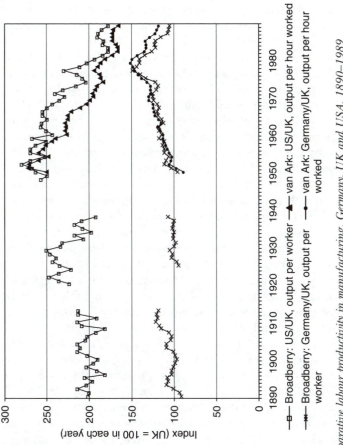

Figure 2.3 *Comparative labour productivity in manufacturing, Germany, UK and USA, 1890–1989*
Sources: Broadberry 1997, Table A3.1c; van Ark 1990, Table C2.

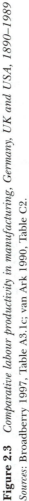

—□— Broadberry: US/UK, output per worker —▲— van Ark: US/UK, output per hour worked

—✻— Broadberry: Germany/UK, output per worker —●— van Ark: Germany/UK, output per hour worked

failure in British manufacturing. Clearly all was not well with British manufacturing, especially in the decade after 1973, when its productivity declined relative to that of the USA, Germany and other European competitors. But for much of the period after 1950 (again excepting the decade after 1973), Britain's labour productivity in manufacturing was roughly 20 per cent below that of Germany, and fluctuated little. It was at approximately the same relative level in the Edwardian years. It is difficult to see how a hypothesis of continuing decline based on poor manufacturing performance is consistent with Broadberry's evidence. Even if relative decline in manufacturing did indeed occur, weak convergence and supply-side weaknesses and the whole idea of a 'British disease' cannot and will not explain why the USA, Germany and a long list of other economies overtook Britain's aggregate output productivity (that is, output of the whole economy divided by the total workforce) in the twentieth century.

As noted above, the main reason why Germany and the USA overtook British levels of aggregate output per worker had nothing to do with manufacturing but lay in the much greater ability of other economies to make big productivity gains by shifting resources out of agriculture. There was also some deterioration of Britain's relative position in services, particularly in financial, distributive and government services, where British productivity leadership at the beginning of the century had been overhauled by the end. In other sectors of the economy (notably in mining and the extractive industries, the utilities and transport) there were very substantial swings in relative productivity, but no obvious trend over the century as a whole. Britain's relative decline is not, therefore, the simple story of manufacturing failure and supply-side weaknesses that dominates the historiography. A good part of Britain's decline relative to the USA before 1950 and to the European economies after was thus 'inevitable', and should not have been the cause for so much breast-beating. The tool kit developed by economists and historians by looking at the postwar period in isolation is positively misleading and unhelpful as soon as the perspective is widened. From this position, it is possible to comment more briefly on other long-run explanations of Britain's relative decline.

Perhaps the single most influential account of the impact of institutions on economic performance has been Olson's (1982) examination of the role of collective interest groups on the pace of economic growth. At the core is a neo-classical analysis of the behaviour of producer groups in the national political economy. Olson contends that such groups will tend to dissolve unless they can find ways of extracting a rent (in very broad terms, to extract more than is put in) from society as a whole, but only for their members. Long periods of social and political stability provide conditions in which collective interest groups can devise such strategies, but rent-seeking diminishes the flexibility of the economic system. Thus politically stable societies are characterised by slow productivity growth. Countries experiencing major socio-political upheaval (revolution, defeat in war, occupation) either have their structure of collective interest groups destroyed, or remade on lines more conducive to flexibility and economic growth. One of the core principles of this theory is that narrow, sectional groups will extract rents, whereas much more broadly based, 'encompassing' collective interest groups will not. Thus, it is possible to have strong producer organisations, which enhance rather than inhibit growth. The analysis applies across the economy, to services and manufacturing equally. Olson's work has been profoundly important in explaining how the Nordic countries, with their strong, centralised unions and employers' organisations, managed to negotiate the turbulence of the 1970s so successfully, and some of his terminology, notably the condition of 'institutional sclerosis', has passed into common usage. There are nonetheless doubts about key aspects of the argument (Pacqué 1996; Booth et al. 1997). In the context of this chapter, its focus on the period since 1945 but its total lack of leverage on the period following the First World War signals great caution. But to most Britons, rent-seeking by organised interests is most familiar as the behaviour of trade unions, a theme which is considered in some depth in Chapter 5, and judgements on Olsonian institutional analysis must be deferred until then.

In the late twentieth century economists began to give new prominence to the role of education and training in national economic performance. In large part, this emphasis arose from a major reappraisal of the economics of growth in the 1980s. The most powerful insight to emerge from this activity was 'endogenous growth theory', which was designed to explain why the diminishing returns predicted by neo-classical theory had not become apparent in the richest nations. It allows the creation of increasing returns to new investment within both the firm and the wider national economy, notably by developing human capital alongside new investment in machinery (for a review, see Boltho and Holtham 1992). This is highly theoretical work, but it has a highly practical application in underlining that improved educational standards, effective R&D or better training can set up the virtuous circle to break through diminishing returns. Governments appear to have taken the implications to heart: everywhere there was renewed emphasis on policies for education, training and industrial research. At a global level, there seems to be a good statistical relationship between human capital as measured by school enrolment rates and subsequent economic growth (Barro 1991). It has, however, been extraordinarily difficult to find an equivalent 'direct' measure of human capital that predicts the more subtle differences in growth rates among the richest nations. As will be seen in Chapters 6 and 7, neither the proportion of the workforce with specific levels of technical and vocational qualifications, nor average years of formal schooling, give statistically significant results. Economists have turned instead to more indirect measures and to the neo-classical assumption that in competitive markets factors of production are paid according to their marginal productivity. Thus human capital can be measured indirectly by relative pay, but this method raises very obvious questions of the direction of cause and effect. Economists take high pay to derive from high levels of human capital, which generates high productivity. But high productivity can equally produce high pay, and in general terms industrial relations research has long insisted that relationships between pay, skill and productivity are highly uncertain in empirical terms (Brown and Nolan 1988). Better education, superior training and more effective R&D are obviously vital to improved economic performance. Intelligent business leaders have known as much for many years. The difficulty is to know precisely how the relationship might work and what other factors might affect it.

The literature on Britain's twentieth-century economic performance is thus profoundly unsatisfactory. It is obsessed with the theme of a failure – the British economy could and should have grown faster – which could have been avoided if fundamental weaknesses in manufacturing had been addressed. This picture misses the point in two important respects. It fails to acknowledge the extent to which relative decline was inevitable and unavoidable. Britain had transferred resources out of agriculture at a much earlier stage than did most competitor nations, so its potential for fast twentieth-century growth was accordingly reduced. The USA, Germany, France, Italy, Japan and many others were certain to grow faster, in some cases very much faster, in the twentieth century than was Britain. Secondly, it vastly exaggerates the role of manufacturing and a supposed catalogue of supply-side weaknesses in industrial organisation. Without question, manufacturing productivity could have been higher, and its growth faster. Weaknesses in the quality of management, the structure of trade unions and the conduct of policy cannot be denied. It is, however, certain neither that Britain was alone among industrial countries in experiencing these difficulties nor that national economic performance was comparatively damaged as a result, except in the difficult decade after 1973. The idea that British manufacturing lost its way either in the 1890s or in the 1950s and somehow experienced a renaissance in Europe in the 1980s, as one recent contributor to the debate has maintained (Owen 1999), sits uneasily with the evidence. It is likely also that the weaknesses of management, workers, investment, the competitive framework and institutions have been exaggerated as influences on the trajectory of British economic development. Stark failures on the supply side are an unlikely cause of subtle but persistent relative decline (from a position of international leadership) in services, which proved a more substantial dead-weight on aggregate economic performance than the shortcomings of manufacturing. This concentration of weaknesses in manufacturing and the supply side has arisen primarily from studies that treat the postwar period as a separate, discrete phase in British (and international) economic history. There are immense methodological difficulties in adopting this narrow perspective. The long-run impacts of the world depression of the 1930s, wartime dislocation and destruction and accelerated structural change during the long boom profoundly shaped national economic performance after 1950 to different degrees. Econometric historians have found it impossible to control for the differential impact of these forces; indeed, precious few have even recognised the problem. Those adopting more literate and descriptive methodologies began to explore the issues in the mid-1960s (see especially Kaldor 1966), but these insights were lost in the 1970s, when the performance of manufacturing did indeed deteriorate relatively. In fact, we cannot be close to understanding the fundamental dynamics of twentieth-century British economic performance if we cannot even decide through which window we should look.

Living Standards and Welfare

The function of economic activity is to improve economic welfare. The picture given above in Tables 2.2 and 2.4 and in Figure 2.1 shows very conclusively that *average* living standards rose more or less continuously throughout the century. It is, however, important to probe beneath this average since questions of income distribution are fundamental to the long-run legitimacy of the socio-economic system. As noted in Chapter 1, the major domestic challenge in 1900 was to integrate a working class that was becoming better organised and more self-confident. It is not possible to gauge all the factors that affect an individual's standard of living, but investigations have been helped enormously by the late nineteenth-century revolution in social statistics, as government and social investigators collected more data on social and economic conditions. The range of such material increased throughout the century, though periodic 'economy campaigns' from time to time checked the expansion of official statistics, and, for the second half of the century, the problem is generally to sort from the plethora of statistical material available. The per capita GDP statistics are the logical starting place.

The data given in column 3 of Table 2.2 show movements in average incomes from all sources (employment, land, financial assets and profits) since 1899. Before 1914 roughly 55 per cent of all income was earned from employment and 44 per cent from capital, broadly defined – investment income, rents and profits (Matthews et al. 1982, Table 6.1). Since capital was very unequally distributed, with huge concentrations in the hands of the super-rich before 1914 (see Figure 2.4), total income was very unevenly distributed.

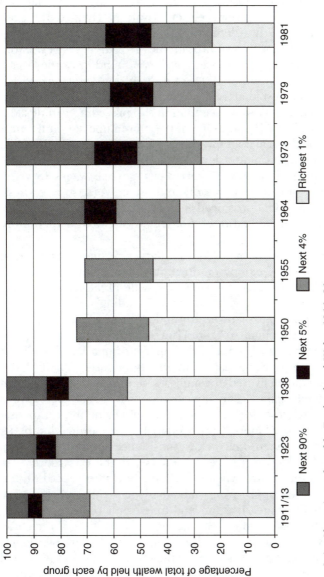

Figure 2.4 *Shares in total wealth, England and Wales, 1911–81*

Note: There are no estimates of wealth-holding below the richest 5% in 1950 and 1955

Sources: Atkinson et al. 1989, Table 1; Westergaard and Resler 1976, Table 16.

Employees receive income as wages or salaries. The contemporary economic statistician A. L. Bowley suggested that real wages were growing relatively quickly from 1882 to 1899 but declined in the Edwardian years (1899–1913) thanks to a rising cost of living and slowdown in the growth of wages. More recently, however, weaknesses have been found in Bowley's estimates (see MacKinnnon 1994 for a discussion), and revised figures now suggest that real wages continued to increase after 1899, albeit at a slower pace than in the preceding two decades (Feinstein 1990c; 1990d). One of the more important influences on the index of real wages was the shift from lower to higher paid employment, which also slowed after 1899 but remained a sufficiently strong influence to carry average real wages forward. Wages are, of course, paid only to those in work, so any assessment of living standards needs to take account of the (ir)regularity of income, and also of household size and expenditure patterns.

As will be seen more fully in Chapter 5, there is little firm evidence on the extent of unemployment before 1913. It is known that underemployment was widespread in Edwardian Britain and that heavy, physically demanding work imposed a substantial burden of ill health and industrial injury upon all categories of manual workers (Harris 1972). Any interruption to income had an instant and significant impact on the living standards of working-class households because benefit levels were low and delivered through a system (the Poor Law) that discouraged claims. The introduction after 1906 of national insurance schemes for unemployment, ill health and compensation for industrial injury improved matters somewhat, but benefit levels remained well below subsistence levels (Hay 1975). Working-class savings were very sparse, so there was little support from this source whenever income was interrupted (Johnson 1984). Although living standards for manual workers had undoubtedly risen since the mid-nineteenth century, concerns were raised (again) after 1890 about the 'condition of England'. The new interest in quantification prompted more systematic observation and in many respects the social surveys of this period set the parameters for subsequent studies of poverty. The most famous were Booth's (1889–1903) investigations into London life and labour and Rowntree's (1901) inquiry into social conditions in York. Rowntree in particular attempted to define rigorously the minimum food, clothing and shelter needs for households of different size and measure the extent to which these needs were met. He found that in 1899 about 40 per cent of the working class (30 per cent of the total population) of York fell below that threshold. About one-third of this group was in (primary) poverty because incomes were insufficient to meet basic needs and the remainder were in (secondary) poverty because, although their incomes were adequate, their expenditure was so structured (for example because of fondness for alcoholic drink or the need to pay off debts) that insufficient remained to meet basic needs. He identified a life cycle of poverty: an individual was most likely to experience poverty as a child, as a parent with several young children, and in old age. Thus, poverty hit a large part of the population, and an even bigger percentage of the children, in the world's richest country.

The First World War brought significant changes. For half a century before 1914, wages and salaries had varied little, at between 50 and 55 per cent of national income. According to Feinstein's (1972, Table 1) figures, income from employment rose significantly during wartime as income from capital declined relatively, and these gains for wage and salary earners were held during the inter-war years. Among wage earners, the inequalities of pay between different levels of skill and different localities also narrowed during wartime, to the benefit of the lowest paid. Working-class living standards were undoubtedly helped by big wartime reductions in unemployment and the expansion of paid work for women, but the acceleration of inflation from 1915–16 worked in the opposite direction. Employees did not exploit their scarcity power to the full, and real incomes were maintained only by longer hours and more intensive working (Pollard 1992a, 31).

Between the wars there were a number of broad influences that allowed disposable incomes to grow at more rapid rates. First, the terms of trade (average import prices compared with average export prices) moved in Britain's favour, adding 0.3 per cent per annum to per capita incomes between 1924 and 1937. This is a relatively small contribution to the growth rate, but Britain imported a significant proportion of its food, and cheaper food prices represented a major gain for wage earners. It was estimated that the average working-class household spent roughly 30 per cent of its income on food, so the fall of imported food prices (by 40 per cent or more during the 1930s) brought real benefits (Glynn and Booth 1996, 25). At the same time, demographic change reduced the relative size of the dependent population. The fall in the birth rate meant that the proportion of the population in the age group 0–14 years had fallen by roughly 25 per cent from 1913 levels by 1939. The fall in the death rate increased the proportion of those aged 65 and over, but they still formed only a tiny proportion of the total population in 1939. There was also considerable growth of the service sector between the wars, permitting further redistribution of the working population into higher paid and more secure employment, though substantial stratification within the white-collar sector became still more apparent. Nevertheless, there are good grounds for optimism about the course of aggregate welfare during the inter-war years.

However, some of the potential for improved living standards was lost in mass inter-war unemployment. Food producing nations were also customers for Britain's exports, and falling prices for their own main exports left them less able to buy manufactures from the UK. The expanded labour supply resulting from demographic trends did not help the unemployment situation. The national improvements in mortality and morbidity between the wars were almost certainly less pronounced in the areas of mass unemployment, though there are good grounds for believing that key evidence was 'doctored' to hide the problem (Webster 1982). There were certainly substantial social class differentials in inter-war mortality statistics. When Rowntree (1941) undertook his second survey of social conditions in York, primary poverty, when measured on a consistent basis, had fallen slightly. The results of the two surveys of York are not strictly comparable, since on this occasion Rowntree used a significantly more generous definition of the poverty threshold, but subsequent researchers have been able to compare the results directly (Piachaud 1988). The life cycle of poverty was still apparent, and almost half of York's children under the age of five were in poverty and nearly a third remained in poverty to the age of ten. The title of his book, *Poverty and Progress*, is an excellent short summary of changing social conditions in inter-war Britain.

The share of wages and salaries in GNP rose again during the Second World War, and once more was held after the war. The war brought full employment and commitments to provide benefits at subsistence level to those after the war whose income was interrupted by ill health, unemployment or old age. Furthermore, family allowances were introduced during wartime and retained into peacetime to help large families stay out of poverty. There may be doubts about the 'generosity' of the benefits planned during the Second World War (see Chapter 6), but the rights of citizenship were extended significantly by the creation of the 'welfare state'. The new benefits made substantial inroads into the traditional causes of poverty, and indeed the increasing employment of married women in peacetime extended economic security among the population. Family size continued its fall since the later nineteenth century, life expectancy increased and infant mortality, a key indicator of social welfare, fell. New consumption patterns emerged, with rapid diffusion of consumer durables, like televisions, motor cars and household appliances, and rising standards of housing space and comfort (Halsey 1972; Bowden and Offer 1994). In the 1950s, Britain woke up to the age of affluence. The rising share of employment incomes in GNP certainly helped, but so too did the upgrading of workforce skills, with a slow shrinkage over time of unskilled work and a parallel rise of semi-skilled, clerical, technical and managerial work. A 'managerial revolution' occurred in twentieth-century Britain, much of it concentrated in the years after 1945, to create a rapidly expanding 'service class' (Halsey et al. 1986). This trend can be seen in the statistics of the distribution of personal income. Over the first 75 years of the century, there was a clear redistribution away from the topmost income earners, but the bottom half of the income distribution made few relative gains (Glynn and Booth 1996, 27, 204). There were, however, attempts to make the tax and benefits systems more progressive (redistributive) between 1964 and 1975, with the result that by 1975 Britain's income distribution was more egalitarian than that of many comparable nations (Stark 1977). At the same time there appear to have been spectacular changes in the distribution of wealth, especially that held by the very rich (Figure 2.4). The apparent, if limited, 'democratisation of wealth' needs to be interpreted cautiously. There were very good reasons for the extremely rich so to arrange their financial affairs as to reduce tax liability, so some part of the reduction of the holdings of the richest represent no more than financial restructuring (gifts to family members, the creation of family trusts, and like initiatives). The rise in the holdings of wealth of the mass of the population (the 'bottom 90 per cent') probably represents the extension of house ownership, which was the fastest growing source of personal wealth after the 1920s (Solomou and Weale 1997, Figure 6).

Despite this trend to higher incomes and more equal distribution of both income and wealth, poverty was rediscovered in postwar Britain. Following the precedent set by Rowntree's second survey of York, the incidence of poverty was measured by a 'relative' rather than an 'absolute' poverty line. In other words, poverty was defined by the standards and culture of the time. Many investigators used the 'official poverty line', or the amount paid by the safety net benefit system for which every citizen was eligible when all other sources of income had failed. There were many problems with this measure and social scientists turned increasingly in the 1980s to measures that defined poverty as a proportion of average or disposable incomes. Piachaud (1988) reworked the findings of earlier studies to try to make some generalisations about the changing patterns of poverty in the twentieth century. His figures for the two periods 1899–1953 and 1953–83 are reproduced in Table 2.6. The first part of the table suggests that poverty fell enormously between 1899 and 1953, with the main cause switching from low pay to old age. A much more generous relative poverty line applies in the bottom section of the table, but there is no doubt that poverty increased after 1973 as a result of rising unemployment and the stagnant real incomes of those in low-paid employment. Roughly one-quarter of all families was in poverty in the mid-1980s, and within that group two-fifths were pensioner families. Other surveys of poverty since the Second World War portray a broadly similar pattern. The most disturbing finding was the discovery that the income of the poorest 10 per cent remained static between 1967 and 1991, during which period average incomes rose by 50 per cent (Goodman and Webb 1994). Inequality of income continued to grow in the 1990s, though at a slower pace than in the previous decade. Among OECD economies in the 1990s, Britain had the highest proportion (one-fifth) of its population in poverty

Table 2.6   *The extent of poverty, UK, 1899–1983*

Changes in poverty, 1899–1953

	1899	1936	1953
Level for couple and one child as a percentage of average personal disposable income per capita in given year	78	79	79
Proportion of persons below this level (%)	9.9	8.1	1.2
Proportion of household below this level because of (%):			
death of husband	28	10	43
old age		24	28
illness	10	5	4
unemployment	3	35	3
other (low wages, irregular work, large family)	59	26	22

The extent of poverty, 1953–83
(proportion of each type of family/household in poverty – %)

	At constant relative poverty levels		
	Over pension age	Under pension age	All
1953	28.8	0.5	6.2
1960	n.a	n.a.	13.3
1973	59.3	6.7	19.4
1975	36.3	5.4	14.2
1979	52.1	9.9	20.3
1983	43.0	17.2	23.3

Note: In the second section figures for 1953 and 1960 relate to households, the remainder to families. To make the figure for 1953 and 1960 comparable they should be roughly doubled.
Source: Piachaud 1988, 341–2.

(using a standard definition); the USA, with the next worst record, had 14 per cent of its population in poverty (*Guardian* 2000). The UK also had much the largest problem of long-term poverty. Thus, the three decades of economic growth at very respectable rates at the end of the century brought no tangible gains to those at the bottom of the income distribution and for whom the quality of life was already impoverished. There is ample evidence of multiple deprivation among the poorest, who are those with the highest danger of unemployment, with the least formal schooling, the highest likelihood of divorce or suicide and with substantially worse health than the better off at all stages of life (Townsend 1979; Townsend and Davidson 1982). It is useful to draw contrasts with the inter-war period. The 'excluded' at that time also amounted to approximately one-tenth of the total population; they experienced extremely severe problems of poor physical and mental health and malnutrition (Whiteside 1987). State support for those at the bottom of the income distribution was sketchy in the extreme and the idea of a national minimum standard had certainly not yet been accepted. Their conditions were objectively far more desolate than those faced by the 'submerged tenth' in the 1980s and 1990s except in one important respect: their incomes, inadequate though they undoubtedly were, did advance in real terms. The falling food prices and 'sticky' benefit levels of the late 1920s and 1930s ensured that the poorest were not totally excluded from *all* the fruits of economic growth, as appears to have happened after 1967. There was indeed a serious problem of relative decline in the twentieth-century British economy and it had nothing to do with British versus French living standards but with the conditions of existence for the poorest from the late 1960s onwards.

Conclusion

Britain's economy certainly experienced relative decline after 1900, in the sense that other countries grew faster and overtook British living standards. The view of the 1970s, that the British economy was on some sort of slippery slope, was, however, badly overdrawn. Britain fell behind the USA in the first half of the century, behind the leading European economies in the third quarter, and then behind some of the Asian tigers in the early 1990s (before their crunch at the end of the century). It was too easy to believe that Britain's decline had been protracted and continuous. The point of a structured comparison is to show the logical fallacy in that view. More countries may have overtaken Britain, but its position relative to its main competitors hardly changed after 1973. Moreover, the speed of Britain's decline relative to the USA and Europe was determined to a very large extent by the speed with which these countries ran down their agricultural sectors, rather than by British economic deficiencies. The other main cause of long-run relative decline was a gradual deterioration of Britain's relative performance in parts of the service sector. The literature on British decline has, however, assembled an analytical tool kit, which was primarily designed to investigate an altogether different problem, a long list of apparently debilitating inadequacies in manufacturing industry. This literature has established a checklist of weaknesses that embraces almost every aspect of British industrial organisation. British manufacturing certainly had its problems in the twentieth century, and it is in obvious need of forensic investigation, but the inquiry does not have to bear the burden of explaining systemic national economic failure. Nor is there anything in the course of British living standards to indicate wholesale failure. There were considerable gains, from both the processes of economic growth and the moves to less inequality in the distribution of income and wealth. The latter were not continuous, as is sometimes assumed, but were concentrated in wartime and the decade after 1964. In the last quarter of the twentieth century, however, a real problem of relative decline did emerge. Those at the bottom of the income distribution were left behind as both markets and governments failed the poorest to an unparalleled extent.

3 Britain's Place in the World Economy

There is no denying the fundamental changes and diminishing influence of Britain's role in the international economy in the twentieth century. Britain began the century as de facto manager of the systems of international finance and trade. At the end of the century the City of London continued to play a major role in the world economy and British multinational companies had carved an important niche for themselves in world production and commerce, but Britain's international standing had waned. We know that the position in 1900 was based upon transient factors that were already beginning to disappear as bigger economies with more natural resources drove towards economic maturity. The question, as with the discussion of the growth rate, is whether Britain's decline needed to be quite so steep and spectacular. Those with experience of the years between 1930 and 1980 will be acutely aware of what external frailty means. Even those whose memories extend only to 'Black Wednesday', 16 September 1992, will recall the sense of national failure that accompanied formal devaluation (also experienced in 1919, 1931, 1949, 1967 and 1972). Rather surprisingly, Britain made fewer efforts to shelter from the dull, continuous ache of external weakness and the public humiliation of devaluation than any of its major rivals. Protectionist sentiment burned less strongly in Britain than in the USA and Europe. One of the questions for examination in this chapter is why the split between those sectors seeking greater national independence *from* the international economy and those seeking more complete integration *into* it should have been won, for the majority of the century, by the free traders. The other main goal is to examine the statistics of Britain's balance of payments to try to understand the main causes of external weakness and why they were not addressed more powerfully.

52

Britain and the World Economy at the Turn of the Twentieth Century

Britain was an important international trader before 1700, and invested heavily in military hardware (primarily, the Royal Navy) to ensure its emergence as the hegemonic naval and commercial power in Europe before the industrial revolution. This effort required heavy taxes and borrowing but the internal stability and global security bought by government expenditure laid the foundation for Britain's domination of world manufactured trade (O'Brien 1997; Cain and Hopkins 1993a). Britain achieved a long-lasting ascendancy in commercial and financial services for international trade, making the City of London an influential manager of the international financial system. The City managed the system informally by granting or withholding access to its main financial markets. Britain also supplied a range of other (non-financial) commercial services (the commodity markets, merchanting, brokering and chartering services, particularly those associated with ocean transport) to the world economy. In terms of goods, the UK concentrated heavily on supplying the world market with a narrow range of basic, unsophisticated manufactures (cotton and wool textiles, iron and steel), heavy engineering products (machinery and transport equipment) and coal. Together these products, collectively known as the exports staples, amounted to two-thirds of UK exports in 1900 (as they had in 1850). The principal imports were food and raw materials, some of which were processed and re-exported. From 1850 to 1914, the barriers to the international movement of factors of production were brought down and trade in goods was also liberalised, albeit with a drift back to protection after 1870. According to the theory of comparative advantage, world efficiency and incomes should be maximised under such conditions, but doubts have been raised about the extent of Britain's own gains from the system (Pollard 1989; Alford 1996).

There were indeed problems in the UK economy in 1900. The reliance on imports for more than half of the food supply left domestic agriculture, particularly cereal-growers, stagnating for the half-century to 1913. For industry, the rise of US mass production posed long-run problems, but, although US manufactured exports grew rapidly in the last quarter of the nineteenth century, in the early years of the twentieth century American industry focused largely on domestic sources of demand. The threat to UK (and French) markets for manufactures came essentially from Germany, which pioneered the path followed by so many twentieth-century late developers of industrialisation, based on the 'heavy-chemicals' sectors behind protective tariffs and facilitated by heavy capital expenditure. Britain's tariff reformers wanted to shield the industries most exposed to competition from German cartels and create stable domestic markets that would allow re-equipment, new investment and the recovery of international competitiveness (Marrison 1996). Tariffs were not, however, universally popular. The export industries feared that a British tariff would merely invite widespread retaliation and the City anticipated that it would be shut out of profitable opportunities overseas if Britain adopted protection. Free trade was also extremely popular with the working class, since the tariff arguably threatened cheap food imports and thus workers' living standards. Joseph Chamberlain's tariff reform campaign failed above all to persuade domestic opinion that tariffs would be used to facilitate, rather than avoid, reconstruction and modernisation. His campaign made little headway, but this left unresolved Britain's response to the changing balance of power in the world economy. These concerns over competitive performance and the social investigations noted in the previous chapter helped concentrate attention on the need for higher national efficiency, in the widest possible interpretation of the term (Hay 1975, ch. 3; Searle 1971). These concerns cut across party-political lines and encouraged a solution in the form of a national minimum standard of life, which would make workers healthier and more efficient and promote the physical quality of recruits into the armed forces. The social reform measures of the 1906 Liberal government were designed to achieve national efficiency and imperial strength. This may appear an indirect method of confronting German manufacturing power, but policy had to balance the different needs of industry, the empire and the City (Gamble 1994, 51–6). In fact, the enormous strength of the British balance of payments before 1913 made it extraordinarily difficult to contemplate government intervention on behalf of any industry, however large or important, in short-run competitive difficulties.

The balance of payments can be thought of as comprising three parts:

(1)   The balance of trade – effectively the difference between the value of goods exported and goods imported. It is sometimes referred to as the 'visibles' account.

(2)   The balance of payments on current account – effectively the 'visibles' plus 'invisible' trade (the difference between the value of services exported and imported) plus the 'interest and dividends' account (the difference between interest and dividends paid to the UK on British-owned overseas assets and those paid from the UK on foreign-owned UK assets).

(3)   The basic balance of payments – the sum of the two previous accounts plus capital movements and balancing items, so that debits always exactly equal credits. This account gives the total acquisition and disposal of foreign currencies and gold, with changes in official reserves or liabilities as the balance.

Between 1850 and the First World War, Britain's balance of trade was almost always in deficit, but was more than matched by growing surpluses on 'invisibles' and 'interest and dividends', leaving the current account in substantial and increasing surplus. This surplus was in turn 'recycled' in the form of short- and long-term overseas lending (a deficit on capital account), so that the basic balance of payments remained in equilibrium. By these methods, London, with Paris and Berlin, supplied liquidity for the growth of international trade. Most private international bills were paid in sterling, French francs or German marks, and these key currencies also comprised one-fifth of the world's official reserves (Foreman-Peck 1983, 168–70). Short-term lending enabled the London money markets to operate extremely efficiently, as small rises in the Bank of England's interest rates quickly attracted funds to London, allowing the bank to operate with tiny gold reserves. Longer-term lending enabled UK investors to build up a massive portfolio of overseas assets. The exact size of this stock of assets is a matter of some debate, but it was approximately £4 billion in 1913 (the debate is surveyed in Feinstein 1990b). This was a prodigious sum, equivalent to almost one-third of the stock of net national wealth in 1913. No country has ever been so committed to overseas investment. Much of it went to transport projects (primarily railways and port facilities) in the empire (Pollard 1989, ch. 2; Edelstein 1994). The *personal* fortunes of City financiers depended heavily on investment in the empire, but economic historians have long debated the *social* costs and benefits of so much overseas investment.

Britain devoted a far bigger proportion of its national income to capital export than its competitors, while at the same time investing a much smaller proportion at home (Figure 3.1). The main point at issue is whether industrial and aggregate economic performance would have been better if capital had not been exported on this enormous scale. By 1913 levels of capital per worker in the UK were well below those in Germany and only one-third of those in the USA – though the estimates are subject to massive reappraisal (compare Maddison 1982, Table 3.5 and idem 1991, Table 3.9). Apologists for capital exports point out that home and overseas investment tended to move in inverse cycles, and total investment (home plus overseas) tended to be higher during the peaks of capital export than when demand was primarily from domestic sources (Edelstein 1982, 177–95). Furthermore, the outflow of funds was less than the inflow of interest and dividends from previous overseas investments, except in the surge of lending immediately before the First World War, and even here the net transfers abroad were very small. The 'burden' on the domestic economy of overseas investment was limited. Industry's demands for capital could be supplied by provincial stock markets and other sources, allowing the London money markets to concentrate primarily on providing funds for overseas borrowers (Edelstein 1994, 188–91). In addition, there were indirect benefits for manufacturing from overseas investment, notably cheap food and raw materials. It was also believed that capital exports boosted foreign demand for British manufactures, as peaks of foreign investment were also associated with booms in visible exports. But this argument is inconclusive and any possible short-run gains must be weighed against delays in restructuring the economy and modernising the export industries. The issues become extremely complex between 1900 and 1913. Capital exports surged during the

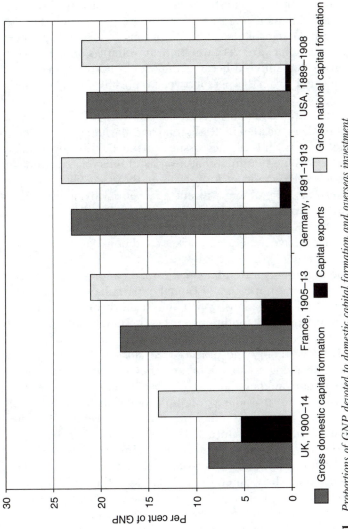

Figure 3.1 *Proportions of GNP devoted to domestic capital formation and overseas investment*
Sources: Kuznets 1966, 236–8; Mitchell 1980, 838; Milward and Saul 1977, 129.

Edwardian years, and exports of cotton textiles and coal also boomed. But Britain's share of world trade began to fall, albeit marginally (Table 1.1, columns 3 and 4, above), and import penetration of the domestic market for manufactures increased – though Chapter 1 argued that import penetration was not necessarily a sign of weakness. Economic historians have been able to bring forward very well-known examples of manufacturing firms that suffered because they could not raise the capital they needed. From this perspective, it is possible to argue that the City ignored industry because of its strong overseas bias and other institutional failings (see Kennedy 1987). Britain's investment bankers, headed by Rothschild and Baring, were geared to capital export and the new issues of the British government. Pollard (1989, 84) argued that a series of interrelated problems (Britain's role as pioneer industrialiser, the availability of empire markets, and the absence of entrepreneurial dynamism that a vigorous growth sector might have engendered) combined to deny the UK economy a substantial wave of domestic investment 'that might have generated market conditions for an altogether different rate of economic growth'.

The arguments for and against capital exports are ultimately unsatisfactory. Supporters of capital exports base their cases on neo-classical foundations, which almost inevitably are some way removed from real conditions in the late nineteenth- and early twentieth-century economy (for a forensic interrogation of the gap between theory and practice, see Pollard 1989, ch. 2). The critics take a longer run and broader perspective, but this almost by definition implies the sort of open counterfactual, such as Pollard's in the previous paragraph, that fails to inspire confidence. UK investment ratios were on the low side by international comparison before 1913, and in that sense the burden of foreign investment was unfortunate. However, low investment ratios continued into the inter-war years, when the attractions of capital export had diminished. Even with the scale of capital export and disappointing levels of domestic capital per worker, the best judgement of the aggregate performance of the UK economy to 1913 emphasises its continuing resilience and competitive strength. Pollard's (1989) assessment that the economy was fundamentally sound and capable of responding aggressively and rapidly to developments elsewhere is most persuasive. The

UK economy reached maturity in 1913: it had not become old, sick and weak.

The Turbulent Years, 1913–51

Signs of weakness multiplied after 1918. The current account was less strong in the 1920s, but still on balance in surplus (Figure 3.2). There are, however, strong suspicions that a balance of payments constraint, so familiar to students of the economy after 1945, emerged first during the inter-war years. There were two main problems. First, UK industrial competitiveness deteriorated enormously over the war period, especially in relation to the USA, and failed to return to pre-war levels (Greasley and Oxley 1996). At the same time, world demand for the products of UK export staple industries was growing slowly. Britain's share of world commodity trade deteriorated markedly (Figure 3.3). After 1918, the German threat to British manufacturers receded somewhat, but competitive pressures intensified on two fronts. US firms invaded markets for which world demand was expanding while lower-wage competitors, like Japan, attacked in Britain's traditional staple export markets. The flow of interest and dividends into the current account was hit by the fall, albeit temporary, of Britain's stock of overseas assets during wartime. London's creditor position also disappeared. During the First World War, Britain had borrowed from the USA to lend to allies, and the overhang of this debt after 1918 damaged City confidence. An even more serious blow came in March 1919 when Britain was forced to leave the gold standard rather than introduce deflation of the economy at a time of enormous domestic political uncertainty. This was the first indication that henceforward domestic and external stability might be less easy to balance than before 1913.

This priority to domestic conditions was, however, short-lived. Having negotiated the political crisis of 1918–19, ministers decided late in 1919, under pressure from officials at the Treasury and the Bank of England, to make restoration of the gold standard the central priority in economic policy. They began to deflate the economy to restore the price level towards parity with the dollar at the pre-war exchange rate. The impact on the

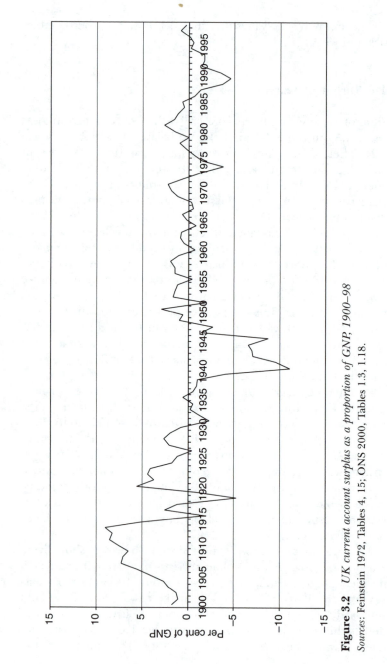

Figure 3.2 *UK current account surplus as a proportion of GNP, 1900–98*
Sources: Feinstein 1972, Tables 4, 15; ONS 2000, Tables 1.3, 1.18.

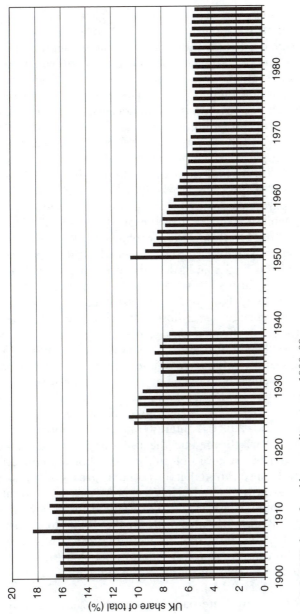

Figure 3.3 *UK share of world commodity exports, 1900–89*
Sources: Maddison 1991, Tables F2, F3, F4; idem 1995, Tables 12, 14.

domestic economy can be judged from the fall in output per head after 1920 that is evident in Figure 2.2 above. In this difficult domestic climate, British industry performed sluggishly in the early 1920s, and policy-makers attributed these difficulties to the failure of international trade to return to pre-war levels rather than to British (un)competitiveness. They sought, with the aid of New York, whose wartime rise had paralleled London's eclipse, to rebuild European and international finance (Kynaston 1999, 59–113). The central step was Britain's decision to return to gold at the pre-war parity, which promised to advance the interests of both manufacturing and the City. However, the reconstructed gold standard of the 1920s worked less well at accommodating balance of payments disturbances and was much more vulnerable to destabilising shocks than the pre-1914 version (Eichengreen 1990, 131–44). Britain's real problem, however, was lack of competitiveness with its seriously overvalued exchange rate. Britain restored the gold standard at the pre-war parity, whereas many of its competitors returned to gold after steep devaluation. There was anyway little real understanding of the need for appropriate exchange rates (those that reflected competitive realities) throughout the system. This disturbing competitive position was weakened further by political considerations. The Bank of England wanted to raise interest rates, but the government was extremely sensitive about interest rates when unemployment was already high, forcing the bank to devise new ways to manage the balance of payments (Moggridge 1972; Sayers 1976, vol. 1, 217–29). UK interest rates were kept just above those in New York throughout the 1920s and money was kept tight. This did not restore industry's international competitiveness, but probably ensured that the economy grew slowly enough to curb the growth of imports and keep the current account in balance. It would, however, be short-sighted to ascribe *all* the problems of British manufacturing in the 1920s to monetary influences. Britain's industrial recovery in 1921–7 was close to the international average and Britain was not alone among European nations in experiencing mass unemployment during the 1920s (Eichengreen 1990).

With frictions in international finance, slow growth in world trade and the great leap forward by US manufacturing, Britain badly needed to shift resources out of the export staple industries. However, this environment made finding a solution to 'overcommitment' difficult. Shipbuilding, coal and cotton shed labour, and many of the home market-based growth industries experienced reasonable expansion, but created insufficient jobs to absorb the unemployed and failed to achieve desired levels of efficiency. In 1935, Britain's comparative advantage remained in essentially the same export staple industries as in 1910 (Crafts and Thomas 1986). The pace of structural change was slow throughout the inter-war years. Inter-war governments might have attempted more radical policies. A more competitive exchange rate was essential, and might have been coupled with monetary expansion, as proposed by Keynes, Lloyd George and others, to accelerate the development of the domestic market. However, the monetary and fiscal policies needed to re-establish the UK's central place in the world economy ruled out expansionist domestic measures, and the political impetus behind alternative policies was limited (Garside 1990, ch. 12). The use of deflation to help restore the international financial system and London's place within it was presented, notably by Keynes, as the sacrifice of British industry on the altar of the gold standard. But, as noted above, recent work suggests that the loss of competitiveness occurred well before the return to gold in 1925. The impact of export weakness was cushioned by substantial favourable shifts in the terms of trade. Compared with 1913, a unit of UK exports paid for more than one-quarter more imports by the late 1920s than before the war, but as noted in Chapter 2 the benefits for living standards were balanced by the costs of higher unemployment.

The great crash of 1929–32 is one of the key events in twentieth-century international economic history. The value of world trade fell by 65 per cent and recovery remained elusive throughout the 1930s. The UK economy was much less badly hit than the international average, but the adverse impact was felt disproportionately by the export staples and the communities dependent upon them (Thomas 1994, 342–7). The precise causes of the crash remain uncertain, but structural weaknesses in the US economy, fragility of the international monetary system, and the increasing dependence of the pattern of international settlements on US lending all played a part (for a discussion, see Eichengreen 1992). The main result of the crash was the fragmentation of world trade and finance. The UK financial crisis broke in July 1931, eventually forcing sterling from the gold standard on 20 September 1931. Empire countries and those with close trading links to the UK also left gold and pegged their domestic currencies to sterling. From these inauspicious beginnings came the sterling area, an informal bloc whose members used sterling for international transactions (Howson, 1980; Cain and Hopkins 1993b, ch. 5). The sterling area had a profound impact on the direction of British trade for three decades. To make sterling attractive, its value had to be stabilised quickly: sterling became a 'managed' floating currency. The impact on British exports was disappointing. British trade was reoriented towards the sterling area in the 1930s but the 'visible' balance with the non-sterling area deteriorated (Table 3.1). Exports did not regain their 1929 value. In the 1930s, and uniquely in peacetime, the UK economy followed a more 'domestic' pattern of development. The share of both exports and imports in national income declined (Figures 3.4 and 3.5). In the 1930s the UK economy enjoyed a long, strong recovery, which compared favourably with that of most competitors (Figures 2.1 and 2.2 above). The pace of recovery was not sufficient, however, to take up into employment all those without work (see Chapter 5).

After the failure of deflation and market-led restructuring in the 1920s, governments of the 1930s intervened rather more, albeit reluctantly. They extended protection by a general tariff in 1931–2 and imposed quotas on imports, especially of foodstuffs. The tariff helped to consolidate Britain's trade within the sterling area and almost certainly provided some short-run security for employment and industry. However, total employment in the newly protected industries continued to contract (in essence, the protection of the home market did not counterbalance the loss of exports). There have been suggestions that any gains in employment were gradually eroded by inefficiencies resulting from industrial collusion behind the tariff (Broadberry and Crafts 1990; but see Kitson and Solomou 1990). There is certainly no evidence of any UK industry using the tariff to modernise and regain overseas markets. In both motor cars and steel, the hopes of using the tariff to restructure the industry came to nought (Foreman-Peck et al. 1995, 76–8; Tolliday 1987). Even with this domestic reorientation of the economy, policy-makers

Table 3.1 *Britain's trade patterns, 1929 and 1937*

	Proportion of exports to: (%)	Proportion of imports from: (%)	Trade balance with: (£m)	Trade balance as a % of exports to: (%)
1929				
European sterling area	5.0	10.5	−79.4	−215.8
Argentina	4.0	7.4	−52.8	−181.6
British empire	39.7	26.4	−4.5	−1.6
Rest of the sterling area	2.9	2.6	−8.0	−42.9
Total sterling area	51.6	46.9	−144.8	−38.5
Non-sterling trade	48.4	53.1	−237.0	−67.1
Total trade	100 (£729.4 m)	100 (£1111.1 m)	−381.8	−52.4
1937				
European sterling area	9.5	11.0	−55.0	−110.7
Argentina	3.8	6.2	−39.5	−196.9
British empire	43.0	32.0	−80.9	−36.1
Rest of the sterling area	2.8	2.3	−7.6	−52.4
Total sterling area	59.1	51.6	−182.9	−59.3
Non-sterling trade	40.9	48.4	−248.4	−116.8
Total trade	100 (£521.3 m)	100 (£952.7 m)	−431.3	−82.7

Source: adapted from Cain and Hopkins 1993b, Table 5.1.

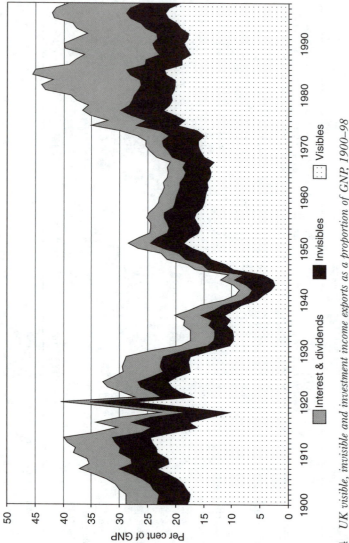

Figure 3.4 *UK visible, invisible and investment income exports as a proportion of GNP, 1900–98*

Sources: Feinstein 1972, Tables 1.4,15; ONS 2000, Tables 1.2, 1.18.

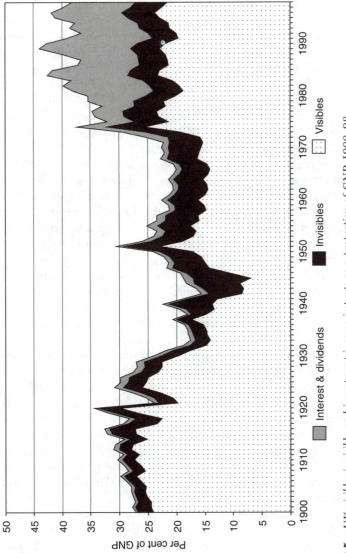

Figure 3.5 *UK visible, invisible and investment income imports as a proportion of GNP, 1900–98*

Sources: as Figure 3.4.

trod carefully in the 1930s for fear of losing the confidence of overseas holders of sterling. The Treasury brought down interest rates, in part to encourage investment, but remained totally opposed to deficit-financing for reasons discussed in Chapter 6. During the 1930s, the British economy's exposure to the forces of international competition was much reduced, but the pace of industrial restructuring continued to disappoint. The government finally introduced an expansionary monetary policy in the later 1930s to accelerate rearmament for defence, and to some extent its reasons for caution were justified. Domestic expansion put pressure on the balance of payments, and Britain's external position weakened substantially (Figure 3.2).

The signs of external weakness in the later 1930s were doubly disconcerting to the Treasury, since Britain's stock of overseas assets was viewed as a major strategic resource, 'the fourth arm of defence', to finance strategic imports in the event of international conflict. Indeed, they were depleted very quickly during the early phase of the Second World War, especially after the German military successes in north-west Europe in 1940. By the end of that year, not only had virtually all the marketable securities been sold, often very cheaply, but much of the gold reserve had also been exhausted (Sayers 1955, ch. 12). The need to conserve 'hard' currency (US and Canadian dollars) during 1939–40 led to the imposition of tough foreign exchange controls for the whole sterling area. Wartime imports from the sterling area were financed by the creation of sterling balances, in effect deposits in accounts at the Bank of England for sterling area countries. After March 1941, imports from the USA were financed by the Lend-Lease system, under which Britain was supplied with massive amounts of military and strategic aid for the duration of the war. The system was, however, so managed by the US Treasury to ensure that the UK emerged from the war with extremely low international reserves and in effect bankrupt. Thus Britain was able to finance a war effort far beyond its current capacity to pay, but at the end of the war the UK gold and dollar reserves stood at approximately £600 million with external liabilities at least six times as great (Sayers 1955, 496–7). The Second World War also had a more damaging impact on the level of current exports than the First (Figures 3.2 and 3.4). The balance sheet for British industry during wartime also contained strongly positive entries. Much of the metals and engineering industry (and, indeed, agriculture) experienced substantial gains from wartime expansion, modernisation and more intensive use of scientific knowledge. By contrast, many of the older industries, both home market-based and export-oriented, suffered from contraction, disinvestment, and loss of skills and expertise (Pollard 1992a, 162–71). Wartime pressures helped to accelerate the pace of structural change and, by bringing government into closer day-to-day relationship with industry, helped provide the experience to nurture new industries during reconversion. The impact of wartime economic policy on British industry is, however, a very contentious topic and will be examined more fully in later chapters.

These structural changes were important because after the war British industry needed to regain its international competitiveness quickly. During the war Britain had committed itself to the US vision of a liberal postwar international order. International finance was to be conducted on the basis of freely convertible currencies, pegged to the dollar, which was in turn pegged to gold. This system, agreed at the Bretton Woods conference in 1944, envisaged short-run borrowing from a new International Monetary Fund (IMF) by countries in short-term current account difficulties and more drastic measures, notably devaluation, for those with deeper external problems. At the same time, Britain was working to end protectionism by phased and co-ordinated reductions in tariffs and quotas. In short, Britain was committed to remove the innovations in policy that had helped ease the potentially dire balance of payments difficulties of the 1930s. Exports of goods and services were urgently needed when war ended. In fact, Britain's postwar export performance was good. The current account came back into surplus more quickly than expected (Figure 3.2). In 1950, the UK also captured a higher share of world commodity exports than had been achieved since 1925, with especially strong performance in manufacturing (Figure 3.3; Table 3.2). But the current account with the dollar area remained weak (Cairncross 1985, 201–4). After the war, North America was almost the sole source of supply for the food, raw materials and capital goods that Europe craved. The US government made dollars available at the end of the war to those countries willing to subscribe to its vision of a multilateral

Table 3.2   *Shares of 'world' manufactured exports, 1900–98 (%)*

	1900	1913	1929	1937	1950	1973	1990	1998
UK	35.5	32.0	23.6	22.0	26.5	9.4	8.8	8.8
France	15.4	12.8	11.5	6.1	10.3	9.9	10.1	9.1
Germany	23.9	28.1	21.6	22.9	7.5	22.9	21.0	18.5
USA	12.5	13.8	21.5	20.2	28.7	16.6	17.0	21.9
Japan	1.6	2.4	4.1	7.3	3.7	13.2	16.1	14.1
Others	11.1	10.9	17.7	21.5	23.3	28	27	27.6

Percentages are based on countries shown in the table rather than 'world' exports.
'Others' are Belgium, Canada, Netherlands, Italy, Sweden.
Figures for Germany refer to West Germany for 1950–90.
Sources: Maizels 1963, Table 8.1; OECD, *Monthly Statistics of Foreign Trade*, various issues.

international order. But these dollars were quickly exhausted as European countries hastened industrial reconstruction (Milward 1984). Despite further US assistance to Europe through Marshall Aid and US overseas defence expenditure, the dollar shortage continued and the US government was forced, albeit reluctantly, to allow European countries to discriminate against the dollar in trade. The sterling area had been a blatantly discriminatory system against the dollar since its inception in 1931 and a prime target for US criticism. In the context of the emerging Cold War, however, the US government saw from the late 1940s virtues in preserving the sterling area on condition that the UK modernised its empire and strengthened its balance of payments, preferably by closer economic ties to Europe (Louis 1985). Britain took the opportunity to strengthen its already substantial quantitative controls against dollar imports, and recovery in the aggregate balance of payments proceeded against a background of weakness in trade with the dollar area.

Ministers urged British industry to export more to North America and Europe, but British managers were pessimistic about their long-run ability to hold many of these markets and looked instead to the protected markets at home and in the sterling area. Whitehall shared part of this business vision. Senior Treasury and Bank of England officials wanted sterling to regain its position as a world trading and reserve currency, and saw in the development of the sterling area a stepping stone towards its re-emergence as an internationally convertible currency. British opinion generally regarded Europe as an area of continuing economic weakness (Cairncross 1985, ch. 10). In the establishment view, Britain could simultaneously head the Commonwealth, lead Europe in economic and political affairs, and remain a great power and potential mediator between the USA and the USSR, albeit from within the US camp (Morgan 1984, 188–284). From this complex of forces emerged a foreign economic policy that was ultimately designed to preserve the Anglo-US 'special relationship' (to ensure continuing access to dollar aid) while demonstrating Britain's capacity for independent decision-making. Dollar-saving import quotas were retained, and exports to North America were vigorously encouraged. Ministers ultimately turned their backs on 'supra-national' institutions in Europe, though the UK became a full member of the European Payments Union (EPU), which dismantled bilateral currency restrictions within Europe, and led the Organisation of European Economic Co-operation (OEEC) trade liberalisation programme (Milward 1984, 335–420). At the same time, capital exports resumed to speed the development of sterling area countries, especially those with the potential to produce dollar-earning or dollar-saving commodities (Cain and Hopkins 1993b, 278–80). Insofar as there was a strategic picture, it was to restore sterling and the export earning capacity of the City while affording British industry the stable markets of the sterling area in which to regroup and modernise.

The Golden Age and After: Britain in the World Economy, 1951–99

Between the end of the Korean War and the commodity price explosion of the early 1970s, the world economy enjoyed a golden age of unparalleled prosperity. Trade, especially between industrial nations, grew faster than incomes, allowing increased specialisation, economies of scale and higher investment in new production techniques. Economists have developed models in which trade performance is the major determinant of the national growth rate, and economic historians have attributed much of the success of the golden age to the liberalisation of trade and payments (Foreman-Peck 1983). More recent work has, however, begun to suggest possible modifications to key aspects of this picture. The role of the IMF and the General Agreement on Tariffs and Trade (GATT) has undoubtedly been exaggerated. Liberalisation proceeded regionally before being extended to a global scale. The EPU and the OEEC trade liberal-isation programme were much more important to European recovery before 1958 than the IMF or GATT. Furthermore, the relationship between trade and growth is undoubtedly more complex than has commonly been supposed. Most of the larger European economies grew during the 1950s by focusing on domestic rather than export markets, so that the causal relation-ship ran primarily from growth to trade (Irwin 1995). For Brit-ain, however, growth of both output and exports appeared disappointing.

After the impressive recovery of the external sector to 1951, the share of all categories of exports in national income sagged until the later 1960s (Figure 3.4). UK exports certainly grew more slowly during the golden age than those of other Organisa-tion for Economic Co-operation and Development (OECD) countries. As a result, Britain's share of commodity exports and manufactured exports fell pretty consistently from 1950 to 1973 (Figure 3.3; Table 3.2). The fall in 'visible' export shares was accompanied by growing import penetration of the domestic market; the balance of trade in manufactures, traditionally con-sidered an area of strength in the current account, also con-tracted consistently between 1950 and 1989 (Figure 3.6). The UK share of world trade in services also fell during the golden age, but less steeply and without the serious import penetration that occurred in manufacturing. There have been attempts to 'explain away' what appears to be weak competitive performance in manufacturing, but they carry little conviction. Rowthorn and Wells (1987) argued that the decline in the manufacturing trade balance was caused by autonomous changes elsewhere in the current account. They suggest that in the early 1950s the UK paid for essential imports of foods and raw materials by a big surplus in manufacturing trade. However, subsequent changes outside the manufacturing balance (greater agricultural self-sufficiency, a growing surplus on invisible trade and the devel-opment of raw materials exports, notably North Sea oil and gas)

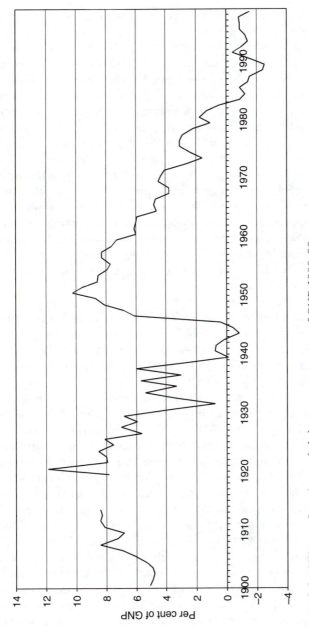

Figure 3.6 *UK manufacturing trade balance as a percentage of GNP, 1900–98*
Sources: ONS 2000, Table 1.3; LCES 1967, Tables K, L; *Annual Abstract of Statistics*, various issues.

implied less need for a manufacturing surplus. But there is no reason why the current account should balance and there were very sound arguments for a continuing current surplus in order to strengthen the reserves. It has also been suggested that the slow growth of exports was caused, at least in the 1950s, by problems in the market structure of UK export demand. Having at long last broken free from overcommitment to products for which world demand was growing slowly, the British economy proceeded to overcommit to the slowly growing markets of the sterling area. It used to be assumed that sterling area markets were 'soft', in that competition was effectively excluded, allowing UK exporters to produce inferior goods at unattractive prices. However, it is now generally accepted that neither argument is convincing (Schenk 1994, 78–87). British manufacturers were losing overseas markets, both inside and outside the sterling area, at a steady pace, but there are disagreements about whether the main causal link ran from poor growth to weak competitive performance or vice versa.

The strongest case for a balance of payments constraint on growth comes in the form of 'Thirlwall's law', which states that 'if balance of payments equilibrium must be maintained, a country's long-run growth rate will be determined by the ratio of growth of exports to its income elasticity of demand for imports' (McCombie and Thirlwall 1994, 234). The argument hinges on calculations of income elasticities of demand for exports and imports, or, on the one hand, the amount of additional UK exports that will flow from a given rise in world incomes and, on the other, the rise of imports from a given rise in UK incomes. It is easy to maintain the pegged exchange rates of the Bretton Woods system if these ratios are similar. However, many hold that whereas the UK import elasticity was similar to that of other countries, the export elasticity was extremely *low* (ibid., 239–43). In order to maintain the current account in balance, policy-makers had to constrain the growth rate of UK incomes, to ensure that imports grew at roughly the same pace as exports. As noted above, the high real exchange rate faced by industry and the unfortunate product mix of UK exports may well have triggered such a mechanism in the inter-war years, but for the postwar period the calculations are controversial. Using different assumptions, the elasticity of demand for UK exports appears at the *upper* end of developed country experience (see Crafts 1991b, 269–70). Despite the doctrinal differences between the Keynesian proponents and neo-classical opponents of the balance of payments constraint, there is common ground on practical points. Both see supply-side weaknesses, which are reflected in poor product quality, as the fundamental problem and argue that devaluation can and did provide at best limited relief.

It is also likely that in the 1950s the domestic economy was overburdened by the cost of the UK's foreign economic policy. The attempt to demonstrate British independence and world power status strained the balance of payments, notably during rearmament for the Korean War (Cairncross 1985, ch. 8). Playing a world role required both increasingly burdensome military and diplomatic expenditure overseas and a disproportionately high commitment of domestic resources to defence. The economic development of the sterling area implied substantial capital exports, but the area did not become the obliging source of demand for UK manufactures and supply of dollar earnings that had been hoped (Schenk 1994, 80–7). The net effect of all this activity was an adverse capital account, inadequate rebuilding of the foreign currency reserves and no obvious reduction in the size of the sterling balances. The US government appreciated the role that sterling could play in the expanding world economy, first as an aid in coping with the shortage of dollars and subsequently as a shield as the dollar experienced its own balance of payments weaknesses. The foreign exchange markets took a less strategic view. Their perspective was dominated by the continuing imbalance between UK international assets and liabilities and the willingness of British governments to contemplate devaluation. The reserves fluctuated between $2 and $3 billion in 1950–70, and the sterling balances showed no real reduction from 1945 to 1958, when they totalled approximately $9.3 billion, and then rose steadily by a further 50 per cent during the 1960s (Cmnd 827 1959, Table 29). Although the sterling balances were held by countries with strong and long-established trading ties with the UK, the markets saw only a mass of volatile and dangerous debt and consistently doubted the ability of British governments to maintain the pegged exchange rates of the Bretton Woods system (Schenk 1994, 33–5). Sterling was devalued in 1949, in effect as part of a general realignment against the dollar to ease the world dollar shortage, but in less than 30 months there were plans for a further move, this time to a floating (downwards) rate (Cairncross 1985). The markets clearly got wind of the plans and drew firm conclusions about sterling's long-run trajectory. Every subsequent hint of external weakness produced bouts of market speculation against sterling, even when the current account was strong. In this climate, the Bank of England's policy of pressing for rapid progress towards convertibility and increasing the exposure of sterling to currency markets was probably ill-judged. The bank considered that the risks were justified. Britain needed exports and the City's invisible earnings potential was enormous.

To reassure the markets governments borrowed from other central banks and the IMF and periodically also reoriented domestic policy to support sterling. This pattern of 'stop-go' became increasingly the focus of widespread criticism of the policy regime, because it appeared to sacrifice long-run domestic growth to short-run external pressures. Keynesian economists argued that a 'stop' in the policy cycle (usually effected by a rise in interest rates or other measures to inhibit investment) left UK firms increasingly uncompetitive. Imports took a bigger share of the domestic market in each successive policy cycle as import penetration increased by a 'ratchet' effect (Alford 1988, 42–6). Again, these arguments are extremely controversial. Whiting (1976) demonstrated that Britain's fluctuations were less acute than those in many advanced countries, but UK cycles were characteristically failures to meet demand, encouraging imports, rather than the oversupply crises more typical of Germany and Japan. Stop-go restrictions clearly resulted in 'patching' or 'defensive' investment (Chick 1998, 165). It would, however, be unrealistic to ascribe all or most of the weakness in the UK balance of payments to stop-go. For much of industry the overriding problems were on non-price, rather than price, competitiveness: delivery times were long; product quality disappointing; after-sales back-up weak; new product development unsatisfactory (Stout 1976). Perhaps for this reason, devaluation proved to be a much less effective weapon than the designers of the Bretton Woods system had imagined. The devaluation of 1949 caused a lasting improvement in trade with the dollar area but had much less general impact (Cairncross and Eichengreen

1983). The devaluation of 1967 had a disappointing and delayed impact on import and export volumes, and clearly did as much to accelerate domestic inflation as to improve competitive performance.

Indeed, the common view of British trade and payments during the golden age is built upon insecure foundations. That picture has two main elements: that current account performance was weak and that manufacturing export performance was little short of dire. The most recent current account figures, however, show an underlying current account surplus even during the 1960s, though the size of the balancing item in the accounts undermines any firm conclusions. Although manufacturing lost markets and produced goods of poor quality, Britain's share of commodity exports in GDP compares reasonably with those of European economies of similar size and stage of development (Figure 3.7). In 1973, Britain held approximately the same share of world manufactured exports as France, a country that had pursued increased market share aggressively by devaluation throughout the golden age (Table 1.1 above). Much has been made of import penetration, but as noted in Chapter 1, import penetration by itself signifies very little. Export markets were undoubtedly lost, in both the sterling area and continental Europe, by firms that attempted to supply inferior products. But there were also under-appreciated and substantial achievements in the export trade during the golden age. UK exports to the tough markets of North America grew respectably during the 1950s. In 1957–9 UK dollar exports were worth roughly two-thirds of those of the EEC 'six' combined, with the motor manufacturers doing particularly well (Black 1962, Table 10). The pattern of Britain's exports was transformed during the golden age towards rapidly growing sectors of the European market in which UK firms had traditionally only peripheral suppliers (Table 3.3). Britain's export performance in the golden age was weak and left considerable scope for improvement, but British exporters do not deserve the very heavy criticism they received at the time and have had to suffer since. In contrast with the 1930s, Britain was now able to combine full employment and current account equilibrium. There were obvious strategic mistakes, but the attempt to pare back the world role, for example, began in the mid-1950s even before the existence of relative

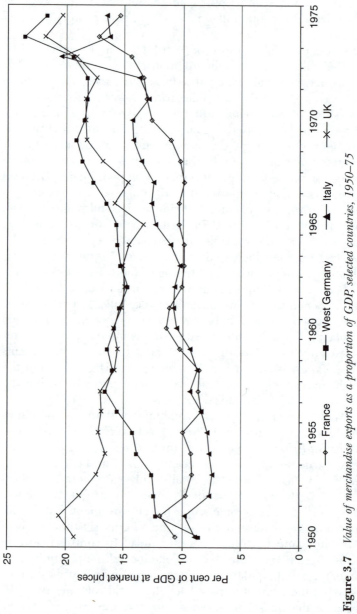

Figure 3.7 *Value of merchandise exports as a proportion of GDP, selected countries, 1950–75*

Source: Mitchell 1992, Tables E1, J1.

Table 3.3 The pattern of British trade, 1938–97

	Percentage of total imports by value from:					Percentage of total exports by value to:				
	North America	Western Europe	(EEC)	Sterling area	Rest of world	North America	Western Europe	(EEC)	Sterling area	Rest of world
1938	21.7	24.0		31.1	23.1	9.3	23.4		44.9	22.4
1946	33.1	14.9		32.8	19.2	7.5	28.3		45.3	19.0
1950	15.0	25.1	(10.7)	38.0	25.9	11.0	28.3	(9.7)	47.8	12.9
1960	20.7	29.2	(14.6)	33.2	16.9	15.3	29.0	(14.6)	40.2	15.6
1970	20.5	37.7	(20.2)	25.3	16.2	15.3	41.1	(21.7)	27.2	16.0
1980	15.0	55.9	(41.3)	11.0	18.0	11.3	57.6	(43.4)	14.4	16.6
1990	13.3	64.8	(52.3)	6.9	15.0	14.4	61.7	(53.0)	9.7	14.2
1997	14.8	59.4	(53.4)	11.9	13.9	13.9	60.1	(55.5)	13.4	12.6

The 1950 EEC entry is for the six signatories of the Treaty of Rome in 1957.
The sterling area is an entirely artificial construct for table entries after 1970. The 1970 *AAS* listed current members of the area. Subsequent table entries indicate the sum of the shares of UK trade held by these countries, where they can be separately identified.
Source: Annual Abstract of Statistics, various issues.

decline had properly registered on the national consciousness (Cain and Hopkins 1993b, 280–91).

Resolving Britain's problems was made more difficult by growing signs of instability in the Bretton Woods system. Shortage of liquidity, particularly of dollars, was overcome in the 1950s by continuing use of sterling and a growing US current account deficit, but the corollary of the US deficit was a continuing current account surplus in Germany and Italy. Surplus countries resisted pressure to revalue their currencies when the main deficit country refused to cut back its imports. These imbalances became potentially destabilising to the system as the volume of private capital movement, especially on short term, increased substantially in the 1960s. US banks moved offshore to escape domestic banking restrictions and created the Euro-currency markets. The growing balances of multinational corporations added to the flow of volatile funds. Speculative activity forced devaluations during the late 1960s (notably sterling and the French franc) and left the US dollar highly exposed. These tensions occurred against a backdrop of rising inflation as developed economies moved into synchronised boom for the first time since the Korean War. Raw material shortages drove up prices, notably that of oil, which quadrupled in 1973. (This episode is popularly known as OPEC1, after the Organisation of Petroleum Exporting Countries, which took the decisions to raise oil prices.) This huge shift in the terms of trade accelerated inflation in the developed countries and created huge current account deficits. The OPEC surpluses increased the instability of the international financial system still further. In the early 1970s the dollar was devalued twice, ending the Bretton Woods system. Britain abandoned pegged exchange rates rather earlier than most. In June 1972, the Heath government allowed sterling to float as part of a growth policy. It was widely believed that floating would end the balance of payments constraint and allow government to concentrate on accelerating growth. The government also made the third UK application to join the Common Market (similar requests having been vetoed by France in 1963 and 1967). Part of the British political elite believed that the European Community (formed by merger of three separate European 'communities' in 1965) could provide more effective answers to its strategic political and economic problems. The EC was known to have strong

US support and membership appeared necessary to reinforce the 'special relationship'. Europe also offered greater international influence than the waning Commonwealth. As noted above, British trade had begun to shift towards the rapidly growing markets of Europe in the 1950s, and it was now recognised that the larger, more competitive European markets offered greater potential than the sterling area for output and productivity growth. Unfortunately, nothing worked as anticipated.

The predicted benefits of a floating exchange rate did not materialise. Supporters of floating rates had assumed that international trade would be dominated by 'visible' items, but the huge flows of volatile capital overwhelmed the visible trade account and quickly became the major determinant of short-term exchange rate movements. Exchange rates frequently 'overshot' the levels needed to balance current accounts. Far from disappearing as predicted, current surpluses and deficits became larger, despite substantial currency realignments: countries needed bigger reserves to cope with larger deficits. These problems were particularly acute for the UK because London handled a significant amount of this highly volatile trade in currencies and short-term assets. The decision to float the currency in 1972 and the steep fall in its value during 1975–6 ended the use of sterling as a world currency and the sterling area, but London's ability to shift into Euro-dollar business improved its position in the market for international financial services (Strange 1986). The relative growth of 'invisible' exports and 'interest and dividend' income since the mid-1970s reveals some of the impact on the balance of payments (Figures 3.4 and 3.5). To effect and consolidate these developments, there were substantial reforms in the regulations and institutions. In the 1980s, the removal of all exchange controls and a government-enforced restructuring of London's money markets attracted substantial inflows of foreign capital and expertise into London. The other side of the coin was the increased volatility of funds in City markets and thus wild fluctuations in the exchange rate. The corollary of such volatility was a perceived diminution (almost the disappearance) of the scope for an independent national macroeconomic policy (Tomlinson 1990, 335). The best example remains the collapse of sterling in 1976, when the sizeable flow of OPEC surpluses into London in 1974 was reversed in 1975–6 as markets became concerned about aspects of UK domestic policy. The markets virtually compelled the UK government to borrow from the IMF and accept unpleasant constraints on domestic policy (Burk and Cairncross 1992, 85). Equally substantial gyrations of the exchange rate occurred throughout the 1980s, and underlined the enormous potential costs of unanticipated inflationary pressures (if sterling's value fell rapidly, as it did during 1984–5) or major losses of competitive strength (as when sterling rose in 1979–81). Manufacturing industry found it much more difficult than financial services to accommodate these costs and demanded more stable exchange rates.

EC members reached similar decisions, and from 1979 they increasingly pegged their currencies to the Deutschmark (DM). British governments did not openly participate in this exchange rate mechanism (ERM), but Treasury disenchantment with floating rates led to unofficial pegging (or 'shadowing the DM') from 1987. The publication of the Delors report on EC economic and monetary union took everything a stage further by setting a timetable for the creation of a single currency for Europe. UK governments had persistent difficulties with the sort of supranational institutions proposed by Delors, but the advantages of greater exchange rate stability persuaded the government to enter the ERM in October 1990. The central exchange rate with the DM was, however, 5–6 per cent higher than the earlier 'shadow' rate and did not reflect fundamental relative competitive strengths. The high interest rates needed to defend sterling's overvaluation as interest rates in the core country (Germany) were rising caused a long and deep recession in Britain and eventually a humiliating exit from the ERM after less than two years. At the time, British ministers claimed that the ERM had internal contradictions, but this did not prevent the steady progress of most other members of the ERM to the creation of the single currency. The single currency is certainly not a riskless enterprise: the ability of the Euro to supply external stability remains unproven; but the UK may be once again a late arrival at the European ball.

The growth potential for UK industry of the larger, more competitive European markets was also difficult to realise. Attempts to measure the impact of the Common Market on member states and in particular on Britain have been dogged by substantial technical problems and offer widely varying results. It is difficult to measure the impact of Britain's membership of the European Community because Britain's trade was growing so strongly with member countries before accession (Table 3.3). Britain's trade patterns clearly shifted decisively towards EC countries, but the effects were somewhat disappointing. The UK share of Europe's imports rose and its share of exports fell after 1970, and a substantial deficit in manufacturing trade with the EC opened after 1975 (Cutler et al. 1989). It is impossible to avoid the conclusion that parts of UK industry failed to respond to competitive forces as hoped. Cutler and colleagues argued that the liberal trade regime within the EC encouraged centripetal tendencies, with manufacturing capacity and employment effectively transferred to Germany, particularly from countries with a lower 'national capacity to organise production' (among which they included the UK). Even the Conservative government of the 1990s, which was not backward in proclaiming successes for market competition, was forced to admit that UK manufacturing had failed to match the competitive strength of its major rivals (Cmnd 2563 1994, 13).

These problems in manufacturing trade did not cause major balance of payments weakness, at least in the short run, because increasing flows of North Sea oil and gas balanced the accounts. The UK recorded an export surplus in oil as a second decisive intervention by OPEC doubled oil prices again in 1978–9 (now commonly termed OPEC2). The inflow of foreign funds to develop the oil and gas fields also helped sustain capital formation at a time when the incentives to invest in home manufacturing were hardly compelling. The effects of the North Sea on the domestic economy were huge: output rose from nothing in 1975 to the equivalent of 7 per cent of GDP in 1984 (Johnson 1991, 268). The impact on the current account was equally remarkable: the oil balance turned from a deficit of £3.9 billion to a surplus of £8.1 billion between 1976 and 1985, but halved in 1985–6 and again in 1988–9. The sharp swing into surplus in oil coincided in 1979–80 with large rises in interest rates to contain the growth of the money supply (see Chapter 6), producing a substantial rise in the exchange rate and fears that the already weak manufacturing sector might be damaged beyond repair. However, OPEC1 and OPEC2 not only made North Sea oil commercially viable, but also stimulated the search for both energy-efficient technologies and non-OPEC sources of oil supply around the globe. Thus, the price of oil became highly unstable, OPEC's control over world oil supply was weakened, but the gains to the UK current account diminished. Both the pessimistic estimates of the damage to manufacturing and the optimistic calculations of the oil 'bonanza' proved to be wide of the mark. The flow of oil undoubtedly provided substantial support for the balance of payments at the margin during the early 1980s, but it left the basic features of manufacturing production and trade substantially unaltered.

Perhaps the most distinctive development of the last quarter of the twentieth century was the increasing globalisation of production. Indeed, among the most paradoxical developments in the late twentieth century was the increasing flow of foreign direct investment into the UK economy at the same time as British multinational enterprises were recording remarkable success overseas. British firms were dominant in multinational activity down to the Second World War, after which balance of payments difficulties reduced the scale of foreign direct investment overseas until the later 1970s (for a discussion of multinational enterprise, see Jeremy 1998, ch. 7, and the literature cited therein). The dominant form of British multinational company before 1913 was the 'free standing company', which had a London head office but carried out its operations overseas in a wide range of activities from agriculture, mineral extraction, manufacturing, the utilities, transport and a host of tertiary activities. Between the wars, the free-standing company declined in relative importance – with a number transforming themselves into major companies – and the number of multinational companies in manufacturing and financial services increased. The inter-war years also saw a significant entry by US manufacturers into the UK to exploit technological and organisational advantages. This was but one aspect of a worldwide effort by US firms to find new markets behind the rising tariff barriers of the 1920s and 1930s. After 1945, and especially after Britain's entry into the European Community, the flow of foreign direct investment into the UK accelerated, and there is little doubt that foreign-owned firms were among the most efficient in the UK. European and Far Eastern companies competed with US multinationals to enter the UK from the 1970s, with oil exploration, engineering, chemicals and electronics being among the most prominent sectors, though the importance of less glamorous activities such as food processing and clothing should not be underestimated. These firms often succeeded in sectors where UK domestic production had failed spectacularly (cars and consumer electronics, for example) by exploiting technological and organisational advantages, though there were also considerable locational advantages in the form of green-field sites, purpose-built factories and generous public subsidies. This may indicate a comparative failure of British managers in these industries, but there was a corresponding and simultaneous expansion of the overseas activities of British multinationals. Indeed, British multinationals tended to switch their focus from the richer Commonwealth and sterling area countries to Europe and North America in the postwar years. They too were able to exploit advantages bestowed by access to the British capital market (as many British firms expanded overseas by acquisition and merger), but British managers were also able to exploit technical and organisational skills that had been honed in British markets. The British economy was certainly not immune to the processes of competition, liberalisation and globalisation at the end of the twentieth century, but it would be misleading to believe that Britain was only on the receiving end of the internationalisation of production. The successes of British multinationals should caution further against the idea of systemic weakness in British manufacturing.

Conclusion

There were three acts in the drama of Britain's changing role in the international economy during the twentieth century. The first covers the first three decades and tells the story of more or less complete integration in the system. Britain lost its leadership in manufacturing production and trade at the start of the play, but retained competitive advantages in sufficient industrial sectors and in international financial services to retain a strong position in the evolving international economy. It needed to rebalance and develop more physical capital- and human capital-intensive sectors of production, but the First World War complicated the process by smashing the sophisticated system of trade and payments and creating conditions in which British industrial export prices moved wildly out of line with those of its main competitors. Rebuilding the international financial system and restoring British industrial competitiveness ultimately failed.

In the second act, also lasting 25–35 years, the action revolved around partial withdrawal from a disintegrating international economic and financial system. Protective devices were created and strengthened, restructuring occurred and the UK economy prepared for reintegration into the world economy. There were two disappointments during this phase. The first concerns the scale and pace of structural change. Although the domestic economy was rebalanced, this was due more to *force majeure* than to conscious decision. The Second World War completed structural shifts that had made only inadequate progress under the regimes of market forces in the 1920s and business collusion in the 1930s. Perhaps as a result, the British economy was insufficiently modernised – the second major disappointment of this phase of inward-focused development. New import-replacing and export industries were created or enormously expanded (pharmaceuticals, oil refining, electrical engineering, for example), but too many established industries interpreted this withdrawal from the world economy as semi-permanent rather than as a temporary breathing space. The extent to which employers, governments and labour unions should take the blame for this will be discussed in the next three chapters. This act, it will be noticed, closes in the period that spans the mid-1950s to the mid-1960s. The strengthening of the sterling area after 1945 and the reorientation of Britain's trade towards the Commonwealth were tactically and strategically rational, given the information available at the time.

It did not take long, however, for the limitations to become apparent and for British producers to shift their focus towards the faster-growing markets of Europe. In this third act of full commitment and exposure to an increasingly integrated global economy, performance was at first better than is normally allowed. The UK is often described as having a chronic payments deficit during the golden age when in fact the current account surplus was substantial. By 1973, British trade had shifted decisively towards the European market and Britain's share of world manufactured trade in the early 1970s compared well with that of France. The real problems emerged after 1973, and reflect the interaction of two distinct forces. The first is international competition and specialisation, which resulted in the contraction of the relative size of the manufacturing sector and the disappearance of Britain's visible trade surplus. Almost every European economy witnessed similar developments, with the major exception of Germany, and even the German position was less powerful than is commonly imagined, as will be explained in the next chapter. The second force was the enormous short-run fluctuation in the value of oil exports, and the implication for the exchange rate and the competitiveness of British enterprise. The gyrations of the exchange rate between 1975 and 1995 can only have handicapped British producers in their quest for a niche in the increasingly competitive and specialised international economy. The partial insulation of multinational enterprise, both British-owned and foreign companies operating in the UK, from the full impact of these forces may explain why British multinationals prospered as foreign direct investment into the UK increased. Again, this is a relatively intricate picture of the erosion of British economic power rather than a simple story of economic failure.

This three-act play of weakening competitive performance interacted in complex ways with Britain's slow loss of international prestige and power. Britain remained a world power, albeit with steadily diminishing status, for the first half of the century, but by the mid-1950s the costs were simply beyond the capacity of the domestic economy. The reappraisal of Britain's world role may have been too long delayed, but meant that final withdrawal was decisive. The end of the world role for the Royal Navy, the pound sterling and the Commonwealth/imperial economic bloc was telescoped into a short, though relatively painless, sequence of major decisions. In retrospect, the pity is that the process did not begin in 1945.

4 Industry, Entrepreneurs and Managers

The two previous chapters have tried to establish three basic points about British economic performance in the twentieth century. First, the historiography has been obsessed with the theme of decline, and deeply entrenched supply-side deficiencies in the manufacturing sector have been presented as the main source of weakness. Second, recent long-run and comparative research on manufacturing performance has undermined the idea that Britain's living standards were overtaken because of British manufacturing failure. There is evidence of weakness since the late nineteenth century, but problems seem to have been addressed sooner or later and signs of the progressive deterioration of British manufacturing are conspicuously absent. Finally, there are some grounds for arguing that British manufacturing trade performance has been rather harshly judged, especially during the golden age. This is not to claim that from 1900 the British economy was dynamic, powerful and successful but rather to try to establish a more balanced framework for judging economic performance. The first step in a more balanced assessment must be to establish the patterns of sectoral and industrial change and the main outlines of comparative performance. This foundation will serve the discussion of this chapter and those that follow. Chapters 4–6 will each focus on one dimension of the criticism of British performance. The present discussion is primarily concerned with questions of the qualities of British entrepreneurs, and in particular their levels of technological sophistication and their openness to new ideas.

The Pattern of Industrial Change

Economists conventionally divide industry (the production of goods and services for financial gain) into primary, secondary and tertiary sectors. The primary sector is concerned with growing or extracting natural products, and includes agriculture, fishing, forestry, mining and extraction of minerals. In the secondary, or manufacturing, sector raw materials are processed into physical goods so that they acquire added value. Everything else falls within the tertiary sector, which is concerned with the supply of all forms of service. Two other terms require explanation. The 'index of production' industries comprise manufacturing, mining, utilities and construction and the 'production industries' are similar but exclude construction. These distinctions are useful, but the boundaries are not always clear, especially between manufacturing and services. As economies develop, the primary sector becomes relatively less important in terms of output, though actual output may continue to grow. The tertiary sector made the biggest single contribution to output growth in most developed twentieth-century countries, though there are uncertainties about this sector's role in the economy, as will be seen shortly.

The main changes in the sectoral pattern of growth are evident in Tables 4.1 and 4.2 and Figure 4.1. As has already been established, from a comparative perspective Britain shifted resources *out* of agriculture long before its main rivals, and *into* services at a rate matched only by the USA (Table 4.1). Figure 4.1 shows that employment in the services exceeded that in manufacturing throughout the twentieth century. It would, however, be misleading to assume that Britain was a 'service economy' from 1899 onwards. Almost half service sector employment in Edwardian Britain was supplying 'producer services' (O'Brien 1983, 81). Only after 1945 did 'services for final output' grow rapidly, and even in this period we must not exaggerate. The postwar growth of consumers' expenditure was dominated, at least until the later 1980s, by five main items: cars, foreign holidays, electronic goods, electric household consumer durables and clothes (Wells 1989, 34). The one service sector item on the list cannot, by definition, be produced in the UK. The real issue is, of course, not the relative size of the sectors, but their relative efficiency. The agricultural labour force and the sector's share in output

Table 4.1 *The structure of output, selected countries, 1900–98*

	UK	France	Germany	USA	Japan
1900–4					
Agriculture	6	38	29	17	34
Industry	38	41	40	26	14
Services	56	21	31	57	52
1910–14					
Agriculture	6	32	23	17	30
Industry	38	41	44	27	20
Services	56	27	33	56	50
1935–9					
Agriculture	4	22	16	10	21
Industry	36	36	50	30	32
Services	60	42	34	60	47
1950–4					
Agriculture	5	13	10	6	23
Industry	47	48	51	39	30
Services	48	39	39	55	47
1973					
Agriculture	3	7	3	4	6
Industry	38	38	51	34	46
Services	59	55	46	52	48
1979					
Agriculture	2	5	2	3	4
Industry	37	35	44	34	42
Services	61	60	54	63	54
1996					
Agriculture	2	2	1	2	2
Industry	28	26	36	28	38
Services	70	72	63	70	60

For UK, 1900–4 is 1901 only; 1910–14 is 1907 only; 1935–9 is 1935–8 only and 1996 is 1995.
For Germany, entries from 1950–4 onwards relate to West Germany.
For USA, 1900–4 is 1899–1908; 1910–14 is 1904–13.
Industry is defined throughout as manufacturing plus mining and quarrying plus electricity, gas and water, plus construction.
Sources: Mitchell 1992, Table J2; idem 1993, Table J2; idem 1995, Table J2; OECD 1995; OECD 1999.

contracted continuously throughout the century, but these trends were not inconsistent with positive growth of output, giving respectable productivity performance, as measured by

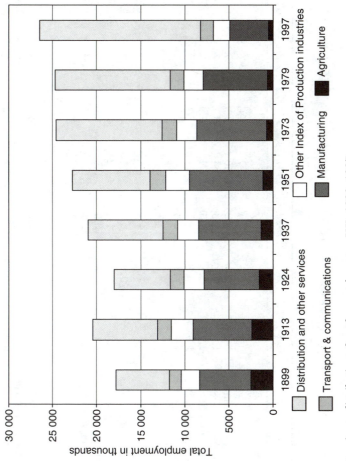

Figure 4.1 *Approximate distribution of employment by sector, UK, 1899–1997*

Source: As for Table 4.2.

Table 4.2 Approximate growth rates of output, employment and labour productivity by sector, UK, 1899–97 (annual percentage growth rates)

	1899–1913	1913–51	1924–37	1937–51	1951–73	1973–9	1979–97	1899–1997
Output								
Agriculture	0.2	0.3	1.4	1.7	2.6	1.6	1.8	1.1
Index of Production industries	1.6	2.0	3.2	2.0	2.9	0.7	1.6	2.0
(Manufacturing)	1.8	2.2	3.3	2.4	3.1	−0.6	0.9	1.9
Transport & communication	2.5	1.7	1.5	2.4	2.9	1.6	3.7	2.5
Distribution & other services	1.9	0.4	1.7	0.4	2.4	1.7	2.4	1.5
GDP	1.7	1.2	2.3	1.3	2.7	1.2	2.0	1.7
Employment								
Agriculture	−0.2	−1.9	−1.4	−0.9	−1.9	−2.8	−1.0	−1.6
Index of Production industries	0.9	0.5	0.8	1.1	−0.4	−1.3	−1.9	−0.3
(Manufacturing)	0.9	0.6	1.0	1.2	−0.2	−1.5	−2.9	−0.3
Transport & communication	1.1	0.7	0.5	0.5	−0.6	−0.5	−0.1	0.1
Distribution & other services	1.4	0.5	2.1	0.2	1.5	1.4	1.9	1.1
Whole economy	1.0	0.3	1.1	0.6	0.4	0.1	0.4	0.4
Output per worker								
Agriculture	0.4	2.2	2.8	2.6	4.5	4.4	2.8	2.7
Index of Production industries	0.7	1.5	2.4	0.9	3.3	2.0	3.5	2.3
(Manufacturing)	0.9	1.6	2.3	1.2	3.3	0.9	3.8	2.2

Transport & communication	1.4	1.0	1.0	1.9	3.5	2.1	3.8	2.4
Distribution & other services	0.5	−0.1	−0.4	0.2	0.9	0.3	0.5	0.4
Whole economy	0.7	0.9	1.2	0.7	2.3	1.1	1.6	1.3

Sources: Output: 1899–1965: Feinstein 1972, Tables 8, 51; after 1965: Blue Book, various issues.

Employment: 1899–1913: interpolations using census data from Feinstein 1972, Table 60.

1920–65: Feinstein 1972, Table 59.

1966–79: *Annual Abstract of Statistics*, various issues. Combines employees in employment and an estimate for self-employment per sector, based on estimates of Feinstein's distribution of self-employment in 1965.

1997: ONS 1999a, Table 7.5, adjusted for self-employment from ONS 1999b, Table 2.5.

output per worker, from 1913 (Table 4.2). The performance of services was a mirror image of that of agriculture. Before 1973 its employment growth was generally faster than for the whole economy but its share of total output was relatively stable, at around 55–60 per cent, apart from the period from the start of the Second World War until the later 1950s when resources were shifted from services into industry. As a result, productivity performance was consistently poor, in part because the service sector tended to become a reservoir for unemployed manufacturing workers during recessions. After 1973 there were more substantial shifts of resources into this sector, with the result that at the end of the century approximately 70 per cent of total output was generated from within the service sector, and approximately 75 per cent of employment was also found there. These shifts were accompanied by profound changes in the gender balance and the nature of employment, which are considered in Chapter 5. The expansion of output and employment in services after 1970 created enormous concern when the trends were first noticed by economists, and led to the notion that Britain (alone) was suffering 'de-industrialisation'. This was, however, another 'declinist' false alarm: Table 4.1 indicates that France, the USA and the UK had practically identical sectoral patterns of output. OECD (1999) data show that Australia, Belgium, Canada, Denmark, Luxembourg, the Netherlands and Sweden also generated at least 70 per cent of their GDP from services. The last column of Table 4.2 gives an indication (and not much more than that as a result of measurement problems) of output, employment and productivity performance over the century as a whole. The poor productivity performance of services stands out clearly. In the longer term, the growth rate of the British economy in the aggregate suffered from transferring resources into a sector with slow productivity growth.

Measured against this service sector yardstick, manufacturing performance was relatively good. Manufacturing output and employment grew until the mid-1960s and the sector also had above-average productivity performance, but there was a big shake-out of labour from manufacturing which began in the 1970s and continued until the end of the century. The suspicion, raised in Chapter 2, that manufacturing met particular problems in the 1970s, seems to be confirmed in Table 4.2, with clear signs of good productivity performance in the sector both before and after this decade but really very poor performance during it. However, employment data give a rather more sombre picture of what happened to manufacturing towards the end of the century. Manufacturing employment fell consistently from the mid-1960s onwards, especially during the slumps of the early 1980s and early 1990s. By 1997, manufacturing employment had fallen below the level of 1899 (Figure 4.2 below); in effect, the price of creditable productivity growth from 1979 was falling employment (Table 4.2). Taken as a whole, the British economy appears to have experienced 'balanced' growth, with similar rates of productivity growth in all sectors, except services, over the century as a whole. Economists and economic historians tend to believe that manufacturing is vested with special properties that make it *the* dynamic sector of modern economies. Productivity growth is more easily achieved in manufacturing than in services and a much higher proportion of manufacturing is exported than tertiary output. Throughout the century British service sector exports were roughly one-quarter of the value of visibles. It is also possible that fast growth of manufacturing *output* will induce fast growth of *productivity* throughout the economy, though this is disputed territory. These expectations of manufacturing were derived essentially from study of the west European economies during their reconstruction/recovery phase of the 1950s and early 1960s. There are many good reasons for believing that this period contained far too many peculiarities that we still do not fully understand to make it a sensible basis for any generalisations about the processes of economic development among the rich nations. As was argued at length in Chapter 2, the idea that the USA, France and Germany overtook Britain as a result of the relative strength of their manufacturing sectors is a myth. A strong manufacturing sector is clearly an asset, but so too is strength elsewhere. It is extremely sobering to recognise that understanding the roles of manufacturing and services in economic development can be achieved only from reliable, long-run, comparative estimates of output, employment and productivity. Only the first steps in assembling this material have been taken so far.

Indications of the changes *within* manufacturing are evident from Figure 4.2 and Table 4.3. Changes in classification again

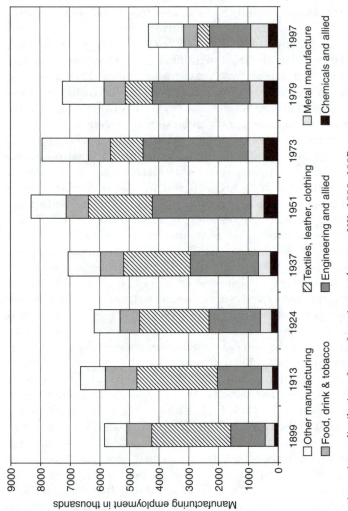

Figure 4.2 *Approximate distribution of manufacturing employment, UK, 1899–1997*
Source: As for Table 4.3.

make long-run measurement extremely hazardous, but for the first three-quarters of the century there appears to be a clear division between those manufacturing industries whose output grew relatively rapidly (chemicals and engineering) and those in relative decline (textiles and the food industries). The trends in productivity performance during the same period are, however, much more mixed. Productivity growth in the expanding sectors was disappointing before 1950 and again in the 1970s, but impressive rates of productivity and output growth were recorded by chemicals and engineering during the golden age. The industries in relative decline clearly made a significant contribution to aggregate productivity growth but also in an uneven pattern. It is perhaps surprising therefore to note that the figures for the century as a whole (the last column of Table 4.3) indicate a very balanced and even pattern of labour productivity growth within manufacturing. Only in iron and steel was performance relatively dismal. The most striking development in manufacturing during the whole century was the huge contraction in employment from the later 1960s onwards and the much slower growth of output after 1973. Rates of productivity growth from 1979 were, however, very creditable, especially in engineering and chemicals. Within services there were examples of very rapid growth throughout the century. Employment grew rapidly in both financial services (3.6 per cent per annum) and health services (3.3 per cent per annum), but changes in classification make this picture at best approximate. There were broad structural changes within services. It seems likely that 'producer services' declined in relative importance until the 1970s. 'Consumer services' (services for final output) grew, in large part from the effects of rising income. The growth of working-class incomes in the inter-war years enabled those working-class households that managed to avoid unemployment to broaden their expenditure on services (and indeed to save to increase their wealth) into a range of leisure activities. It is a mistake, however, to believe that all parts of the service sector expanded during the twentieth century. Private domestic service disappeared as a separate classification during the golden age, but its contraction from the peak in 1913 was a protracted process lasting well beyond the Second World War (Figure 4.3). The growth of state activities (Chapter 6) fostered the growth of 'public sector services'

Table 4.3 *Approximate growth rates of output, employment and labour productivity for manufacturing, UK, 1899–97 (annual percentage growth rates)*

	1899–1913	1913–51	1924–37	1937–51	1951–73	1973–9	1979–97	1899–1997
Output								
Chemicals & allied	4.0	3.1	3.1	4.8	6.1	1.8	2.2	3.6
Metal manufacture	1.4	1.9	3.3	2.3	1.4	−2.6	−0.8	0.9
Engineering & allied	2.9	3.6	4.4	3.8	3.4	−1.0	1.2	2.6
Textiles, leather, clothing	1.3	−0.1	1.7	−0.4	1.8	−1.5	−1.8	0.2
Food, drink, tobacco	0.7	1.5	2.8	1.7	2.7	0.8	0.9	1.5
Other manufacturing	1.5	2.7	3.9	2.2	3.8	−0.9	0.7	2.2
Manufacturing	1.8	2.2	3.3	2.4	3.1	−0.6	0.9	1.9
Employment								
Chemicals & allied	2.6	2.3	1.4	4.2	0.1	0.3	−2.6	0.8
Metal manufacture	1.6	1.1	0.7	1.0	0.7	−2.3	1.7	0.7
Engineering & allied	1.6	2.2	2.1	2.7	0.3	−1.2	−4.7	0.2
Textiles, leather, clothing	0.2	−0.6	−0.3	−0.4	−3.0	−3.2	−4.5	−1.9
Food, drink, tobacco	1.7	−0.9	1.4	0.1	0.0	−1.2	−2.2	−0.6
Other manufacturing	0.8	0.9	1.7	0.5	1.2	−1.6	−0.9	0.5
Manufacturing	0.9	0.6	1.0	1.2	0.2	−1.5	−2.8	−0.3
Output per worker								
Chemicals & allied	1.4	0.8	1.7	0.6	6.0	1.5	4.8	2.8
Metal manufacture	−0.2	0.8	2.6	1.3	0.7	−0.3	−2.5	0.2
Engineering & allied	1.3	1.4	2.3	1.1	3.1	0.2	5.9	2.4

Textiles, leather, clothing	1.1	0.5	2.0	0.0	4.8	1.7	2.7	2.1
Food, drink, tobacco	−1.0	2.4	1.4	1.6	2.7	2.0	3.1	2.1
Other manufacturing	0.7	1.8	2.2	1.7	2.6	0.7	1.6	1.7
Manufacturing	0.9	1.6	2.3	1.2	2.9	0.9	3.7	2.2

Sources: Output: 1899–1965: Feinstein 1972, Table 51.

1965–97: Blue Book, various issues.

Employment: 1899–1913: interpolations using census returns in Mitchell and Deane 1962, labour force Table 1b.

1920–65: Feinstein 1972, Table 59.

1965–97: *Annual Abstract of Statistics*, various editions, with adjustments for self-employment as in Table 4.2.

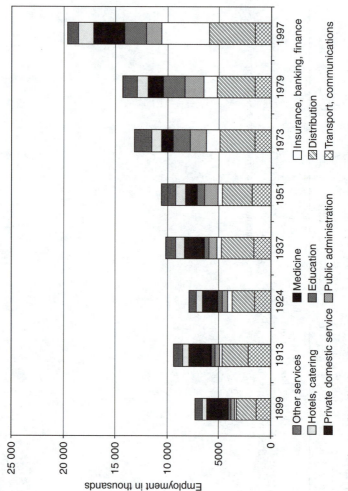

Figure 4.3 Approximate distribution of service sector employment, UK, 1899–97

Source: As for Table 4.2.

throughout the twentieth century, especially in the social services (Lee 1994). There was a remarkable growth in producer services in the last decades of the century, with major developments in distribution and a later explosion in specialist business services as many manufacturing firms contracted out to specialist suppliers service activities previously supplied 'in-house'. To take the discussion further, however, it is necessary to set this national picture in an international framework.

Comparative Productivity Performance

From very small and slow beginnings, the study of comparative productivity performance has begun to expand in recent years. The focus continues to be firmly on the period since 1945 and on manufacturing, but the longer-run and more broadly based estimates of Broadberry on Anglo-German and Anglo-US productivity differentials offer very new insights into British performance throughout the twentieth century. The broad pattern of UK/US and UK/German productivity performance has already been described in Chapter 2. The US economy surpassed British levels of total output per worker during the 1890s; Germany overtook the UK during the 1960s. Whereas the Anglo-US productivity gap began to fall from the 1960s, the German productivity lead continued to grow until the late 1970s, when it too began to close. Most explanations of these trends have been framed within a 'convergence' hypothesis centring on manufacturing, but Broadberry has demonstrated that both the USA and Germany overtook the UK's aggregate productivity levels essentially by switching resources out of agriculture and by making small but definite relative productivity gains in the service sector. The Anglo-US and Anglo-German comparisons of manufacturing productivity reveal a substantial US lead over European levels, and substantial swings in comparative productivity levels, but no tendency for divergence or convergence in the longer run.

For individual industries, Broadberry and Crafts compared British productivity levels with those of comparable industries in Germany and the USA for both the inter-war period (Broadberry and Crafts 1990) and the years 1954–63 (idem 1996). The different methods of defining and classifying industries in the three countries means that some industries can be studied more fully than others, but in broad terms they demonstrated that the gap between UK productivity levels and those of Germany and the USA tended to be wider for the heavy industries than for the lighter. Textiles emerge as a relatively good performer to 1939, food, drink and tobacco in both periods, and pharmaceuticals after 1951. In heavy industry, iron and steel and motor manufacture perform relatively badly. After 1970, however, these differences disappear and both heavy and light industries suffer similar productivity gaps (van Ark 1993, 198–201). Broadberry and Crafts argue that the persistence as much as the size of these productivity gaps requires explanation. It is not easy to do justice to this body of work briefly, not least because there are differences of emphasis within it, but broadly they argue that the pace of productivity growth in the UK and the size of the productivity gap with the USA and Germany are jointly determined by 'economic fundamentals' (which tend to explain the size of the gaps) and the 'bargaining environment' (which explain persistence). The list of 'economic fundamentals' varies, but includes market size, growth of capital per worker, human capital endowments and rate of growth of output. The factors in the 'bargaining environment' also vary, but generally include some measure of the monopoly power of firms, the extent of trade union organisation and the impact of economic policy. They find that in both the inter-war and postwar (1954–63) periods, the size and persistence of the productivity gap between US and UK manufacturing industries is best explained by a combination of superior US human capital development and larger US markets (which together provide more productive workers, longer production runs and greater division of labour) and Britain's weak competitive environment. Collusive firms in inter-war Britain and powerfully organised labour after the war blunted the pressure to invest and modernise production. Two of their three factors are, however, extremely difficult to measure. The problems associated with human capital were noted in Chapter 2. In the Broadberry and Crafts equations, human capital is statistically significant only when measured indirectly by relative wages and hardly at all when direct measures of workforce or managerial skills are measured. The competitive environment is virtually impossible to measure. Broadberry and Crafts use the share of industry output taken by the three biggest firms in each industry, but in the twentieth century British and other manufacturing firms developed an array of ways to manage their markets, all of which limited effective competition (see below). Logically, this is also a comparative variable, but Broadberry and Crafts only measure it on a national basis. The authors are very aware of these difficulties and they supplement their statistical results with a mass of case study evidence, both comparative and descriptive. Broadberry's (1997) book on comparative productivity performance contains even more descriptive microeconomic material. This, however, is not their forte and their reading of the evidence and conclusions have been vigorously challenged (Tomlinson and Tiratsoo 1998). There is also the more fundamental problem that the case studies and the quantitative evidence give very different pictures of Britain's relative performance, but Broadberry and Crafts are somewhat blind to the implications. The statistical evidence suggests that in three of the important benchmark years for twentieth-century economic performance (1909/07, 1937/35, 1973 – for an explanation of the esoteric choice of dates, see Broadberry 1997, 19–33) Anglo-American productivity differentials were roughly similar. In the Anglo-German case, the productivity gap was almost identical in 1911 and 1973, but rather smaller in the 1930s (see Figure 2.3 above). This seems to suggest that the sizes of the Anglo-US and Anglo-German manufacturing productivity gaps were very similar at the end of the Edwardian period, in the later 1930s and at the top of the long postwar boom. However, Broadberry and Crafts produce a very different interpretation of their data: they detect a substantial deterioration over the century in Britain's relative performance in manufacturing. In the Edwardian period, they suggest that British manufacturing was adjusting rationally to competition from abroad (Broadberry 1997, 209). In the mid-1930s, they find disappointing performance, with uneven failures caused essentially by the growth of collusion (Broadberry and Crafts 1992, 554). At the end of the golden age, the assessment is unequivocal: British manufacturing had performed badly since 1950. British manufacturing had pursued 'Fordist' production systems, without success, but at the same time had destroyed the craft-based technologies that had been successful in the past and

upon which German manufacturing continued to depend
(Broadberry 1997, 393). It is not easy to see immediately quite
how the comparative productivity figures support this case. As
Figure 2.3 above shows, British productivity levels in manufacturing fell relative to those in Germany (and, indeed, relative to
other European countries) during the 1950s and 1960s, but this
deterioration was scarcely drastic (by less than 10 per cent in
relation to Germany between 1952 and 1973) and really does
not deserve such a condemnatory judgement. The case study
material and the theme of decline that permeates it has unduly
coloured this interpretation. What follows assumes that the
Broadberry/Crafts figures are more reliable than the case study
material through which they have been filtered. Their work has
thrown up an agenda for judging economic performance, having
emphasised the importance of choice of technique, levels of
physical and human capital investment, market size and the
bargaining environment. We begin with those matters related
to entrepreneurs.

Entrepreneurs: Theory and Performance in the Edwardian Years

The focus on the entrepreneur as the dynamic element in modern capitalism owes much to the writing of the Austrian economist Joseph Schumpeter (1939; 1954). In Schumpeter's vision,
entrepreneurial activity acts as the primary agency of economic
transformation in the capitalist economy. The role is essentially
strategic, to identify new and profitable areas of production, but
it follows that not all business leaders can be classified as entrepreneurs. Those who interpret their role as being to create
structures and goals to ensure that existing areas of production
are undertaken profitably and efficiently might best be classed as
managers. The literature has struggled with definitional difficulties (for a good survey see Pollard 1994, 62–4), but the role of the
manager in industrial performance cannot be overlooked. It is
common to distinguish between macro- and micro-inventions,
that is between a major breakthrough and gap-filling improvements in existing knowledge, while recognising the blurred
boundary between the two. Economists suggest that most

productivity gains are generated by small-scale improvements, but these effects may be most intense when the firm is subjected to especially fierce pressures. Thus, the distinctions between strategic vision and the routine implementation of change are blurred in the real world, where the short and long term constantly interact. We now turn to this real world.

The controversy over entrepreneurial performance before 1914 is one of the classic set-pieces of Anglo-American economic historiography, with robust damnation matched by vigorous defence (for a review, see Payne 1974). New perspectives drawn from other social science disciplines have consistently invigorated the topic, and the evidence has been reappraised regularly. Signs of consensus remain weak, however. There remain sharp dividing lines between optimists, who tend to be neo-classical and focus on the short run, and pessimists, who are usually of a neo-Schumpetarian cast with longer-term perspectives.

The main criticisms are that British entrepreneurs failed to accept technical innovation and remained wedded to the small, family firm as US manufacturing developed larger-scale, more intensively managed corporations. Size prevented British firms from developing the internal research and development facilities that successful German and US companies had already pioneered. The examples are legion. British steel-makers produced approximately 44 per cent of the world's output in 1870 but only 11 per cent at the outbreak of war (Pollard 1989, 27–31). They fell behind US producers in the size of blast furnaces, the use of materials handling equipment, electric power and the technique of 'hard driving' and behind the leading European firms in fuel economy and the use of by-products. They made inadequate use of scientifically trained managers and did not switch to the rich East Midlands ore field before 1914 (Elbaum 1986). In shipbuilding there is a similar story, with British yards failing to modernise methods and equipment (again, especially materials handling equipment and the use of electric power) and remaining committed to craft-intensive production techniques (Pollard 1989, 23–5). In cotton, British firms entered the twentieth century using machines that were rapidly becoming antiquated in other countries. They maintained their competitive position by reducing product quality rather than by restructuring into vertically integrated firms using more capital-intensive methods, as did their rivals in the USA (Lazonick 1986). In chemicals, German firms developed a commanding lead by rigorous and large-scale application of scientific knowledge in industrial research laboratories (Reader 1979, 156).

Naturally enough, very diverse lessons have been drawn from this evidence. The iron and steel and chemical industries undoubtedly contained some poorly run firms. However, a defence case can be made in both industries. In iron and steel, some part of the alleged technological conservatism resulted from the structure of demand. British steel-makers concentrated on plates, which were best produced by the open hearth method. US producers, still facing huge demand for rails, utilised the Bessemer technology, which was not only ideally suited to rails but also had superior scale advantages (McCloskey 1973). The greater throughput in US Bessemer led directly to innovations in management, which were not transferable to open hearth technology (Elbaum 1986, 80). The openness of the UK domestic market for steel (because of Britain's free trade regime) and greater dependence on varied export markets inhibited British firms from investing and restructuring, but they were much better able to import semi-finished steel and work it up into more complex, higher value products like ships, tinplate or galvanised sheet. In chemicals the defence is rather simpler: not even the USA could rival Germany (Reader 1979). In shipbuilding and cotton, British firms continued to dominate export markets despite apparent technological backwardness. Both industries relied heavily upon relatively lavish supplies of relatively cheap skilled labour, giving British firms unrivalled flexibility in production and greater ability to withstand the slumps in highly cyclical industries, since they did not carry the high fixed costs of more capital-intensive competitors (Pollard 1989, 24–5; Sandberg 1970). Both industries were highly specialised, giving the best firms sensitivity and responsiveness to changing market conditions. Thus, British cotton producers simultaneously sent high-quality yarn to protected European markets and cheap piece goods to the developing markets of empire countries.

Evidence of market success cannot satisfy the critics of entrepreneurial performance. Alford (1996, 55–71), for example, argues that technical conservatism piled up difficulties for the future. Much of the problem, it is argued, resulted from insufficient progress towards the larger-scale, more bureaucratic company adopted in the USA and Germany. British firms continued to be led by 'practical men' and the economy remained inflexible. Large-scale bureaucratic companies certainly did exist in Britain in 1900, notably in the railways and in banking after 1900, but they were not seen as the model for manufacturing firms, in sharp contrast to developments in the USA (Chandler 1977, chs. 3–6). There may have been institutional constraints. British common law became distinctly more tolerant of collusion by industrialists as the US Sherman Act of 1890 took a fiercely anti-cartel position. British law was, however, less encouraging to monopoly and industrial collusion than continental legal codes. Collusive arrangements between British business leaders were far from robust before 1914, tending to be temporary anti-recession initiatives, but they may have been enough to frustrate any ideas of radical industrial restructuring. The strength of these institutional forces should not, however, be exaggerated. Large-scale companies did indeed appear in the textile finishing trades at the turn of the century. These were horizontal associations of family firms in a holding company structure, rather than the vertically integrated corporations emerging in the USA. In textiles, the emergence of large companies on the US model was frustrated in the UK less by the law and more by the extent of specialisation and vertical disintegration that in turn flowed from the intensely competitive nature of the industry (Lazonick 1986). The extent of structural inflexibility can also be exaggerated. Rising working-class living standards translated into growing demand for a range of consumer goods industries, such as newspapers, food processing, the production of cheap household goods ranging from pottery to soap, cosmetics and bicycles. Many of these industries were developed to the mass production stage by British firms, some of which had to resist strong overseas competition. It is also easy to exaggerate Britain's technological conservatism. Foreman-Peck (1999) attempted to construct a balance sheet of trade in high technology products. Britain moved from virtual self-sufficiency in 1870 to become a 'follower' economy in new sectors in 1901–13, but a follower that adapted quickly. He argues strongly that British delays in developing capacity and exports in its weakest areas should be

explained not by entrepreneurial failures but by an inappropriate regulatory regime. The Post Office's monopoly interest in the
telegraph constrained the expansion of the telephone system; the
development of the British motor car industry was held back in
part by regulation that limited speeds on the highway to 4 m.p.h.
in the interests of safety. In 1914 British industry was behind the
USA in research and development; Britain certainly had no
equivalent of the major industrial laboratories already established by companies such as General Electric, Bell Telephone
and Kodak. British chemicals producers were also behind their
German rivals, but lack of data means that this comparison cannot be extended further. There is no doubt, however, that the
amount of research undertaken by British firms has been badly
underestimated (Edgerton and Horrocks 1994; Edgerton
1996a). Taken together, this material goes some way to weaken
the case that the strategic decision-taking by British entrepreneurs was poor in the years to 1914. There certainly were badly
run companies and some technological conservatism, but the
argument for systematic errors of judgement and technological
blind spots looks much weaker than when originally articulated.

Entrepreneurship in Difficult Conditions, 1914–39

The outbreak of war in 1914 created huge disruption, especially
for the export staple industries. There were also major opportunities, especially for those supplying domestic or military demand.
Despite high taxes on wartime profits, many firms evaded the
regulations and accumulated substantial reserves. New industries
were created and given protection for military-strategic reasons.
The Ministry of Munitions promoted mass production of
standardised products by automatic machinery and improved
techniques of labour management throughout the engineering
and metal-working industries (Wrigley 1982, 46–52). Stronger
and broader links were forged between university science and
industry (Barnett 1999). Government established a new Department of Scientific and Industrial Research to promote a more
active research effort by British industry. The state came to control an ever-expanding segment of national economic life and
relations with manufacturing industry were transformed (Blank

1973, 13–15). In similar conditions after 1939, government and industry found ways of expanding the manufacturing base, as is evident from Table 4.1, but there were no lasting, parallel developments from the First World War. The opportunities for restructuring evaporated. The modernising potential of wartime profits was lost in high dividends to shareholders and inflation. Employers did not exploit the new US technologies. The poor climate of industrial relations during the war and early postwar periods may not have helped, but the unions suffered major defeats in the 1920s (see Chapter 5), which managers failed to exploit fully (see below). The plans to project closer government–industry relations into peacetime collapsed with the military defeat of Germany; Britain looked to blunt German competitive power by the peace treaty rather than by domestic industrial reorganisation (Cline 1982). In these conditions, firms rushed to be free of government (Lowe 1978; Cline 1982). Europe-wide postwar restocking and port congestion gave a huge short-term boost to British exporters (Figures 3.2, 3.4 above), but the dramatic world slump of 1920–2 and the huge postwar overvaluation of sterling (Chapter 3) left British manufacturers in an intensely difficult trading climate.

For most employers in the early 1920s, the cost of labour was the most weighty and potentially controllable element in variable costs. The labour-intensive export staples had particular need to reduce labour costs but many employers had made wartime concessions on job control and were looking to regain lost ground (McIvor 1996, 146–79). The collapse of the postwar boom and rapidly rising unemployment gave employers their opportunity. Money wages were forced down, notably in agriculture, iron and steel, shipbuilding, mining, textiles and engineering – in broad terms the industries most exposed to foreign competition, but also in building (Clegg 1985, 330–45). Employers regained control only after bitter confrontation. In coalmining miners were locked out in 1921 to enforce lower pay and the restoration of managerial rights after wartime government control. The engineering employers locked out their workers in 1922 to reimpose the 'right to manage'. Despite the falls in money wages and the pushing back of the frontiers of control, the real cost of labour rose sharply for industrial employers from 1922 to 1935 (Dimsdale 1984), but, despite their success on wages and control, employers could not claw back the reduction in the length of the standard working week granted in 1919 (Dowie 1975; Broadberry 1990). There was some offset in falling material costs, but this compensation was only partial and profits in the export sector and closely related industries (textile machinery, steam engines and marine engineering, for example) tended to be disappointing, though individual firms might perform well. There were, therefore, big incentives to raise labour productivity, but weak profits limited the ability of firms in the more depressed industries to achieve their goals (Hart 1965, 70).

There are in theory alternative stimuli for industrial reconstruction, whether from the firm's bankers or from stock market pressures on under-performing public companies. The retail banks certainly did lend to industry, usually on short term, but such loans, as before 1913, could be continued to become medium-term finance (Ross 1990). However, British banks remained aloof from questions of industrial restructuring. The bank with most interest in restructuring was the Bank of England, via its own commitments to the ailing armaments firm Armstrong-Whitworth and its concern for the wider banking structure in the depressed areas, where industrial depression threatened local banks. But the bank's policy was to preserve a limited relationship between the banks and industry (Kynaston 1999). The promise of managerial restructuring was strongest in the later 1920s, when a big merger wave coincided with a public debate on the need for industrial rationalisation (Hannah 1976, 99). However, rationalisation failed to become as important a force for restructuring as in Germany, and hostile takeovers (to eject under-performing management teams) were unknown in Britain before the later 1950s (Roberts 1992, 183–4).

Even allowing for the institutional difficulties, the managerial response to cost pressures appears to have been half-hearted. Engineering employers, for example, used their newly won power after the successful lock-out of 1922 to intensify the pace of work, but the extent of restructuring towards standardised mass production by semi-skilled operatives was disappointing (Melling and Johansson 1994). But there were formidable demand-side problems. In mechanical engineering, for example, most machine tool makers did badly because the old staples postponed new investment (Gourvish 1979, 142–3). Nor was disappointing productivity performance of firms in heavier manufacturing with expanding demand incompatible with technological progressiveness. In an important article, Edgerton and Horrocks (1994) have demonstrated that the research effort of many UK firms was better than had previously been supposed. US firms retained their international lead in 'routinised R&D', but there is no evidence that British manufacturing lagged behind German (or other European) competitors. Many leading UK firms in growth sectors, like electrical engineering and chemicals, concluded international agreements to share scientific and technical information, and something like an international technological community existed in chemicals- and engineering-related fields. This effort was concentrated by firm as well as by industry, with foreign-owned and larger-scale producers in the expanding manufacturing industries being much more committed to organised R&D than the average. Technological conservatism seems more elusive than previously imagined.

In the very severe competitive conditions created by overvaluation, firms attempted to manage markets with as much energy as they attempted to reduce costs, most obviously by demanding protection and imperial preference. Support for free trade dwindled rapidly among British business leaders. For the export industries, there was enormous pressure to form cartels to limit production and set prices but equally strong incentives for rogue firms to ignore such agreements. The staple industries consistently failed to make cartels work until the government was dragged in as reluctant enforcer during the 1930s, and even then only the most limited schemes were attempted (Roberts 1984). For the industries with expanding demand, the balance of market-managing activity tended to be somewhat different. International cartels thrived in electrical engineering, chemicals, tin cans and steel, establishing market-sharing agreements in addition to the agreements on processes, patents and equipment noted above (Prais 1981, 245–6; Wurm 1993). In fact, even in home-market industries, cartels were rather hit- and-miss affairs with a tendency to instability (see Cook 1958). Thus, conditions encouraged other methods of maintaining prices and sustaining profits. Resale price maintenance, or producer control over the price at which retailers might sell, grew rapidly in the inter-war years (Mercer 1995,

18–19). Branding, advertising and other marketing techniques flourished. The branding of consumer goods had begun long before 1914, and parts of the chemicals industry and food, drink and tobacco firms were notable early exponents of this sort of product differentiation (Westall 1994, 220–1). There is no reason to believe that British entrepreneurs were alone in managing markets. Much is made of the anti-trust environment in the USA, but most new marketing techniques came to Britain in the inter-war years from North America, and British subsidiaries of US firms were enthusiastic users of consumer marketing (Jeremy 1998, 474–84). Since the impact of all these systems of market management was to establish barriers to entry and limit competition, it is almost certainly misleading to suggest that the British competitive environment was distinctly weak (or that the extent of competitive pressure can be measured easily and conveniently).

It is moreover likely that these constraints on effective competition strengthened parts of British industry, despite apparently weak productivity growth. This can be illustrated by reference to the chemicals industry, which is presented by Broadberry as a relatively poor performer in the inter-war years. The story begins with the difficulties of the British chemicals industry under free trade to 1914. Government recognised that weak parts of the industry had a vital military-strategic role, and all parts of the industry were protected during and after the war. Leaders of the British chemicals industry sought parity with Germany, which led them to the formation of ICI in 1926 and to international cartels. The impact of cartelisation is uncertain. Broadberry (1997, 216) implies that productivity performance was sacrificed by collusion, but Reader (1979, 173) insists that without the international cartels the industry in Britain would have contracted steeply, since British firms were hopelessly outclassed in scale and scope in the early 1920s. ICI certainly improved its international position during the 1930s, thanks to its own breakthroughs and information acquired through the cartel system. The ICI board appears to have considered itself the guardian of the UK's capacity to produce chemicals and decisions were taken as much on national strategic grounds as to secure a return for shareholders. Productivity growth in ICI was moderate, but by 1938 and especially by 1945 the British chemicals industry was much stronger than in 1914, and it is difficult to see how this could have been achieved without the tariff and international cartels. The industry would have been smaller, and it is by no means certain that the resources released by a smaller chemicals industry would have flowed to more productive uses. Mention has already been made of the lavish use of labour by manufacturing industry despite the heavy cost pressures it faced. The other likely reservoir for unemployed industrial labour was distribution and miscellaneous services, where productivity levels and growth rates were very poor indeed. Thus it is a mistake to assume that collusion always impaired inter-war industrial or national performance. Collusion could be a rational, long-term entrepreneurial strategy: ICI is one of only two firms praised by Barnett (1986, 181–2) for wartime performance. There may well have been insufficient pressure on inter-war industrialists to use the breathing-space in the 1930s to pursue efficiency and competitiveness more vigorously, but that is essentially a problem of government or governance, which is taken up in Chapter 6.

Entrepreneurship after 1939: War, 'Americanisation' and 'Japanisation'

If there are signs of 'redemption' for entrepreneurs extending now to the inter-war years, the judgement on postwar performance is still vigorously condemnatory, with criticisms of the poor quality of industrial leadership, its inability to adopt the most efficient managerial structures and its weakness in organising effective 'technological activity' (defined below). Barnett's (1986) 'audit' of British economic performance during the Second World War offers a truly scathing indictment of all aspects of British economic organisation, particularly of the inability of entrepreneurs to organise production and harness technology effectively. His book was hugely influential, but has met equally forceful criticism from economic historians. A significant step in Barnett's argument is to demonstrate that it required two-thirds more labour time to build the Spitfire than the equivalent German fighter aircraft (1986, 59, 147), thus illustrating the inefficiency of British industry in the modern, technologically advanced sectors. However, Barnett's figures are at best debatable and at worst positively misleading: the German wartime aircraft industry was notoriously inefficient (Edgerton 1991a, 79–81; Edgerton 1991b; Overy 1984, 148–85). Barnett's critique of British entrepreneurs has some merit, but his picture of a society incapable of utilising technology is overdrawn.

Equally, many of the long-standing complaints about the intellectual capacity of British business leaders are inconclusive. Ackrill (1988) compared the academic qualifications of British senior managers very unfavourably with those of their US counterparts, and Keeble (1992) painted an equally compelling picture of undereducated and undertrained managers. However, when comparisons between like and like are attempted, the gap between British and US qualification levels becomes much less, and narrows over time, and there is almost no difference between academic attainments in Britain and Germany (Broadberry and Wagner 1996, 257–60). One of the few rigorous comparative surveys of senior managers found that British and US managers were similar in their responsibility, intelligence and even knowledge of technical matters, but US managers tended to be more democratic in their leadership style (Heller and Porter 1977). At lower levels, it has traditionally been easier to enter management without formal educational qualifications in Britain than elsewhere, and those calling themselves 'managers' tend to be only marginally better qualified than the general population. But the effects on the quality of decision-taking are difficult to ascertain, as there are so few reliable investigations of lower-level managerial decisions. The shortage of qualified managers in engineering has frequently been a cause for complaint, but again the one attempt to make rigorous comparisons found little basis for the view that British industry was undersupplied with graduate engineers when compared with Germany (Prais 1995, Table 2.2). The debate on the level of qualifications of British managers is infuriating, with general historical sweeps insisting upon a deeply entrenched British problem offset by specific and rigorous studies that show nothing of the sort. However, the latter are usually snapshots of a single year or small span of years and are of unknown wider relevance. This literature amounts to a very thin foundation upon which to build a thesis of systemic managerial failure.

The criticism that British managers failed to adopt the Chandlerian deep managerial hierarchies and vertically integrated business structures (noted above in connection with Edwardian entrepreneurs and in Chapter 2) has also returned, but equally inconclusively. British firms did not adopt the Chandlerian multidivisional form in any great numbers until the mid-1970s (Channon 1973, 67–9), but there are good reasons for believing that the relevance of the Chandler thesis to the UK may have been overstated and even for doubting the accuracy of its picture of US manufacturing (Foreman-Peck 1994, 396–8). There was certainly no clear association in twentieth-century Britain between organisational structure and market performance nor even between organisational structure and managerial strategy (Gourvish 1987, 40).

The discussion of the 'technological activity' of British firms is no more conclusive. This term embraces the range of practices, such as design, R&D and production engineering, that help to establish a technological lead in product markets and are crucial in non-price competitiveness (Patel and Pavitt 1987, 72). However, 'technological activity' cannot be measured directly, only by means of such indirect indicators as the proportion of value added directed to R&D or the taking out of patents. For what it is worth, the R&D statistics show that the amount of research undertaken by British firms increased between 1945 and 1965, but tended to be concentrated in a relatively small number of firms in chemicals, aircraft and electrical engineering. In 1967, Britain stood second only to the USA in the proportion of GDP devoted to R&D, and second also in R&D funded by industry itself, which excluded military and civil prestige projects (Edgerton 1996a, 62–3). It has been argued that Britain devoted too much R&D to military projects, but even this apparently self-evident fact has no real substance (Edgerton 1996a, 63). The main problem in this whole area is, however, that there is no statistical association between R&D expenditure and economic performance (Edgerton 1996b, 78–9). Both Germany and France overtook Britain's GDP before 1970 while undertaking less R&D. Again, the evidence for obvious British failure is uncertain.

Given the lack of definite conclusions in the literature on these weaknesses, it might be useful to turn to the debate on the impact of 'Americanisation' on British industry, since it illuminates many aspects of managerial competence. The comparatively recent rediscovery of the reports of the Anglo-American Council on Productivity and its offshoots, which in the late 1940s and early 1950s undertook detailed examinations of British industry in the light of US practice, has fostered an interesting debate on the reaction of British firms to US methods of production and organisation. Zeitlin (1995) and Broadberry (1997) defined Americanisation as the use of mass production and systematic management techniques which spread only slowly and was fundamentally inappropriate for the UK. On the other hand, Tiratsoo and Tomlinson (1998a; 1998b) argued that Americanisation was less a 'model' of production than a series of limited and discrete improvements to production and management methods that offered real benefits to British industry, but was met largely by apathy or rejection. Finally, John Dunning (1998) revisited his (1958) work on the transfer of management practices to UK affiliates of US-owned firms and reaffirmed his conclusion that the UK's indigenous business culture *was* transformed for the better by US multinationals. Unfortunately none of the items on this menu is totally satisfying.

The Zeitlin/Broadberry case is that too many British manufacturing industries chose, or were steered towards, US mass production, or 'Fordist', methods of production when more flexible, skill-intensive methods of production geared to smaller, more fragmented European and overseas markets would have been better. The case is best understood by looking at Lewchuk's (1986; 1987) assessment of British-owned motor manufacturers. He argues that 'Fordism' was introduced into Britain before the First World War, but British firms lacked the managerial capacity and experience to organise mass production in exactly the same way as their US mentors. Instead, they introduced systems of payment by results (piecework) for shopfloor workers to place on manual workers much of the responsibility for the detailed organisation of work flows and processes. Instead of managers driving workers to higher effort, workers would push each other to maximise piecework earnings. This British hybrid was much less managerially and capital-intensive than US Fordism. The system worked, according to Lewchuk, until full employment after 1945 shifted the balance of power on the shopfloor from management to labour. Workers used their new bargaining strength to drive up piece rates and frustrate management attempts to increase the pace of work. When management finally tried to regain control of the pace of work, it merely worsened already confrontational industrial relations. This has been a highly influential argument, but it oversimplifies by neglecting the market and demand sides of manufacturing activity. Manufacturers not only have to produce cheaply and efficiently, they have to sell profitably. During the long boom, the motor producer with the most intractable difficulties in organising production and industrial relations was BMC, especially at its Austin factory at Longbridge. However, Austin's production engineer until the early 1950s was a genius, Frank Woollard, who took the automated systems pioneered by Ford (Detroit automation) to new levels at Longbridge. Despite its strike-proneness production at Longbridge was highly successful in the 1950s, because BMC produced a series of outstanding models for which demand was strong, enabling Longbridge to produce in long production runs (Williams et al. 1994, 137–45). However, the small-car market, in which BMC specialised, was highly competitive and margins were low even on the best models. BMC also had a large, exposed equity base and needed high dividends to retain shareholder loyalty, but this in turn limited the company's ability to invest. Not all of BMC's sprawling production system was as efficient as Longbridge. BMC had too many factories, operating at very varied levels of efficiency. It might have been sensible for BMC to close these less efficient factories and concentrate production at an expanded Longbridge site, but demand for cars was highly volatile. BMC needed to keep Longbridge working at full capacity and adjust to variations in demand in its less efficient plant. There was also an effective limit to BMC's domestic sales as the British car market was split into two. In the 1950s and 1960s, BMC dominated that part which came from private purchasers, and usually represented small cars with low profit levels. However, the rapidly growing market segment of larger cars for commercial users (fleet sales) was dominated before the 1980s by Ford, and then shared between Ford and Vauxhall. BMC needed much higher sales volumes to solve its problems of low profits, but could not generate these sales either at home, because of the peculiarities of the UK market, or overseas, because its profits were simply too low to fund the creation of an export sales network (Williams et al. 1983, 235). The firm could make reasonable profits as long as it could generate exciting new models, like the Morris Minor, the Mini and the Austin 1100, but two unrelated developments undermined its great strengths. First, the problems of the international economy in the 1970s slowed the growth of the private purchasers' market for new cars, thus hitting profits. Secondly, the new environmental regulations introduced by the US government in the 1970s and followed elsewhere raised the costs of new model development. BL, as BMC became in the later 1960s, simply could not generate sufficient profit to compete and the company produced a string of awful, but cheap, new models in the 1970s. BMC/BL's goose was well cooked before its much-publicised problems of the later 1970s and 1980s by this combination of market, financial and production problems (Williams et al. 1987, 1–4). To insist that the company simply chose the wrong technology, and then failed to change, is to underestimate the quality of management in a company that was capable of world-class production, design and marketing.

There is much more force in the Tiratsoo/Tomlinson approach to Americanisation as a series of limited initiatives (better materials handling, more rigorous deployment of work study, more standardisation, simplification and specialisation, use of statistical techniques of quality control, the human relations approach to labour management and inter-firm efficiency comparisons), each of which was relatively cheap and yet promised significant productivity gains for UK firms. These techniques were heavily promoted by US productivity agencies in the UK and elsewhere, and promised real if not always spectacular efficiency gains. British managers were, however, slow to take up the ideas, revealing the traditional amateurism of British industrial management. The difficulty with the analysis is to assess its significance. All factories at all times in all countries could make some efficiency gains by adopting at least some of these practices. Interestingly, it was obvious in the debates on automation in US industry in the mid-1950s that many *American* firms could also have benefited from the Americanisation agenda (Booth and Bufton 2000). Tiratsoo and Tomlinson's evidence suggests that the best British managers were willing and able to employ these techniques, but the majority were not. There is therefore a pathology of British relative industrial decline, with a small head of efficient firms and a relatively long tail of inefficient (Tiratsoo and Tomlinson 1997, 57). This is not an unfamiliar conclusion. Broadberry and Crafts (1990, 385–8) reached the same conclusion by a different route. There is, however, only equivocal empirical support. Census of Production material in both countries in the 1950s shows very similar dispersion of productivity by size of firm (Booth and Bufton 2000). Britain's levels of productivity in manufacturing were well below those obtaining in the USA, but there is no evidence of a comparatively long tail of British poor performance. By itself, this evidence does not redeem the postwar British entrepreneur, but it does reveal yet another area where the case for failure cannot survive modest empirical probing.

In the period of slower growth after 1979, the pace of technical change appears to have quickened and stimulated important changes in the management of manufacturing production. Much of the change was associated with the diffusion of micro-electronics into new areas and the different work practices that the new technology made possible. The spread of computer control to new areas of manufacturing encouraged a change from the mass production of standardised goods to more specialised and flexible systems of production; from 'Fordism' to 'flexible specialisation' (Piore and Sabel 1984). By the end of the century it was much cheaper to produce a greater variety of specifications in relatively small batches and thereby possible to respond more quickly and effectively to subtle changes in market demand. Accompanying these trends was a growing appreciation of the qualities of Japanese managers, and leading representatives of British industry visited Japanese firms to learn the new techniques, just as they went to the USA in 1948–52. The influence of 'Japanisation' was as carefully examined in the 1990s as was the impact of 'Americanisation' in the 1950s. Just as in the 1950s, 'Japanisation' appeared to be both a whole model of business organisation and a series of discrete improvements to production methods, many of which sought familiar goals with new techniques (total quality control, quality circles, flexible working, group working, statistical process control, just-in-time production). Together they constituted 'lean production', with the firm seeking constant improvements in its products and production processes while utilising all its resources more efficiently (Oliver and Wilkinson 1992, 20–39). It is probably too early to judge the response of British industry to these stimuli, but even though Britain's comparative investment record improved after the 1970s, there remain suspicions that new technologies diffused comparatively slowly to many parts of manufacturing (Gospel 1992, 123–4). It is also clear that 'Japanisation' spread more slowly in British firms than managers had anticipated (Oliver and Wilkinson 1992, 316–18). The problems in controlling inventory levels, where very substantial cost and space savings were possible, were particularly acute. However, British managers were not alone, as western firms in general appeared to be less good inventory managers than the Japanese, and most Japanese firms were less good than Toyota (Oliver and Wilkinson 1992, 319–22). Evidence is mounting that British manufacturers secured their productivity gains less by new technologies and methods and more by driving their workers harder in the 1980s and 1990s (Edwards and Whitston 1991). We do not yet have data from competitor countries to put these admittedly very tentative conclusions into perspective, but there are parallels with conditions in the inter-war years when managers implemented limited change to technology and work practices and used their enhanced power over production primarily to intensify worker effort (Gospel 1992, 124).

Conclusions

One of the most self-evident truths in the story of Britain's supposed economic decline has been the alleged technological amateurism of British managers. This was at the centre of the critique of late Victorian entrepreneurs and re-emerged in the debates on postwar 'Americanisation'. However, thanks to the work of David Edgerton, the picture of Britain as technologically incompetent looks dangerously overdrawn. Somewhat mischievously, Edgerton (1991a) awarded Britain the epithet of 'technological nation', which may just be appropriate to the period up to 1970 but is probably less so thereafter as Britain slipped to become a middle-ranking investor in R&D in the 1990s. There were some stunning British technological failures, notably in rubber tyres, motor cycles, consumer electronics, motor car manufacture and office machinery. But the rapid emergence of world-leading pharmaceutical and biotechnology industries and the continuing vitality of aerospace undermine so much of that traditional criticism. It is unrealistic to believe that only Britain suffers such reverses. The USA, for example, had much of its metal-using industry severely damaged by imports in the 1970s and 1980s. A number of celebrated South Korean and Japanese motor producers failed even more spectacularly than did the Rover Group. Periodic failure in some branches of manufacturing is an integral part of the fast-moving, competitive, unified world economy, not conclusive diagnostic proof of the British disease. If the case for ingrained technological incompetence is unsatisfying, so, too, is the idea that British managers simply chose the wrong production system. In the hands of Broadberry and Crafts, this argument comes dangerously close to damnation for not introducing more Fordist systems before 1939 and equal damnation for having done so after 1945. The criticism that British managers were poorly qualified by international comparisons must also be treated as unproven until more systematic data and definitions can be found. This aspect of the human capital debate is in urgent need of greater analytical rigour. The question of the bargaining environment also seems to be less decisive than is frequently claimed. Just as neo-classically inspired economists claim that only intense competition can maximise efficiency in the long run, so business strategists have pointed out that the successful companies are those which exploit new markets first and then erect barriers to entry to protect their positions (see Porter 1985, 6). Protection appears to have been decisive for the development of some industries in twentieth-century Britain, but it is also easy to understand why British policy-makers wanted to expose British industry to more intensive competition from European firms in the early 1960s. The impact and potential of competition, collusion and protection seems to be a question of evaluating specific contexts rather than of applying simple rules. The firmest conclusion to be drawn from this survey of entrepreneurial performance is the absence of compelling evidence for failure, either at a specific time (apart, perhaps, from the 1970s) or in a specific aspect of their functions. British firms and even industries failed, but without leaving an obvious pathology of failure. The debates on the performance of British entrepreneurs will no doubt continue, since there are examples enough of competitive weakness, but surely the time has come to recognise that there is no simple key to unlock the secrets of market success and failure.

5 The Labour Market, Unions and Skill

The second element of the 'British disease' to attract attention has been the British labour force, with its distinctively decentralised and fragmented structure, its apparently antagonistic attitudes to management and its vigorous exploitation of bargaining strength during the long boom. This chapter begins by sketching the broad outlines of change in the labour market during the twentieth century and then looks in turn at debates on unions and pay, productivity and skill. The chapter concludes with a brief overview of unions and the 'British disease'.

Employment and Unemployment

The broad outlines of the main changes in employment are set out in Figure 5.1. The uneven growth of civil employment after 1920 is very clear, with obvious crises in the early 1920s and early 1930s and during the Second World War, and a generally less stable picture from the mid-1960s, with no obvious growth and quite substantial fluctuations. The other very obvious feature to emerge from Figure 5.1 is the changing gender balance of employment. The fall in the male and rise in the female shares of civil employment during the Second World War is clear enough and is well understood. Male (and female) workers were recruited into the armed and auxiliary services during wartime and were replaced in the civil workforce increasingly by females. Similar changes took place in 1914–18, but there are no reliable figures to provide a clear illustration. In both world wars, the number of married women in the workforce increased dramatically. At both armistices, however, women, especially married women, returned from the factory to the home, and

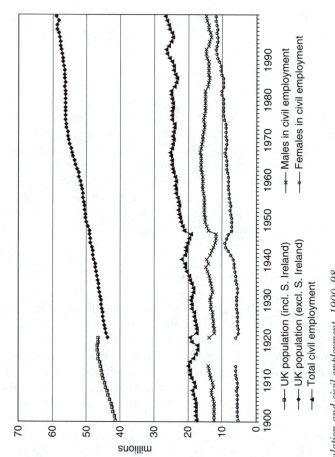

Figure 5.1 *UK population and civil employment, 1900–98*

Sources: LCES 1967, Table E; *Annual Abstract of Statistics*, various issues. There are no estimates for the gender division of employment in 1914–20.

Legend:
- ━□━ UK population (incl. S. Ireland)
- ━◆━ UK population (excl. S. Ireland)
- ━▲━ Total civil employment
- ━✕━ Males in civil employment
- ━○━ Females in civil employment

the longer-run impact of wartime developments on the gender balance of the labour force was limited. From the mid-1950s, however, the number of female workers began to rise more noticeably and to offset the falling number of males, which peaked in 1965 but then went into more or less continuous decline. Figure 5.1 measures workers in employment; if the focus had been 'workforce jobs' (allowing for the tendency of some part-timers to hold more than one job), it would have shown more female than male employment in the 1990s. Two obvious questions suggest themselves: what caused these substantial changes, and why did they occur after the 1950s and not before?

The most obvious driving force was the changing economic structure, what is popularly described as 'de-industrialisation', though, as has been argued above, this term is less than helpful. Manual, heavy industrial work has traditionally been the province of the full-time male worker. The decline of some parts of this sector since the mid-1960s hit male employment hard. Over the century as a whole, employment expanded only in the service sector (Table 4.2 and Figure 4.3 above), where females constituted a disproportionate part of the workforce. This does not mean that there was rigid gender segregation between a female service sector and male manufacturing – far from it – but the changing structure of the economy was the main cause of the dramatic change in the gender balance of employment. This also helps to explain why this gender shift did not occur in the inter-war years. Employment growth in services was comparatively modest before 1951, and the impact on the female labour market was dampened by steady contraction in clothing, textiles and private domestic service, all of which had traditionally been very heavy employers of females.

The other major change that accompanied the restructuring of work in the second half of the century was the enormous expansion of part-time employment. The dimensions can be seen in Table 5.1. The growth in all employment between 1951 and 1998 was less than the increase in the number of female part-timers. Part-time employment grew particularly strongly in distribution, hotel and catering, financial services, local authority and health service work, all of which had a long history of employing women on low-paid, insecure work (Dex 1985). Part-time workers were

Table 5.1 Growth of part-time employment in the UK, 1951–98 (thousands of employees in employment)

	Males				Females				All
	Full-time	Part-time	All	% part-time	Full-time	Part-time	All	% part-time	
1951	13 438	45	13 483	0.3	5 752	754	6 506	11.6	19 989
1961	13 852	174	14 026	1.2	5 351	1 892	7 243	26.1	21 269
1971	12 840	584	13 424	4.4	5 467	2 757	8 224	33.5	21 648
1981	11 511	718	12 164	5.9	5 321	4 141	9 462	43.8	21 105
1991	10 432	1 015	11 447	8.9	5 962	4 738	10 664	44.4	22 112
1998	11 360	1 006	12 366	8.1	6 169	4 869	11 038	44.1	23 404

Sources: Robinson 1988; ONS 1999a, Table 7.2.

attractive to service sector employers on cost grounds. Until 1994 employers paid lower statutory and occupational welfare contributions for part-timers than for full-timers, and by using part-time workers employers were able to extend their hours of opening without incurring overtime and premium payments. At the same time, part-time employment was attractive to those women with childcare or other responsibilities who were unable to commit to a conventional working week. Most part-time workers were married or single parents (Robinson 1988). However, part-time workers have low pay, minimal skills, few opportunities for training or promotion and little job security.

Before 1939, on the other hand, distinctions between full- and part-time work were less stark. Whiteside and Gillespie (1991) demonstrated that in a number of industries (dock work and coalmining, for example) casual labour systems had long operated and many workers valued the flexibility of these arrangements. In others (notably, cotton textiles), short-time working was the normal reaction to trade recession. Casual labour systems tended to exert downward pressure on wage rates, and short-time working in recessions (especially when it could be subsidised by state unemployment insurance benefits for laid-off workers) allowed some employers to adjust labour costs without permanently losing their skilled workers. Indeed, in the less depressed parts of the inter-war economy employers began to take a keener interest in the training and retention of their workers (Gospel 1992). Despite these developments, under-employment, an intermediate category between full-time employment and un-employment, was common in Britain before 1939. For a variety of reasons, governments were keen to eradicate these arrangements after 1945 and to modernise work arrangements, not infrequently against the wishes of employees. The tight labour market during the long boom also encouraged employers to hoard labour, for fear that their firms would be short of skilled workers as demand expanded, and then to develop much more sophisticated methods of retaining and developing the skills of the company's core workers. However, there is a pervasive belief that these 'internal labour markets', where firms recruit their workers into a limited number of grades and then rely on training and promotion to fill higher positions, should have been taken further, especially in recent years. Thus, the main changes in employment during the twentieth century were the erosion of the role of the male breadwinner after the mid-1960s and the re-emergence of inter-war patterns of stronger job security for some co-existing with temporary work on part-time contracts for many.

The most obvious reason for the return of greater job insecurity in the last quarter of the century was the return of mass unemployment. While the unemployed are easy to define as 'those willing and able to work but unable to find it', it has proved to be extremely difficult to operationalise definitions of both unemployment and the workforce. Indeed, the question of definition became acutely politicised in both the 1930s and the 1980s, when governments were accused of 'massaging' the unemployment statistics (Glynn 1991, 20–5). In practice, historians and social scientists have tended to work with official statistics of unemployment in which definitional problems have been subjugated to administrative convenience. Some of these series are given in Figure 5.2. The only continuous data for the late nineteenth and early twentieth centuries were produced by a number of trade unions that made returns to the Board of Trade, but estimates of unemployment in the wider economy cannot be drawn from so unrepresentative a base. The national insurance scheme, introduced in 1911 and extended to cover most manual workers in 1916 and 1920, provides much better coverage for the inter-war years (Garside 1990, 34–8). The scheme applied to only 60 per cent of the workforce and insurance figures exaggerated the extent of unemployment in the wider economy. Most of the excluded groups were non-manual workers and much less likely to suffer unemployment than insured workers. Attempts to use other information to estimate the scale of exaggeration vary from one-fifth (Feinstein 1972, 220–2) to approximately one-third (Metcalf et al. 1982). The postwar unemployment insurance statistics were accepted as a reasonable indicator of actual unemployment after 1948, but it became increasingly clear that there were substantial differences between different countries' methods of defining and measuring both the number of unemployed and the size of the workforce. There are many different ways to standardise definitions, and one attempt is given in Figure 5.2 in the series compiled by Maddison. It confirms the general impression that the inter-war unemployment insurance

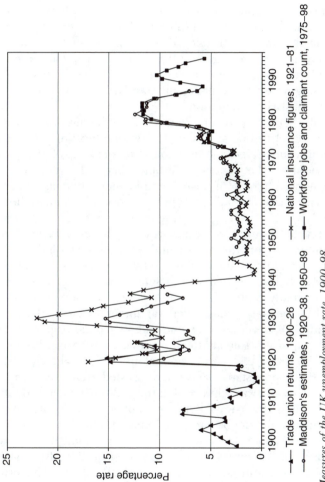

Figure 5.2 *Measures of the UK unemployment rate, 1900–98*

Sources: Insurance figures and trade union returns: DEP 1971, various tables; Annual Abstract of Statistics, various issues; claimant count: ONS 2000, Table 3.4; Maddison's estimates: Maddison 1991, Table C6.

figures exaggerate 'standardised' unemployment, but that the postwar insurance figures are underestimates, especially to the mid-1970s. For these reasons, revisions were planned in the way that British unemployment statistics were compiled, but they were overtaken by political interference as the Conservative governments of the 1980s, in a period when unemployment was rising rapidly, made a series of substantial revisions to definitions, almost all of which had the effect of lowering the rate of recorded unemployment. From the later 1980s the government's annual survey of the economy produced several estimates of unemployment, using both an internationally standardised basis and various different British definitions.

After this lengthy prologue, some generalisations are possible about the level of unemployment in twentieth-century Britain. We know comparatively little about the working of the pre-1914 labour market, but it is certainly likely that the underemployment inherent in casual employment systems (where workers are hired at traditional spots to work for a limited duration and which encouraged gross oversupply) was as bad as unemployment caused by variations in the business cycle. With only limited support for the unemployed, there was little alternative to irregular employment (Whiteside 1979). The First World War helped regularise and standardise the employment system in many industries, but the steep recession of 1920–2 ushered in the age of mass inter-war unemployment. Between 1921 and 1938, never less than one million manual wage-earners were unemployed. Initially unemployment was spread broadly, but the distinctive pattern of regional and industrial concentration on the export staples and the depressed areas emerged by the late 1920s and was reinforced in the 1930s (Glynn and Booth 1983). Although inter-war unemployment occasionally provoked social unrest, it did not become a dominant political issue, in part because the Labour Party was reluctant to exploit it (Garside 1990, part 5). Unemployment disappeared quickly after 1939, and by 1943 a 'labour famine' had developed and forced government to innovate a sophisticated method of allocating contracts for work to firms with workers available. From the successful postwar demobilisation in 1945–6 until the 1970s, the British economy enjoyed full employment, no matter what definitions of 'workforce' and 'unemployment' are chosen. In the early part of the period, job vacancies comfortably exceeded the number of unemployed, but the pressure of excess demand gradually eased and there was a tendency for unemployment to rise slightly at each business cycle recession. However, perspective is needed. Unemployment remained below 4 per cent on Maddison's standardised basis until the early 1970s, and even in the 1970s unemployment remained well below inter-war levels. It is worth remembering also that, even though full employment was difficult to manage, a buoyant labour market was compatible with both an aggregate surplus in the current balance of payments and modest inflation. During the 1970s governments struggled to balance rising inflation and unemployment, until the early 1980s, when the Thatcher government sacrificed domestic employment in its effort to squeeze inflation (Chapter 6). Unemployment rose rapidly in the early 1980s and responded only slowly to macroeconomic recovery. It was already clear that unemployment was concentrated on a relatively small part of the workforce, so the rise in unemployment in the 1980s caused its duration to rise and regional concentration to increase. The echoes from the 1930s were deafening. In many respects the problem of long-term unemployment was more substantial and durable in the 1980s than in the 1930s (Table 5.2). The inter-war division between a prosperous 'inner Britain' and the 'depressed areas' was replicated in an equally stark 'north–south divide' (Table 5.3). As in the inter-war years, recorded unemployment was heavily concentrated among males. Unemployment fell in both the later 1980s and the later 1990s, but the slump of the early 1990s was almost as steep as that of 1979–82 (Figure 5.2). Finally, there were new features in the 1980s in the shape of a youth unemployment problem and high rates of unemployment among some ethnic minorities (Glynn and Booth 1996, 287–8). The unemployment of the late twentieth century was less severe than that of the inter-war years, but it nonetheless came as a very rude shock to the economic system and stimulated major changes in economic analysis and policy, as will be seen in Chapter 6.

All markets are socially constructed, and none more so than that for human labour. Britain's labour market at the beginning of the century was conditioned by institutions (socially constructed rules and conventions) that had developed slowly, in

Table 5.2   *The duration of unemployment in the UK, 1929–98*

Percentage of the total unemployed in each category (all workers, September figures to 1951, July thereafter).

	up to 4 weeks		4–26 weeks	26–52 weeks	more than 52 weeks
1929		65.0		32.1	4.8
1937		65.7		10.1	24.2
1948	41.7		34.0	10.3	14.0
1951	50.0		28.9	7.6	13.6
1974	31.9		34.3	12.1	21.6
1979	24.0		36.3	15.2	24.5
1986	11.6		28.1	19.2	41.1
1990	16.1		34.8	17.5	31.7
1997		50.1		14.8	35.1

Note: Data before 1939 and after 1994 do not distinguish a separate category 'up to 4 weeks'.
Sources: 1929 and 1937: *Ministry of Labour Gazette*, vol. 38 (1930), pp. 6–8; vol. 45 (1937), p. 400.
1948 and 1951: DEP 1971, Table 175.
1974–90: *Employment Gazette*, various issues.
1997: DEE 1998, Table C1.

some cases over several centuries, in the areas of wage levels and differentials, work practices and relationships and employment contracts (Fox 1985). Many have argued that during the twentieth century the labour market was a prisoner of the past, prevented from adjusting sufficiently to meet new challenges by the conservative forces of history and tradition. The remainder of this chapter is concerned with the role of rules and rule makers in the 'British disease'. Three areas of concern are identified: pay, productivity and the provision of skills. We begin with pay.

Wage Bargaining in Twentieth-century Britain

At the turn of the century, British industrial relations were in an embryonic state. A few employers recognised trade unions through employers' associations, which negotiated and administered collective agreements on wages and conditions of work (Gospel 1992). Procedures for handling disputes between

Table 5.3 Regional unemployment rates in the UK, 1923–98 (average percentage rates)

	1923–9	1930–8	1948–64	1965–73	1974–9	1980–9	1990–6
London	7.3	9.4	1.1	1.6	2.6	6.3	7.8
South-East	6.3	9.4		2.1	3.0	6.6	6.3
East Anglia				2.5	3.9	7.3	7.3
South-West	8.6	12.0	1.6	2.1	3.5	10.5	8.8
W. Midlands	9.6	13.7	1.1	1.9	3.0	8.0	7.8
E. Midlands				2.5	3.5	10.0	8.9
Yorks & Humber	14.0	20.7	2.7	4.3	5.2	12.9	10.6
North							
North-West	12.8	21.2	2.1	2.7	4.6	11.4	9.4
Wales	15.9	30.0	2.9	3.7	4.8	11.2	8.9
Scotland	13.2	21.6	3.3	4.1	4.9	11.3	8.8
UK overall	12.2	16.5	1.8	2.2	3.6	9.0	8.4

Note: Regional boundaries were redrawn during the period, and changed drastically in May 1997.
Sources: DEP 1971, various tables; ONS 1997, Table 3.3.

employers' associations and unions tended to be national and industry-wide, but wages and conditions were settled at local level. In broad terms, the historiography is divided between those who argue that employers were fragmented, prevaricating and weak in dealings with powerful craft unions, and an alternative view of employers' associations as powerful and effective agents of the employer interest (for a recent review of the debate, see McIvor 1996). In part, the differences hinge on interpretations of the effectiveness of unions and employers in manipulating government.

The British labour movement was weak in 1900. It suffered a major reversal in the courts in 1901 with the Taff Vale decision, which limited union powers to conduct successful strikes (Clegg et al. 1964), and it was also hit by a downturn in the business cycle in 1900–5. Some employers remained vigorously anti-union, and even those who bargained with unions fully exploited their market power. These were years of slow growth of earnings and retail prices (Figure 5.3) and almost static trade union membership (Figure 5.4). The weakness of the economic upswing which began in 1905 and growing frustration at the inability of the new Labour Party to exploit its parliamentary position created tensions that boiled over in one of the most explosive periods in twentieth-century British industrial relations. Between 1910 and 1920, trade union membership more than trebled (Figure 5.4). Density, or the proportion of the workforce belonging to trade unions, increased slightly faster, and this growth in trade union strength was accompanied by surges in industrial unrest, both before and after the First World War (Figure 5.5). This period has been a magnet for historians and social scientists and has provoked classics in historical and socio-political writing (Dangerfield 1935; Phelps Brown 1959; Middlemas 1979). The key features are now well established. Rising industrial unrest was accompanied by an explosion of working-class interest in radical ideas, especially related to workers' control of industry. Ideology almost certainly had no more than a marginal impact on the scale and nature of unrest at the national level, but in specific industries and areas (notably in the South Wales coalfield and parts of the transport sector) the ideas of industrial unionism and workers' control tapped into and channelled patterns of discontent (Holton 1976; Egan 1996). Most disputes concerned the 'bread

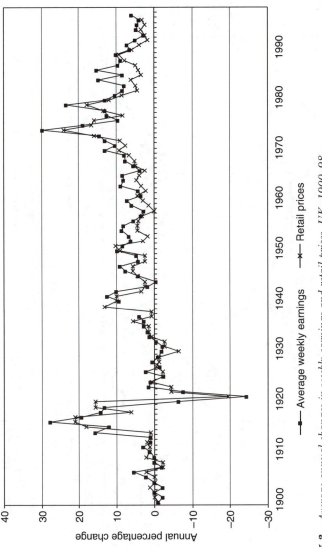

Figure 5.3 *Average annual changes in weekly earnings and retail prices, UK, 1900–98*

Sources: both series to 1965, Feinstein 1972, Table 65; prices since 1965; ONS 2000, Table 2.1; earnings since 1972, *Annual Abstract of Statistics* various issues. There are no earnings figures for 1939–40.

136

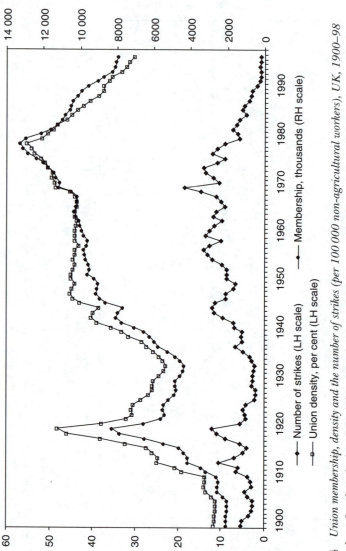

Figure 5.4 *Union membership, density and the number of strikes (per 100 000 non-agricultural workers), UK, 1900–98*

Sources: number of trade unionists: DEP 1971; *Annual Abstract of Statistics*, various issues; civil employment (for density): Figure 5.1; strikes; Flora et al. 1987, 749–57, and *AAS*.

137

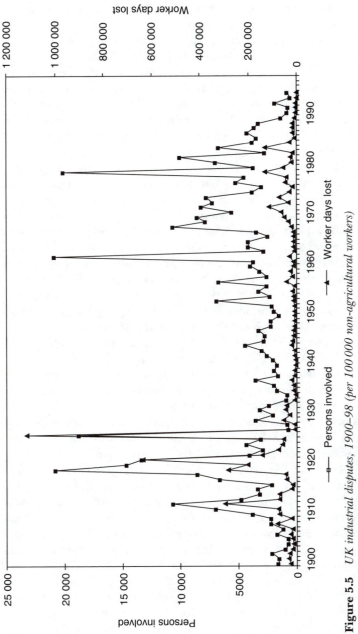

Figure 5.5 *UK industrial disputes, 1900–98 (per 100 000 non-agricultural workers)*
Sources: Flora et al. 1987, 749–57; *Annual Abstract of Statistics*, various issues.

and butter' issues of pay, hours and conditions, even though a number of union labour leaders were profoundly influenced by the radical ideologies of syndicalism and other forms of workers' control. Politicians and leading civil servants became increasingly perturbed at the scale of confrontation and state efforts to conciliate between employers and their workers expanded enormously. Lloyd George, in particular, tried to bolster the moderates on both sides of industry by admitting them into policy-making circles and steering government policy towards their legitimate demands. These developments helped to foster the slow emergence of national pay bargaining, between representatives of national employers' associations and national unions.

The First World War accentuated the difficulties of an already uncertain situation. The labour market tightened as a large proportion of the male workforce enlisted. Accelerating inflation (evident from Figure 5.3), especially when coupled with higher profits in the munitions industry and rising rents for workers in the main engineering districts, heightened the sense of grievance over wages that had already festered before 1914. In these conditions, trade union membership and density grew spectacularly (Figures 5.4 and 5.5), as did membership of employers' organisations. Growth of national collective bargaining not only accelerated but also broadened and grew in sophistication, with strong support from the government. In effect the new Ministry of Production came, via its control of compulsory arbitration, to determine wage rates in engineering and many other sectors (Wrigley 1987a). Running parallel were major changes in shopfloor bargaining. Full employment and the need for production at almost any cost gave great power to the shopfloor workgroup and led to an enormous expansion of workplace bargaining over a wide-ranging terrain (Hyman 1987; Hinton 1973). These two levels of bargaining increasingly came into conflict, and the wartime government machine did everything possible to legitimate the position of national union leaders. Despite these tensions levels of industrial unrest fell and wage rates barely kept pace with inflation. The operation of the wartime 'system' of industrial relations bore heavily in many ways on the position of the relatively well-paid, skilled worker. Pay differentials narrowed. Union leaders accepted that, for the duration of the war, skills could be 'diluted'; that is, semi-skilled workers could perform work normally regarded as the preserve of skilled workers. The system of 'leaving certificates', designed to keep essential workers in those firms undertaking work of national importance, prevented manual labourers from exploiting their market position. The increases in wartime earnings visible in Figure 5.3 came from longer hours and more effort. Thus, the huge deterioration in Britain's export competitiveness noted in Chapter 3 did not arise from bald trade union exploitation of labour scarcity during wartime. Employers, on the other hand, viewed wartime extensions of trade union organisation and heavy taxation of their profits with concern, and many were deeply troubled by the lengthening tentacles of the wartime state. These mutual antagonisms and frustrations boiled over in 1919–20. With continuing full employment and substantial inflation, unions won a sharp reduction in the length of the normal working week without reduction in pay and pressed for higher wages, greater control at the workplace and a reconstruction programme similar to that adopted in 1945 with a militancy and independence that disturbed leaders of industry, government and formal trade unionism.

However, in the slump which began in 1920 prices collapsed, and earnings followed as unemployment rates soared, short-time working spread and most of the postwar increase in union membership evaporated very quickly (Figures 5.3, 5.2, 5.4). Workplace organisation crumbled in many industries, especially engineering. Employers' associations pressed home a vigorous counter-attack (Wigham 1973, 110–25). The wartime experiments in state control of industry were unravelled in ways that weakened the more radical demands for workers' control and nationalisation. The miners suffered particularly severely as the return of the industry from state control to private ownership implied big pay cuts, which were accepted only after bitter disputes (Wrigley 1987b, 81–7). Earnings and wage rates fell during the slump of 1920–2. However, a curious, and to contemporaries increasingly perplexing, change overtook the labour market as the slump eased. Money wages stabilised; they did not continue their slide, despite high unemployment. Some employers attempted to break this 'stickiness' of wages after 1922–3 (evident from Figure 5.3) by *force majeure*, with the coal owners in the van. Industrial relations in coalmining were dire, and had widespread ramifications. The mineworkers frequently called upon the wider trade union movement for support, and owners tried to enlist the government's powers of mobilisation, persuasion and news management. Economic conditions favoured the owners, however, and a planned sympathy strike by the railway and transport unions collapsed in 1921. Confrontation continued and boiled up again in 1925–6. The coal owners, faced by evidence of obvious lack of competitiveness in export markets and losses also on domestic coal, demanded lower wages and longer working hours. The union insisted that cost reductions should come from efficiency improvements, not labour costs. The government's attempts to mediate merely delayed the confrontation from July 1925 to May 1926. Both sides went to war at the head of more powerful forces. The Trades Union Congress (TUC) called a national sympathy strike for the miners, the general strike, and the mine owners were greatly aided by the decision of the government to treat the strike as a threat to the constitution rather than a trade dispute. The general strike of course collapsed quickly, but the miners remained out for months and were effectively starved into submission. The costs of enforcing wage reduction in coalmining far exceeded any benefits of lower wages. Indeed, wage rates remained remarkably stable after 1926. Trade union organisation remained remarkably resilient in the face of extremely adverse economic conditions. The slump of the early 1920s brought a major collapse in membership and density, with further reductions after the general strike (Figure 5.4). But organisation held up pretty well in the downturn of 1929–32 (the worst effects of which were felt in the established union heartlands of coal and manufacturing) in part because of greater support for orthodox trade unionism among many employers. Others, however, were worried about the impact of unions on wages and unemployment (Casson 1983).

Contemporaries and some later economists have seen sticky real wages as the principal cause of inter-war unemployment. Beenstock and colleagues (1984) argued that the rise in unemployment in 1929–32 was caused by a rapid rise in the real wage and, conversely, that the growth of employment after 1932 was the result of moderation in wage growth. However, further investigations have suggested that rising real wages made some contribution to changes in employment, but employers were driven more by falling demand for their products than by the rising cost of labour when shedding employees (Hatton 1994, 378–9; Dimsdale 1984). Although high wages were probably not the prime cause of the unemployment problem, real wages became more rigid in the inter-war years. The halving of union density from 1920 to 1933 (Figure 5.4) makes union resistance an unlikely cause. Employers in the export trades reshaped collective bargaining to meet their competitive needs and reversed wartime centralisation (Gospel 1992, 89–90). Contemporaries also argued that the extensions in the national insurance scheme, noted above, made wages less flexible downwards, by giving employees an alternative to grudging acceptance of wage cuts (Casson 1983). This argument has also been taken up more recently and has formed the foundation of a substantial reinterpretation of the functioning of the inter-war labour market (Benjamin and Kochin 1979). These arguments are best discussed as one aspect of a more general critique of the economic effects of British social welfare policy (see Chapter 6), but it is sufficient at this point to note that they carry little conviction. Union strength, generous welfare benefits and inflexible wage bargaining institutions are unlikely to have caused Britain's (comparatively modest) inter-war unemployment problem, especially as, on a European scale, mass unemployment clearly resulted from deficient demand (Feinstein et al. 1997, 138).

The flexibility of British institutional arrangements for wage determination was strikingly evident during the Second World War. Although wage bargaining nominally remained free, the British labour market became more centralised and neo-corporatist. When Ernest Bevin became Minister of Labour in 1940, he acquired enormous power over labour allocation, work conditions and the conduct of industrial relations, but these were used sparingly on the understanding that national leaders of trade unions and employers' associations would control their members. It was also understood that prices of essential goods would be controlled and that the distribution of both consumer goods and raw materials for industry would be 'fair'. These methods and a sympathetic and intellectually coherent macroeconomic policy helped control inflation much better than in 1914–18 (Figure 5.3). Wage pressures remained a constant concern for policy-makers, especially in engineering and coal-mining, hardly surprising given the scale of excess demand for and massive redistribution of industrial labour (Howlett 1994). But wartime policy helped create conditions for relatively stable wages and prices. This system was much less efficient at defusing industrial discontent. Just as in 1914–18, wartime over-full employment gave new power to the workgroup and fostered the growth of workplace trade union organisation, which was frequently at odds with the national leadership (Hinton 1994). Workplace radicals became fierce critics of managerial inefficiency and strong advocates of a greater managerial role for organised labour. Wartime controls also generated friction, with engineering workers again concerned about the dilution of skilled labour and coalminers upset by the essential work orders, which effectively prevented them from quitting for less arduous, better-paid work elsewhere in the war economy (Harris 1984, 64–70). Thus, strike frequency was high, but relatively few workers were involved and strikes were comparatively short (Figures 5.4 and 5.5).

Given the huge deterioration of Britain's balance of payments during the war, there was a strong case for retaining much of this system into peacetime, but the unions objected to state regulation of the peacetime labour market even though their own recon-struction policy envisaged far-reaching government economic controls. They were certainly not opposed on principle to the idea of responsible behaviour in pay bargaining, but they expected that the burdens of moderation would be spread equally and the grounds for it fully explained (Panitch 1976, 15–20). The TUC firmly opposed government demands for wage restraint during 1947, but strained to make a 'voluntary' wage freeze work from the spring of 1948 (Jones 1987, 35–7). TUC leaders found themselves caught between government pressure for tighter discipline and the growing frustration of ordinary workers as profits and prices continued to rise. The Attlee pay policy, which was really only exhortation and arm-twisting, crumbled in 1950 and made union leaders suspicious of repeating the exercise. It is customary to portray this collapse as evidence of the failure of British decentralised institutions, but Britain's inflation rate during this exceptionally difficult period was comparatively low, despite excess demand for labour and unfavourable movements in the terms of trade.

British inflation remained roughly at the OECD average until 1970 (Woodward 1991, 191), but there was a growing sense that British performance was relatively poor and that the trade unions were primarily to blame for the steady rise in underlying inflation from the late 1950s. Conservative ministers began to attack union 'greed' and search for new anti-inflationary policies in the later 1950s (Booth 2000). Trade union leaders were finding it increasingly difficult to maintain the discipline of their workplace organisation. Official strikes, signifying the breakdown of formal negotiations between employers' organisations and central union leaderships, were comparatively rare, but 'unofficial' or 'unconstitutional' stoppages began to increase (Taylor 1993, 116–18). During the long boom, four phases of industrial unrest can be identified: a period of postwar peace, lasting from 1946 to 1952; the return of the strike during the remainder of the 1950s; the period of the shopfloor movement, which extended to 1968; and the high tide of rank-and-file militancy in the early 1970s (Durcan et al. 1983; Lyddon 1999). Disputes tended to be heavily concentrated in three industries, the coal mines, the docks and motor cars. For different reasons, each of these industries could be presented as particularly important to national economic performance. The coal industry was consistently strike-prone, and the picture of very disturbed industrial relations in a nationalised industry gave Conservative ministers much ammunition to use against the unions. Problems over piecework for coalface workers, the high demand for coal and growing insecurities caused by mechanisation and pit closures generated grievances that tended to produce many short strikes involving small groups of workers. The National Coal Board eventually found a technological solution to some of its problems in the greater use of power-loading equipment and the consequent ending of piecework (McCormick 1979). In the docks, the situation was equally complex and centred on the gradual loss of authority of the Transport and General Workers' Union (TGWU) as a result of its efforts to 'decasualise' the industry through the Dock Labour Scheme, which was established in 1947. Although decasualisation had been a long-term objective of the union, its operation constrained the traditional freedoms of dockworkers to choose whether or not they attended for work and whether they would accept work that was offered. In the eyes of some dockworkers, the union began to act almost as an agent of discipline rather than as a bargaining agent of the workforce. The union's authority slowly crumbled and rival unions began to recruit and challenge the TGWU's position. This confused position was almost guaranteed to produce rather than settle conflict and, given the importance of the docks to the export drive, the persistent conflict and confusion in the ports gave the critics of British unions ample ammunition (Phillips 1996). Perhaps the most important centre of industrial conflict was the automobile industry, which was in many ways the central manufacturing industry during the long boom. Its problems were to a considerable extent inherent in its organisation and structures. As will be seen below, there is a tendency for industrial conflict to increase as the scale of production rises. The industry suffered in two ways. First, the companies in British ownership tended to use piecework systems to drive workers to higher effort. It has been argued that in the tight labour market, managers lost control of the system with enormous penalties on costs and productivity (Lewchuk 1987, ch. 9), but as was evident from Chapter 4 there are doubts about this analysis. Nevertheless, this decentralised bargaining system generated a steady undercurrent of small-scale strikes. The companies in US ownership tended to rely on more centralised payment systems, but Ford in particular had serious problems in industrial relations in the later 1950s and early 1960s (Turner et al. 1967; Lyddon 1996). The industry as a whole was subject to strong cyclical changes in demand, and all companies were liable to experience major industrial unrest during downswings in the cycle. To outside observers, industrial relations in the industry could appear chaotic, and shop stewards, who were the central actors in workplace bargaining, tended to be portrayed as agents of chaos. Fred Kite, the character played by Peter Sellers in the British film *I'm all right Jack*, was in many ways the personification of the disruptive, over-powerful shop steward. The tendency to see the unions as agents of disruption and greed increased in the 1950s as strikes over wages became more prominent (Cronin 1979, 213). Thus, the trade union movement could be portrayed by its enemies as the cause of both industrial conflict and the gradual increase in wage pressure. At the same time, economists attempted to explain inflation in terms of the degree of union aggression on wage demands. Mainstream Keynesian analysis also began to insist that union power was an important and independent inflationary force. British commentators became much more interested in incomes policy to secure both short-run competitive advantages and more stable, longer-term growth of production and incomes. But British incomes policy, either as informal exhortation or, from the 1960s, as formal and statutory measures, was very different from the European pattern. British governments typically resorted to incomes policy hurriedly to sustain confidence in sterling in the midst of a balance of payments crisis. The first phase of pay policy was usually tough but would be eased significantly once the external crisis had abated. The third stage usually witnessed collapse, as catch-up claims were pressed by workers who had been particularly ill served by the hurried introduction (Brittan and Lilley 1977). Much of the blame for slow acceleration of inflation and the simultaneous rise in strike activity (Figures 5.3, 5.4 and 5.5) during the 1960s was thus laid at the door of workplace trade unionism, and in particular of the shop steward, who became the focal point of popular criticism of British unions.

The broad thrust (though not the detail) of this criticism was underlined in the most authoritative survey of postwar industrial relations, the Donovan report (Cmnd 3623 1968), which famously concluded that Britain had two systems of industrial relations, one at the industry level conducted by full-time officials of employers' associations and trade unions and the other at the workplace conducted by shop stewards and line managers, and they were in conflict. The report directed most of its criticism at management for its failure in many cases even to develop the idea of an internal pay policy. Even this apparently firm evidence of institutional failure was almost certainly overdrawn. The driving intellectual force was Hugh Clegg, Professor of Industrial Relations at Warwick University, who subsequently conceded that this conclusion was somewhat exaggerated (Clegg 1979, 232–40). Government ministers tended to see the Donovan analysis as insufficiently vigorous and wanted more immediate and substantial reform of Britain's voluntary (that is, not subject to legally enforceable rules) system of industrial relations. The Labour government introduced a white paper, *In Place of Strife*, which proposed limited state intervention to limit strikes and lockouts. However, it created enormous tension between the unions and the government and within cabinet, and its proposals were not enacted (Taylor 1993, 151–73). Nevertheless, the Donovan report's specific recommendations had much greater influence in company boardrooms than in the cabinet. Many companies withdrew from industry-wide collective bargaining, created company- and plant-level negotiating frameworks, and strengthened their personnel management resources accordingly. Progressive firms had already moved in this direction before the Donovan report, but the pace of change accelerated in the mid-1970s and again in the later 1980s. By the early 1990s, the role of employers' organisations in pay determination had diminished significantly as single employer collective bargaining had spread rapidly.

These observations apply to the private sector. Public sector pay bargaining had its own trajectory, with a much less important role for workplace bargaining but a much more substantial impact, often adverse, from government pay policy. Throughout the postwar period, governments always implemented pay policy more severely in the public than in the private sector, with the railways (in the 1950s) and local authority workers (in the 1970s) as the prime targets for 'informal pay policy'. Since public sector pay bargaining was conducted at the national level, disputes could lead to big strikes. The rise in indicators of strike activity in the early 1970s and in the mid-1980s reflects the sharpening of conflict in the coal mines, and the peak in 1979 owes much to the radicalisation of public sector manual and non-manual workers who bore the brunt of pay policy during the decade (Gilbert 1996, 143). There were, however, no major disputes in the public sector after the defeat of the miners' strike in 1985, even though governments continued to use public sector pay to indicate their views to the private sector on tolerable increases in wages.

Private employers faced much more favourable conditions in the labour market after 1979. The big rise in unemployment noted above clearly weakened labour at the shopfloor level, just as in the inter-war years. Major changes to industrial relations law to discipline the unions were also introduced by the Conservatives after 1979. Union membership and density fell consistently in this unfriendly environment (Figure 5.4). Some employers also 'de-recognised' trade unions for collective bargaining purposes. Despite these changes, wages continued to rise strongly, especially in manufacturing where unemployment was most concentrated, and Britain's unit labour costs rose rapidly at roughly the international average (ONS 2000, Table 1.22). Some commentators have suggested that union strength was resilient, despite adverse legislative and labour market conditions (Metcalf 1991). In part, this hypothesis is confirmed by continuing evidence of a 'trade union mark up', or higher pay for trade unionists than non-unionists for the same work, though the whole concept is fraught with measurement problems (Stewart 1990; 1991; Parsley 1980). The other main explanation of the continuing rise of wages during the sharp contraction of manufacturing employment has been the 'insider power' of those in the internal labour markets discussed in the first section of this chapter. Those in relatively secure 'core' employment had firm-specific skills, which the firm would want to retain, develop and reward. The unemployed, on the other hand, experienced deterioration of their own skills and the increasingly long spells of unemployment noted above. Internal labour markets and insider power are statistically associated with trade union presence, but trade unionism is not a necessary condition. Thus, the internal labour market offers a plausible explanation of trends in the labour market towards the end of the century, but commentators differ widely on the extent of internal labour markets in Britain.

In sum, labour market conditions of the last quarter of the twentieth century might call into question much of the received opinion about the impact of unions, employers and institutions on British economic performance. The pace of institutional change during the last 30 years was remarkable. The prime movers in much of this were the employers, who did not simply jump onto the first passing bandwagon but implemented a variety of labour management policies suited to their specific needs (Ackers et al. 1996, 25–6). These experiments were very clearly beginning in the late 1960s, long before the explosions first of inflation in the 1970s and then of unemployment. It is also pretty clear that Britain had, in government attempts to manage public sector pay, something close to a permanent postwar incomes policy, albeit loose, informal and somewhat uneven. The case against British institutions in the management of pay and competitiveness is much less strong than conventionally believed.

Surprisingly, the same can be said about the impact of unions on the pace of productivity change.

Unions and Productivity Growth

Nichols (1986) drew attention to the 'British worker question' – the idea that British workers were lazy, limited their work effort and had too much power over production through their unions – which was a fundamental part of postwar political culture. There is not much evidence of the unions as threats to productivity growth before 1939 (apart from the period 1910–20), and during the Second World War trade unions at both the workplace and national levels were clearly identified with the cause of higher production (Hinton 1994). In the later 1940s the TUC was a strong champion of faster productivity growth, in part to deflect some of the pressure for stronger control over wages. But in the 1950s, Conservative ministers found it expedient to blame unions for causing inflation (see above), and successive governments from 1966 attempted to reform either the trade unions or the wage bargaining process. The Thatcher governments perfected the technique of populist 'union bashing', and the identification of the unions as 'the enemy within' certainly struck a chord in some quarters of British society. Allen (1979, 61–8), Barnett (1986, 199–200) and others claimed that the endemic labour troubles in large-scale British industry slowed the diffusion of labour-saving plant and resulted in low investment and chronic overstaffing. In effect, class-war mentalities still pervaded British industry. However, Britain appears in the middle of international tables of postwar industrial unrest, performing consistently worse than Germany, Sweden and the Netherlands, but consistently better than Italy and Australia and better than the USA until the mid-1970s (Gilbert 1996, 131–3). However, inconvenient facts should not be allowed to get in the way of a good argument. Several authorities suggested that Britain might have had a much lower strike rate that the USA, for example (typically about one-third of US rates of industrial conflict between 1945 and 1970), but the small scale and unpredictability of British strikes and the preoccupation with job demarcation were more damaging for productivity growth (Alford 1988, 71; Phelps

Brown 1977). This seems a wholly implausible argument, but indicates the determination to pin down a trade union responsibility for what appeared to be weak British economic performance. There are good grounds for circumspection. Even in the strike-prone years of 1971–3, 98 per cent of British plants remained free of stoppages in any one year, and 95 per cent were strike-free for all three years (DoE 1976, 1219–24). The improvement in British industrial relations after 1985 (Figures 5.4, 5.5) may reflect the belated disciplining of British unions by the reforms to industrial relations law by the Thatcher government, but most other OECD countries experienced similar improvements at the same time without Thatcherite legislation and conflict (Gilbert 1996, 133). British industrial relations were not *uniquely* coloured by the overhang of class conflict from an earlier industrial era. The largest British factories were strike-prone, but the tendency for strike-proneness to increase with plant size was common to other developed economies, especially during the 1970s (Prais 1981, 261–3). However, the example of Longbridge, cited in the previous chapter, suggests that labour relations problems and high efficiency were certainly not incompatible in very large plants, provided that design, marketing and production engineering were of a high standard. Perhaps the econometricians have been looking at the wrong variables, and even the wrong direction of causality, to discover why the largest British factories underperformed.

The idea that British workers developed a culture of low effort, overmanning and systemic inefficiency is another part of popular mythology allegedly given academic solidity. Pratten's (1976) much-quoted study undertook three paired comparisons (of the UK with North America; Germany; and France) of labour productivity levels within different plant of international companies. He found that, on average, the British branches tended to have lower productivity in all industries. The causes were divided more or less equally between 'economic fundamentals' (such as differences in product mixes, lengths of production runs, levels of investment per worker) and 'behavioural factors' (such as the incidence of strikes and major restrictive practices, manning levels and effort). Nichols (1986, 55–63), however, exposed enormous methodological flaws, notably a substantial bias in the data and the total absence of objective observation in Pratten's analysis. Another highly influential report, the government's Central Policy Review Staff's survey of motor manufacturing, concluded that British firms were driven to both overmanning and underproduction by failings on 'the labour side' (CPRS 1975). Similarly, Caves (1980, 179) concluded that Britain's productivity problem lay 'in long-standing attitudes of the workforce that sustain hostility to change and co-operation'. In both cases, Nichols (1986, 40, 74–105, 243–52) demonstrated that what was presented as objective economic evidence was little more than untested managerial prejudice. The argument that British workers were uniquely obstructive and antagonistic to changes lacks convincing academic support. It is worth noting that when worker attitudes to technical change and higher labour productivity were measured directly in the mid-1980s, workers and their unions were strongly in favour, since such changes usually resulted in higher earnings (Daniel 1987, 182–209). This is, in fact, the only piece of hard evidence on worker attitudes to technical change; there are no well-documented cases of British unions uniquely frustrating technical change since 1945. Even in the allegedly notorious case of worker resistance, the printing of national newspapers in Fleet Street, the British position was far from unique. US and German national newspaper publishers had similar problems and also needed to force through technological change by confrontation (Prais 1981, 200–2). Looking back on industrial relations and technical change in what used to be called Fleet Street (itself a measure of change in the industry), the British record now appears to be much less distinctive than it seemed during the years of most intensive national self-preoccupation in the 1970s.

There is nonetheless a strong theme in the literature on British industry that identifies trade union power, particularly that exercised by craft workers, as the main cause of Britain's alleged productivity failure. Braverman's (1974) study of the close control by US managers of the pace and methods of production (or the labour process) stimulated comparative studies. Kilpatrick and Lawson (1980) suggested that British craft workers' control over the labour process prevented British firms from introducing the mass production methods pioneered by US manufacturers. Most of their examples were drawn from the nineteenth century, but they have since been supplemented by studies inspired by

Braverman and Chandler of cotton textiles (Lazonick 1986), steel (Elbaum 1986) and motor cars (Lewchuk 1986; 1987). They tell a common story of workers exercising formidable constraints upon entrepreneurial and managerial action. The analysis is, however, vulnerable because in a whole range of industries British firms were faced by a more varied pattern of demand than their US counterparts and needed the flexibility that craft-intensive methods provided (Kirby 1992). This radical literature inspired by labour process studies has been supplemented by more orthodox institutional accounts, which have also found the cause of Britain's apparent productivity problem in the craft origins of its national labour movement. The work of Olson noted in Chapter 2 inspired a number of studies linking national rates of labour productivity growth to the structure and durability of national labour market institutions. The best-known is that of Batstone (1986), which demonstrated an apparently strong link between national institutional characteristics and the pace of labour productivity growth during the long boom. However, his link disappeared in the 1970s, and in subsequent decades many countries experienced evolutionary institutional transformation. The basis of this whole analysis was that institutions, once established, could be transformed only by major social upheaval. In countries where institutions adapt to changes in political and economic circumstances, the present cannot be a prisoner of the past.

Despite these recent basic problems with the main strands of institutional analysis, the tendency to blame unions for Britain's manufacturing productivity gap increased after 1980, primarily because an upswing in the economy coincided with obvious reductions in trade union strength at the workplace and in national politics. The availability of much more detailed data on output, inputs and matters relating to industrial relations from individual establishments, the workplace industrial relations survey (WIRS), stimulated an explosion of research in labour economics, which still seems to point an accusing finger at British trade unions. The most succinct summary came from Gregg et al. (1993, 906), who suggested that unionised firms had, on average, a lower level of labour productivity than their non-union counterparts around 1980, particularly in large workplaces with a closed shop. Then during the 1980s, unionised companies narrowed and quite possibly eliminated or even reversed the favourable productivity edge previously enjoyed by non-union companies. Productivity growth was fastest in unionised companies, particularly in those which 'de-recognised' unions for some aspects of collective bargaining. The idea that productivity growth accelerated as union power at the workplace declined is widely held, but its application to Britain after 1979 is problematic. Productivity growth in unionised firms came in two bursts during the 1980s. The first occurred in the early 1980s and is consistent with the 'bargaining power' approach, but the second, in the late 1980s, is not (Gregg et al. 1993, 899–903). Furthermore, studies by industrial relations specialists reveal a more fragmented and uncertain picture. Managers certainly demanded higher effort from their workers, but they also improved the technical organisation of work and secured greater worker commitment to the firm (Edwards and Whitston 1991, 598). Managers continued to offer financial rewards to their workers to accept major changes in work organisation. In fact, there were comparatively few major changes to the way that the British labour market functioned, despite the big shifts in workplace bargaining power (Blanchflower and Freeman 1994). Bean and Crafts (1996, 156–8) offered a variant of the crude 'transfer of power' hypothesis in suggestions that the British pattern of multi-union bargaining may hold the key to differences in productivity growth. In 1954–79, productivity growth was higher under single-union bargaining than where employers had to bargain with several unions simultaneously. In effect, each union held the employer to ransom and the employer's incentive to invest in productivity-enhancing change was reduced. The acceleration of productivity growth after 1979 is explained, as above, by shifts in crude bargaining power and the spread of single-union agreements. This is an interesting hypothesis, but it is as yet at only a preliminary stage of development. It is, for example, possible that Crafts and Bean picked up industrial, rather than industrial relations, characteristics and simply found another method of identifying the poorly performing heavy industries of the 1930s (see Chapter 4), where trade union power or fragmentation was not really an issue.

Econometric work on the British 'productivity miracle' has shown a wide variety of stimuli to faster productivity growth after 1979, but efforts to identify a 'British worker problem' have proved essentially unconvincing and rather bluntly conceived. Even a minimal historical perspective cautions against such crude theorising. The collapse of trade union power after 1920 scarcely provoked a productivity miracle, and it is likely that efforts to portray the Thatcher revolution in industrial relations as a turning point in British economic history are equally wide of the mark. Even the tiniest awareness of developments elsewhere suggests that other European countries experienced similar positive changes without having shared Britain's conflict and polarisation.

Workplace Skills and Productivity Growth

The importance of human capital formation to the processes and pace of economic growth has been emphasised in previous chapters, as have the difficulties of definition and measurement. The importance of skilled workers to the trajectory of Britain's economic development scarcely needs emphasising. The high level of skill among manual workers was a decisive advantage in Britain's industrial revolution and the shortage of skilled workers in those countries seeking to follow Britain's lead was almost certainly a decisive disadvantage (Pollard 1981, 147–8). British skilled workers were a match for the more capital-intensive methods of competitors in many Edwardian industries, as was evident in Chapter 4, and skill shortages were a perennial problem for British manufacturers after 1945. Even during the phase of higher unemployment after 1979, many manufacturers complained that they could not fill vacancies for skilled and technical workers.

An insight into the importance of workforce skills is available in the work of a research team at the National Institute of Economic and Social Research (NIESR), which since 1979 has undertaken comparative studies of skill and economic performance (for an overview and assessment, see Prais 1995). This is action-oriented research, without a sense of historical development. But it has tried to identify the precise relationships between education, training and levels of output and productivity that have been so elusive for those who have identified human capital formation as a key variable in economic development. In their study of matched (by type of product, size of firm, scale of production) firms in the British and German machine-tool industries, Daly and colleagues (1985) found that German productivity levels were 50–80 per cent higher than the British. German firms operated more sophisticated machines, but the simpler British equipment tended to break down more frequently and required more maintenance workers. German workers tended to control more machines, thanks to automatic materials-handling devices. The authors identified three basic differences between firms in the two countries. German firms used more production engineers to ensure that work flows and handling equipment were fully utilised. Such high-levels skills were in short supply in Britain. German supervisory staff tended to be better qualified than British and were much better at ensuring that machines were properly set up and used for the most appropriate tasks and that workers were adequately directed. Finally, German firms had proportionately twice as many skilled workers. German workers could more easily undertake the basic cleaning and maintenance tasks that were beyond British semi-skilled staff, and the failure to clean machines was the biggest cause of breakdowns, with breakdowns being the biggest cause of the productivity difference between British and German firms. In a similar comparison of matched firms in the furniture trade, German firms made higher-quality products at higher efficiency levels (Steedman and Wagner 1987). Firms in both countries had access to the same technology, but German workers were able to operate more complex production methods and again secure smoother operation and fuller exploitation of the machinery. German advantage in this case resulted less from vocational (work-based) skills but from higher attainment in mathematics at school and continuing education that enabled German workers to operate computer-controlled machines that could not be used in Britain. These are fascinating studies, but they are small in scale, do not control for the state of market demand, tend to show a productivity gap that is above the average for Anglo-German comparisons for manufacturing as a whole, and have unknown relevance to the wider twentieth century. Indeed, these micro-studies that show an unequivocal link between education, training and productivity are only weakly confirmed in economy-wide data collected by the same research team (see Chapter 7 and the discussion of Figure 7.1). This work does, however, establish a list of important influences for study, starting with the education and training of skilled workers.

International comparisons of workforce skills are at best approximations, and even the best data cover only apprenticeship at different dates throughout the century (Broadberry and Wagner 1996, 249–57). Figure 5.6 presents some of the results in the form of a comparison between British and German apprenticeship in the key metalworking sector during the twentieth century. US data are also available, but on a different basis. The position is, however, reasonably clear-cut: in the USA the traditional apprenticeship had all but disappeared by 1900 apart from a small number of industries and urban centres (Gospel 1994, 510–11). In Europe, apprenticeship had more substantial institutional and market supports and survived more strongly. Britain tended to produce more apprentices than Germany before 1914, but the position was reversed in the inter-war years. Apprenticeship contracted in both countries after 1945, and they appeared to be converging during the long boom. However, from the early 1970s onwards apprenticeship gradually disappeared in the UK, whereas it strengthened in Germany. Broadberry suggests that after 1945 Britain conducted a failed experiment with Fordism whereas Germany placed renewed emphasis on craft production (Broadberry and Wagner 1996, 245–6; Broadberry 1997, 393–4). This is, however, an unpersuasive reading that overlooks the similar trends in both countries in 1950–70 and the extent to which employers and their workers were in conflict over the number of apprentices, the content of their training and the nature of their tasks within the firm.

This latter point may be illustrated with reference to McKinlay's (1991) study of British engineering apprenticeship. In theory, apprenticeship bound together the boy, his guardian and his employer in a formal written contract that guaranteed stability of employment and adequate technical training. Before 1939, however, British employers and skilled workers fought vigorous battles over apprenticeship. The introduction of American semi-automatic machine tools in the 1890s and still more the demonstration during the First World War that semi-skilled 'dilutees' could perform craftwork pushed employers to neglect the

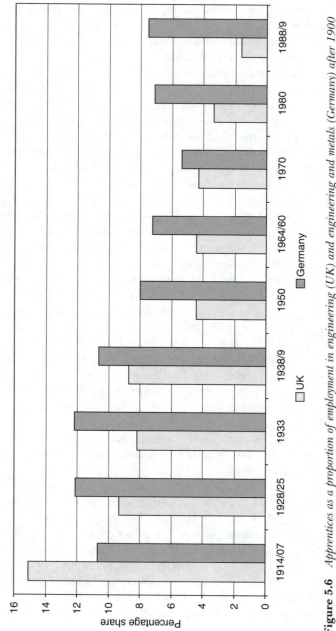

Figure 5.6 *Apprentices as a proportion of employment in engineering (UK) and engineering and metals (Germany) after 1900*
Source: Broadberry and Wagner 1996, Tables 6.2 to 6.5.

content of skilled training. Especially after the engineering employers' success in the lockout of 1922, firms in the newer mass production sectors were able virtually to dispense with apprenticeship and adopt informal patterns of skill development within the firm. In the older sectors, producing in small batches for more varied markets, employers tended to see apprentices more as 'productive boy workers' than as 'learners', and tried to replace fully qualified craftsmen with cheaper apprentice labour. Disputes over the number of apprentices and the nature of their work continued throughout the inter-war years and left the apprenticeship 'system' in a state of near anarchy. During the Second World War, 'dilution' of skilled work proceeded more easily than in 1914–18, and more employers became disenchanted with the general skills provided by apprenticeship training and concentrated on imparting firm-specific skills (Parker 1957, 388). In the much tighter postwar labour markets, skilled workers regained some of the control over apprenticeships that they had lost during the inter-war years, and were accused by the Donovan Commission of restricting entry and inculcating defensive attitudes into new craftsmen. At the same time, the tightness of the labour market and legislative changes were forcing up the rates of pay for juvenile workers closer to those for adults, persuading even progressive employers that they could not afford to train younger workers (Prais 1995, 103). Juvenile workers increasingly preferred higher-paid semi-skilled work to apprenticeship. The narrowing of wage differentials for skill, in part a by-product of incomes policies that imposed flat-rate pay increases, caused some skilled workers to move into higher-paid, semi-skilled work. The contraction of manufacturing employment in the process of de-industrialisation also eroded Britain's stock of formal skills. Thus, Broadberry's technological determinism misses most of the fundamental and contextual problems of British apprenticeship.

It is equally misleading to assume that German engineering firms examined and rejected 'Fordism' in favour of more skill-intensive, flexible indigenous technologies. German entrepreneurs were fascinated by Fordist mass production. Even before 1925 they made pilgrimages to Ford plants in Detroit, bought Ford's autobiography in huge quantities, and devised popular lecture courses on 'Fordismus'. In the VW Beetle, Germany produced one of Fordism's most original creations, extremely large-scale production of a single car based on a single body shell (Abelshauser 1995). Indeed, Abelshauser suggested that Germany's macroeconomic framework after 1945 was well suited to the introduction of 'Fordist' mass production techniques. Whereas other nations tended to produce in increasingly small-scale plant, only Germany's vehicle and component industries continued to produce in large-scale, large-volume factories (Williams et al. 1994). By 1970, the logic of the mass production of motor vehicles and other consumer durables led both Germany and the UK to increasing reliance on semi-skilled, machine-minding labour and a similar diminishing commitment to training skilled labour (Figure 5.6). More German than British firms shifted into higher-quality, smaller-batch production systems after 1970. They took greater advantage of the opportunities afforded by the increasing application of computing to industry, driven in large part by higher wage costs (Streeck 1992, 169–96). There is little evidence to support Broadberry's idea that trends after 1970 were conditioned by strategic decisions made in the early 1950s.

The apprenticeship is, however, only one type of 'intermediate' qualification. Britain has had a wide range of such qualifications issued by organisations like the City and Guilds of London Institute, the Royal Society of Arts, and many others. This decentralised, free market approach to technical and vocational education has frequently been overlooked by those with a narrow focus on apprenticeship. But it was capable of rapid and impressive responses to demands for new skills. Pollard (1989, 194–213) illustrated the huge rise in demand for scientific and technological qualifications just after the turn of the century, as British society first appreciated and struggled to come to terms with the competitive power of German and US industry. However, the steam was already being taken out of the vocational education movement, and technical education became an under-resourced service when compared with other developed countries (Sanderson 1988). These issues are more easily examined in Chapter 7, but the shortcomings of British training for industry were noted regularly. The Labour governments of 1964–70 attempted to reform the system with the Industrial Training Act of 1964. It imposed a levy on all firms which was reimbursed if they

provided training, but British manufacturing firms were enter-
ing a period of difficult financial performance in the 1960s and
resented such additional costs. More sustained efforts were made
to reform training for industry from the mid-1980s, but in part as
a method of coping with the rise of juvenile unemployment
noted in the first section of this chapter. The new training initiatives were designed to ensure that school-leavers received an
extended period of more or less compulsory vocational training.
Equally, reforms of the secondary school curriculum were
designed to ensure, *inter alia*, that education for industry played
a more substantial part. There was a genuine attempt to remedy
some of the deep-seated deficiencies in the system of technical
and vocational education, but much was frankly experimental
and resulted in frequent changes of both regulations and the
institutions through which training was organised and delivered.
An important goal was to reduce the wage expectations of the
young unemployed. The long-term unemployed were also
offered more or less compulsory training and retraining to ease
them back into employment. Thus, there were two parallel, and
not easily compatible, goals, to improve training and reduce
unemployment, with the unfortunate result that training was
provided cheaply and introduced quickly to have the maximum
short-run impact on unemployment (Begg et al. 1991). It is too
early to judge the impact of the initiatives of the 1980s and 1990s,
but interim judgements have given only qualified approval (Finegold and Soskice 1988; Keep and Mayhew 1988).

With apprenticeship on the decline almost from the 1920s and
formal vocational education and training fragmented, much
rested on employers to equip their workers with the necessary
skills. The mass producing engineering firms began to move in
this direction in the 1920s, as noted above. A number of inter-war
firms found that special training programmes within the firm
were the best and most cost-effective method of developing
workforce skills (Gospel 1992, 66). There was also growing reliance on night schools and day-release courses in technical colleges (see Chapter 7). After 1945, the situation was again patchy:
some firms had an excellent reputation for providing training
for both apprentice and non-apprentice labour, whereas the
majority were much less good (Gospel 1992, 157). Comparatively
little changed after 1979 and the 'productivity miracle' in

manufacturing. The shift of workplace power to employers was accompanied by intensification of work but also by accelerated training and retraining of workers (Gallie 1996, 138). These very recent developments mirror inter-war changes, when leading British firms improved their training, while many more responded to increasing competition by tougher management regimes and a faster pace of work, with an eye only on the defence of short-run profitability.

Conclusion: The Labour Market and the British Disease

The summary of the argument on the back cover of G. C. Allen's (1979) account of the 'British disease' contains two points that relate directly to the themes of this chapter. 'In Britain security and preservation have been put before the economic growth necessary for welfare and amenity' and 'Trade unions and management should abandon their present obsolete institutional arrangements and learn from countries where industrial relations are harmonious.' Allen was doing little more than voice very commonly held views of the late 1970s. It was widely believed that the attitudes of British workers were dominated, except when demanding higher pay, by stubborn defensiveness derived from the nineteenth century and passed on to successive generations of workers by sectional, fragmented trade unions. The evidence is rather less convincing. The alleged obstructiveness of British unions to new technology rests upon a tiny base of evidence from industries that were conflictual in all developed countries and econometric studies that fail to carry conviction. Countless statements by union leaders and ordinary workers (in response to questionnaire surveys) show readiness to accept technical change for the higher wages and greater job security that follow, but these are generally overlooked. Equally, there is no satisfactory and convincing academic support for the proposition that British workers were idle or work-shy. Indeed, one of the universal findings of workplace industrial sociology is the desire for workgroups to create their own rules and practices (Thompson 1989, 153–79). Perhaps the most surprising conclusion to emerge from this survey of the working of the various aspects of the British labour market in the twentieth century is the flexibility of arrangements. Decentralised bargaining permitted a range of responses to problems, for example, of setting wages and delivering training for skills. Evidence that unions and managers were imprisoned by obsolete institutional arrangements overlooks the extent to which firms sought new methods of organising their multiple relationships with workers throughout the century. To say that employers had a free hand in shaping the way that they managed their workers is clearly an exaggeration, especially for the period of the long boom, but there is no doubt that managers had more latitude than has been generally supposed. Gospel (1992, 188) concluded his study of the management of labour in Britain thus: 'Taking a long-term perspective, the best interpretation of [changes in the management of labour] is one that stresses market and technological contexts, corporate structures and managerial capabilities, and employer choice of strategies.' Union or worker resistance was relatively unimportant.

6 Government and Economic Policy

The twentieth century saw a major expansion of the role of government, both as a producer of goods and services and as a regulator and stabiliser of the national economy. Controversy has raged for more than 250 years over the proper role of government in British political economy, and it was especially fierce during the twentieth century. These ideological, doctrinal and sectional struggles left unresolved, however, even the basic question whether the state is fundamentally the solution or the cause of national economic problems. The summary of Allen's (1979) polemic, to which attention has already been drawn, heaps particular criticism on politicians, civil servants and the structure of state policy as causes of the British disease. There have been equally strong appeals to the state as the only force powerful enough to reverse decline. Before examining this literature, it is essential to grasp the different ways of measuring the pattern of public sector growth.

Long-term Growth of Government

It is not easy to measure the size of the public sector. The most common method uses current money *values* of both total public expenditure (TPE) and GDP, as in Figure 6.1. TPE rose faster than final output consistently throughout the century, but this does not mean that the state pre-empted an ever-larger *volume* of national resources. The state's use of resources is measured by that part of TPE that represents goods and services consumed by the public sector and at constant prices. A very different picture emerges (see Figure 6.2), with remarkably similar rates of growth for public sector consumption (1.9 per cent per annum between

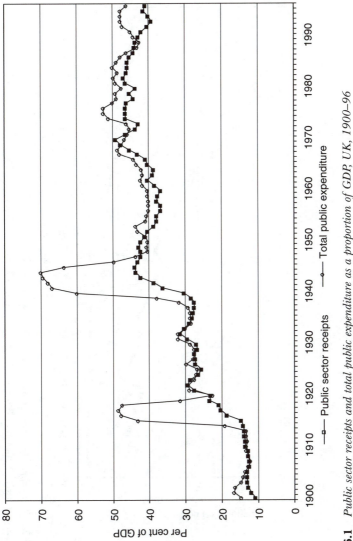

Figure 6.1 *Public sector receipts and total public expenditure as a proportion of GDP, UK, 1900–96*
Sources: Feinstein 1972, Tables 4, 14; Blue Book, various issues; ONS 2000, Table 1.2.

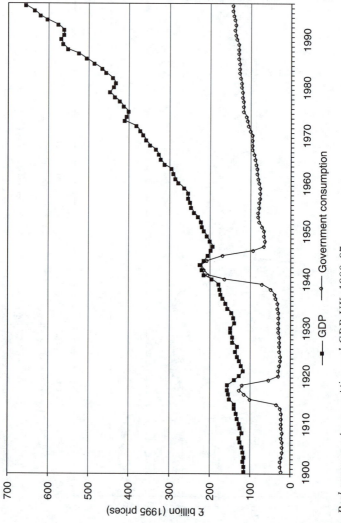

Figure 6.2 *Real government consumption and GDP, UK, 1900–97*
Sources: Feinstein 1972, Tables 4, 5; Blue Book, various issues; ONS 2000, Table 1.2.

1900 and 1997) and for real GDP (1.8 per cent per annum) (see also Hatton and Chrystal 1991, 55–6). The reason for the big difference between the two series is the relative price effect to which attention was drawn in Chapter 4. Costs in the public sector rose faster than costs generally, perhaps twice as fast. The services provided by the state (health, education, defence, law and order, etc.) are labour-intensive and not easily amenable to rapid, labour-displacing productivity growth. The trajectory of TPE in Figure 6.1 arises from this relative price effect and the state's role in transferring resources from one consumer to another by such means as interest payments to holders of the national debt, state welfare benefits and subsidies to industry. Levels of transfer payments were modest until the First World War, but the wartime explosion of the national debt and the growth of the state's welfare role in the early 1920s (see below) produced big increases. Further substantial increases occurred in the late 1940s and in the 1980s and 1990s, and at the end of the century transfer payments represented approximately 20 per cent and TPE 45 per cent of the value of GDP (Figure 6.3). In international terms, Britain's public spending tended to be slightly below the average for the richest nations before 1913 but slightly above thereafter (Middleton 1996, 94–5). This judgement applies to both the TPE and total public consumption measures. British levels were, however, very similar to those of Germany and somewhat below France for most of the postwar period when, as will be seen below, controversy over the role of the state in the economy was most intense. The difference between volume and value measures of public expenditure makes it hazardous to generalise about the size and economic effects of the public sector in the twentieth-century economy. The public sector did grow, but more slowly and to a much less potentially damaging size than popularly imagined. Governments had to finance the growth of both public sector consumption and transfers and needed to become more and more skilful at raising revenue and loans (Figure 6.1).

Figure 6.1 reveals starkly that wars had a major short-run (and possibly longer-term) impact on the growth of TPE. In both world wars, public expenditure exploded as governments took a commanding role in the economy (see Figure 6.2 especially). The return of peace saw falling TPE, though not to pre-war

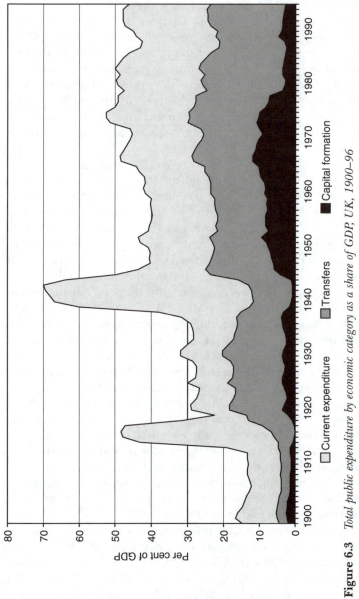

Figure 6.3 *Total public expenditure by economic category as a share of GDP, UK, 1900–96*
Sources: as Figure 6.1

levels, and the share of taxation in GDP followed a similar path. Peacock and Wiseman (1961) argued that wars increased public expenditure by two mechanisms: they exposed new socio-economic problems or presented old problems in a new light, favouring new spending commitments when peace returned. This was only possible because war also made higher taxation more tolerable, an effect that extended into peacetime. War thus exerted a 'displacement effect'. As soon as Peacock and Wiseman's book appeared, underlying conditions changed. Great efforts had been made to control the growth of public expenditure in the aftermath of the Suez crisis of 1956, but the purse-strings were relaxed in time for a big expansion of public spending before the 1959 general election, and TPE continued to grow more rapidly than GDP until the later 1960s. This rapid peacetime growth of TPE undermined Peacock and Wiseman's analysis, and scholars with widely differing research agendas subsequently proposed alternative models (see the review in Middleton 1996, 114–24). However, the very complexity and ambiguity of the concept of public expenditure resulted in diverse treatments. Alt and Chrystal (1983) focused on the slow, steady expansion in the volume of public expenditure on goods and services; others were more interested in modelling the growth of transfer payments. US economists developed public choice theory, a much-discussed alternative approach. In this view, self-promoting bureaucrats enhanced their personal status by increasing their departmental budgets in the less austere postwar fiscal climate (Buchanan and Wagner 1977). However, public choice theory had almost no impact on the UK, where a very different administrative culture held sway (Clarke 1998, 190–212).

An Outline of British Economic Policy

The question of the proper, legitimate role of the state in economic affairs was certainly not new to the twentieth century. O'Brien (1994) commended the efforts of the eighteenth-century mercantilist state to provide stability and security at home and overseas, despite the relatively heavy cost in taxation and conflict. To others, however, the costs and the potential for corruption in this mercantile system attracted far less favourable comment, notably in Adam Smith's *Inquiry into the Nature and Causes of the Wealth of Nations* in 1776, which is widely regarded as the greatest book ever written on political economy. Even as mercantilism was being disassembled during the nineteenth century, a tide of small-scale state regulation in economic and social affairs was becoming evident. However, the assumption that the market would determine the allocation of resources and that the state would exert a broadly neutral influence on the economy had become entrenched by the nineteenth century. In many ways, the role of the state was conceived as *facilitating* economic and social activity. The main function of economic policy was to ensure that the national economy adjusted smoothly and quickly to the network of markets which extended far beyond the boundaries of the nation state. As has been seen in earlier chapters, this market system was challenged in the later nineteenth and early twentieth centuries by German and US industrial power and by the rising social and political power of organised British labour. Governments came under pressure to provide *support* to the casualties of market capitalism, and in the early twentieth century supportive measures began to acquire a class dimension, beginning with ways to help the 'respectable' unemployed without encroaching too far onto the workings of the labour market (Harris 1972). The more adventurous political and administrative spirits soon became involved in supporting employer and trade union leaders against the threat to both from the workers' control movements of 1910–22 (Chapter 5 above). Tripartism (policy-making involving leaders of business and trade unions as well as ministers and their officials) formed one of the main supports of state policy during the First World War, when government took on a more *directive* role and relied on leaders of business and labour as its agents in making and implementing policy. As was seen in Chapter 4, some business leaders were keen to continue this close government–industry relationship to improve industrial competitiveness, but the sudden collapse of Germany and postwar inflation allowed a rapid reconversion of most of industry to a normal peacetime relationship with government. Government sought to reintegrate British industry into the complex of international markets under essentially the same terms as before the war. The most important features were noted in Chapter 3: the reconstruction of international finance under the gold standard and Britain's continued support for free trade.

However, the internal challenge from labour and the external challenge to British industry were intensified by wartime developments. The Russian revolution of 1917 and intense social friction in Britain during and immediately after the First World War revealed the potential threat from labour, and ministers made concessions, notably by extending the franchise to all adult males and women over the age of 30 in 1918 and then moving to full adult suffrage from 1928. But policy-makers also vigorously opposed labour's industrial and economic demands (Lowe 1987). From 1922 a more coherent system emerged in Baldwin's policy of conciliating moderation and strongly opposing any kind of radicalism. One of the most striking features of the policy regime of the inter-war years is the growth of state expenditure on the social services (Figure 6.4). In fact, almost all areas of social expenditure (education, health, unemployment and other welfare benefits) expanded significantly in the inter-war years, but that on unemployment grew fastest (Middleton 1996, 335).

British prices did not adjust to foreign competition as anticipated (indeed, they could not without devaluation) and ministers had to extend their supportive policies in the labour market. The real level of unemployment benefits rose steadily (and relative to wages), but government controlled the impact on TPE by aggressively limiting benefit entitlements for the most vulnerable (Deacon 1987). With that prop to the labour market in position, ministers sought new ways of speeding adjustment to world market conditions. Ministers favoured lower interest rates to encourage industrial investment, and relations with the Bank of England became difficult, as noted in Chapter 3. Governments also became involved in industrial policy, with legislation to re-organise the railways in 1921, intervention in the intractable problems of the coal industry, and major initiatives in such expanding industries as electricity supply, radio broadcasting and civil aviation (Foreman-Peck 1994, 404–7). They intervened behind the scenes in iron and steel and other export staples. Ministers generally encouraged employers to invest in modern, large-scale plant through which scale economies could be

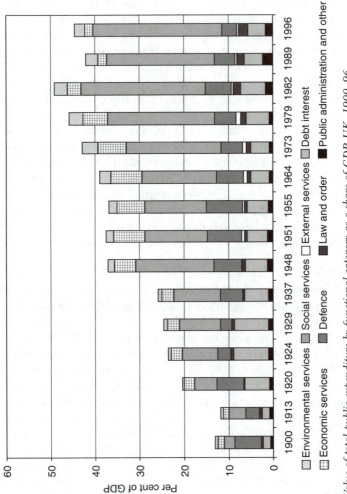

Figure 6.4 *Value of total public expenditure by functional category as a share of GDP, UK, 1900–96*
Sources: as Figure 6.1.

achieved to speed the pace of adjustment to world market conditions. They championed any policy that held some prospect of promoting adjustment, finding new markets or retaining existing customers. Many new microeconomic policies were implemented, but within a tough macroeconomic framework. Budgets remained relatively small and balanced, exchange and interest rates were relatively high, and government borrowing was controlled once immediate postwar crises had been overcome.

The slump undermined the whole basis of the economic policy of the 1920s. The great cornerstones of the market order – free trade, the balanced budget and the gold standard – were smashed or severely threatened by international and domestic market contraction. But this new environment also offered opportunities, as Treasury officials were quick to realise. The collapse of the gold standard allowed Britain to undertake a unilateral devaluation, which in turn gave the Treasury the scope to achieve a long-standing goal and lower interest rates. As interest rates came down, so the burden of interest payments on the national debt diminished, which was perhaps as well since the relative cost of the social services continued to rise during the 1930s (Figure 6.4). Lower interest and exchange rates also permitted greater scope for purposive economic management. Treasury officials quickly set about the creation of an economic environment in which British entrepreneurs might be able to achieve modest price rises and rebuild profits, investment and growth of output (Booth 1987). Leading officials believed that the biggest threat to their objectives lay in accelerating inflation provoked by currency collapse, as had occurred in central and eastern Europe in the early 1920s. To preserve foreign confidence in sterling, budgets were balanced, at least according to the conventions of the time (Middleton 1996, 360–2). At one level, the effort was successful. Britain enjoyed a more substantial recovery than most democracies during the 1930s. However, the policy regime was criticised, both at the time and after 1945, for its caution and for featherbedding British industry.

The first criticism is essentially doctrinal. The leading academic critic of government policy in both inter-war decades was Keynes. His central concern was the failure of policy to cut back the permanent core of unemployment, of roughly one million idle workers. Whereas contemporary economists focused on the real wage and the market for individual workers, Keynes gradually constructed an alternative perspective that invented the concepts of aggregate supply and demand. Keynes demonstrated that the unemployment rate depended upon the level of aggregate demand, the sum of total consumption and total investment. Keynes's favourite remedy to reduce British unemployment was to expand investment by a programme of public works, which would create additional consumption by the workers employed, and further waves of consumption and investment as new incomes were generated and additional expenditures made at each round. Keynes's programme made little headway at the time, not least because public works had been relatively unsuccessful against rising unemployment during 1929–32, but it has been controversial ever since. The closest approximation to a public works programme in the later 1930s was deficit financed rearmament, which certainly stimulated demand for workers (Thomas 1994, 356) but also undermined an already weak current balance of payments (Chapter 3). The present consensus appears to be that Keynesian policies did not offer a unilateral solution to Britain's unemployment problem in the 1930s but that a more ambitious fiscal policy could have alleviated some of Britain's inter-war difficulties, though economic historians disagree about the scale of potential benefit (for a review, see Thomas 1994). The second criticism concerns the failure of governments of the 1930s to arrest the trend towards producer collusion. To radical critics, government policy gave industrialists too much scope to protect profits, especially as recovery gathered momentum. Profits certainly recovered, especially after 1935 (Hart 1965, 70). More recently, the weakening of competitive forces in the 1930s was presented as the sacrifice of long-run efficiency for short-term political expediency (Broadberry and Crafts 1990). However, it is difficult to argue that collusion created particular problems in the 1930s, when, as noted in Chapter 4, comparative productivity levels were little different from those under the very different policy regime before 1914.

The mood of the electorate, which had sustained cautious pragmatism in the 1930s, changed dramatically in the early part of the Second World War. The prudent conservatism of the 1930s was blamed for leaving the country (apparently) unprepared for war: the inability of inter-war policy to deal with unemployment was now seen as the single most damning inadequacy of the Baldwin years (Addison 1977). After the collapse of the Chamberlain government in May 1940 it was certain that British politics and policy could not return to the 'safety first' of the inter-war years, but it was by no means certain how the landscape of postwar policy would be redrawn. To some extent, the success of the centralised war economy pointed to a bigger role for the postwar, peacetime state. As in the First World War, the state took a directing role during wartime. State control went further than in 1914–18, as the Chamberlain and Churchill governments effectively conscripted labour and wealth for the war effort, and economic policy revealed a coherence and sophistication that it had not displayed in the First World War. Significantly, macroeconomic management was much more successful than in 1914–18, thanks in part to the intellectual coherence given to Treasury thinking by Keynes. Churchill made Ernest Bevin, the leading personality of British trade unionism since the early 1920s, Minister of Labour with major responsibilities for organising war production. He brought unions further into government and gave greater confidence to workers than in 1914–18. Employers, on the other hand, were pushed back onto the defensive. As in 1915, there was a munitions 'scandal' early in the war, which stimulated fierce attacks on 'Blimps in the boardrooms' (Hinton 1994, 30–2). Public opinion certainly moved leftwards after the entry of the USSR into the war, with repercussions for postwar planning (Calder 1992, 524–50). Addison suggested that this 'low politics' of reform prepared the ground for decisive shifts in the British political climate after 1945. Labour ministers in the wartime coalition government dearly wanted to exploit the shifting currents of mass opinion; Conservatives in turn wanted to focus the wartime coalition narrowly on wartime problems. However, they were forced to compromise on committing postwar governments to the imaginatively presented but ultimately limited reforms suggested by Beveridge for improved and better co-ordinated welfare support, by disciples of Keynes for postwar macroeconomic management, and by other non-party specialists in areas ranging from education policy to land use planning. Addison's thesis has been much discussed and the general view is that he exaggerated the extent of wartime consensus between the parties but that major changes in British politics certainly occurred during the 1940s (see the essays in Smith 1986). Almost every aspect of postwar planning was also dependent upon a satisfactory postwar international settlement. For the British, Keynes drew up plans to stabilise postwar currencies (to encourage trade, exchange and economic growth), expand world liquidity (to provide the main foundation for the expansion of trade and exchange) and promote quick and fair adjustment of short-run balance of payments problems after the war. He recognised that Britain's postwar external position would be weak and that full employment would be possible only with an expanding world economy. He strove almost single-handed to convince a sceptical British policy-making elite of the need to accept US plans (van Dormael 1978, 268–85). By the end of the war, therefore, British governments were committed in principle, if not in detail, to full employment, a big programme of postwar social reform, a phased liberalisation of international trade and payments while simultaneously undertaking the international responsibilities of a victorious power at the end of a devastating international conflict. It had to manage these commitments with an astonishingly weak export sector and the worst balance of payments deficit of any nation in history (see Chapter 3).

Demobilisation and reconstruction were handled smoothly and effectively, despite continuing problems in the balance of payments (Chapter 3). These achievements were made by a government that nationalised the 'commanding heights' of the economy and preached higher efficiency to private industrialists at every opportunity. It also created a welfare state to make good the effects of market failure on ordinary workers and extend to all citizens the right to social security (Lowe 1993). The economic policies of the Attlee government have attracted enormous interest from historians and its policies have been more thoroughly investigated than those of any other government. The tone of this assessment has been broadly supportive, though the failure to reform private industry and to question whether Britain could afford its postwar international responsibilities has attracted unfavourable comment (Cairncross 1985; Tomlinson 1997). There were also problems in industrial policy. The government ran the economy with high, and probably excessive, levels of demand, in part to encourage industry to invest and in part to ensure full employment. This put a strain on building and the capital goods industries, compelling manufacturing to delay investment decisions or make sub-optimal choices (Chick 1998). Excess demand arose from the very breadth of the goals pursued by the government. Ministers wanted lower taxes, lower interest rates, and food subsidies at a time of severe world food shortages. Dalton, the Chancellor of the Exchequer, believed that in the short term, the system of controls and subsidies would control inflationary forces, but the twin crises of 1947 (a shortage of fuel in the spring and of dollars in the late summer) helped push the Treasury towards greater efforts to reduce excess demand, though the process was not complete until the early 1950s (Howson 1993, 96–152).

Equally important changes occurred in the Conservative Party during opposition as it, too, adapted to the new social democratic agenda (Gamble 1974). There were comparatively few major alterations in the framework of economic policy when the Conservatives came to power in 1951. Bank rate was unfrozen after nearly two decades of cheap money, especially to meet pressure on the balance of payments, but changes in the conduct of monetary policy were limited. There were two 'privatisations', of steel and the road haulage industry, but the Conservative government left the main boundaries of the expanded public sector intact (Burk 1988). The main parameters of industrial relations policy were unchanged (Davis Smith 1990). Historians have, however, rather discounted the claims made in the 1950s that the policies of the Labour Chancellor, Gaitskell, and the first Conservative Chancellor, Butler, were more or less identical (giving rise to the term 'Butskellism'), citing differences over taxation, controls and monetary policy (Rollings 1994). But there were continuities at a deeper level. The most trusted economic adviser to successive Chancellors of the Exchequer from 1948 to 1961 was Sir Robert Hall, head of the government's small cadre of specialist economic advisers and probably the world's leading practitioner of applied Keynesian economics during the 1950s. Treasury ministers and officials had reservations about the use of economic analysis, especially Keynesian theory, in policy-making, but Hall's ability to interpret economic trends gave him enormous influence and brought a 'liberal Keynesian' colour to British macroeconomic policy in the 1950s (Tomlinson 1995). The usual description of liberal Keynesian policies is to liken policy-makers to Pavlov's dogs, responding equally to two stimuli: a run on the gold and currency reserves brought cuts in the pressure of demand, and rising unemployment induced macroeconomic expansion (Brittan 1971, 455). There was also a vigorous debate among economists about whether policy stabilised or destabilised the aggregate economy (see Tomlinson 1990, 258–9). But the real issues for policy-makers were how to deal with sagging confidence in sterling and with the evidence of faster growth in other European countries.

A major policy reappraisal began in the middle 1950s, reaching its zenith in the early 1960s. It began with efforts to strengthen the balance of payments, notably by containing the growth of public spending, pushing unemployment to the very limits of political acceptability and arranging that the public sector would give strong signals on wage moderation to private employers. Monetary policy was reviewed by the Radcliffe Committee and fiscal policy by a whole series of ad hoc and formal bodies, culminating in the Plowden Committee. From this process, government acquired a wider range of policy instruments but also more demanding policy goals (Gamble 1994, 118–19). There appeared to be a new emphasis on growth and on the medium term, after so much intense preoccupation with short-term pressures. The Conservative government of the early 1960s established the National Economic Development Council (NEDC) and its many offshoots, but at the same time the Treasury was deliberately holding a very tight grip on domestic demand in the search for export-led growth (Booth 2000). The Labour government elected in 1964 went further, with a new ministry of the medium term (the Department of Economic Affairs), a new 'state investment bank' (the Industrial Reorganisation Corporation), an explicit incomes policy and a much more vigorous technology policy, but it walked an even more difficult path between expansion and external crisis (Tomlinson 1994). There were obvious implications for public spending, and steps had begun to be taken in the early 1960s to plan public expenditure more clearly over the medium term. By general consent, however, the new approaches of the 1960s failed and left an undertow of rising public expenditure fuelled increasingly by public borrowing (Tomlinson 1990, 246–8). In the government's defence, many of the problems lay at least as much in the realm of governance as in the capacity of the state to make coherent policy. The leaders of industry, labour and the financial sector were reluctant to see power gravitate to the central state: the resistance to a *directive* role for government was powerfully entrenched (Lowe and Rollings 2000). The making of economic policy became increasingly fractious as the international economy became more difficult from the mid-1960s onwards (see Chapter 3). The tragi-comic slide of the 1964–70 Labour government from promises of faster growth to devaluation and ultimately to major retrenchment marked a key stage in the development of postwar economic policy. Sections of both main parties and many informed public commentators concluded that managed social democracy was incapable of delivering improved economic performance. The search for fundamentally different approaches had begun.

The strategic alternatives to the social democratic consensus were the free economy favoured by the new right and the alternative economic strategy (greater centralised control and state ownership) of the Labour left, though both strategies came in many variants and drew on different traditions of political economy (Gamble 1994). The free market conservatism of the new right had its roots in the tradition of British liberal political economy that stretched back to Smith's *Wealth of Nations*, with strong overtones of Austrian neo-liberalism and Chicago monetarism. The gurus of the new right were Friedman and Hayek and their political priorities not only differed from those of the neo-classical British tradition but also were not always compatible with one another. Four key issues came to dominate the new right agenda: the need to abandon Keynesian economic management and concentrate instead on control of the money stock; to cut back the size of the state, as measured by the share of state spending in GDP; to reduce trade union power; and to find ways of preventing democratic pressures from demanding policies at variance with the needs of the market economy (Gamble 1994, 147–85). The Labour left, on the other hand, drew on the traditions of social imperialism and the socialist critique of economic policy to demand greater insulation from the world market and greater state direction of industrial modernisation. Both alternative perspectives developed rapidly in the very difficult economic conditions of the 1970s.

In this decade, economic policy began with strong strategic vision but succumbed eventually to preoccupation with day-to-day crisis avoidance – and that description might equally serve for the 1950s and 1960s. In opposition, what became the 1970–4 Conservative government had been influenced by the first indications of the liberalising agenda, and on taking office was committed to reform industrial relations, sharpen the market disciplines on British industry and disengage the state from the economy. The government applied to join the European Economic Community in the hope that the bigger 'domestic' market and sharper competition would push industry towards higher productivity and competitiveness. This was liberalisation within the social democratic vision, but the government began its programme just as inflationary pressures mounted in the international economy. The British inflation rate rose dramatically, diverging from the OECD average for the first time in the postwar period, and the disturbed macroeconomic environment caused both industrial relations and unemployment to deteriorate. Perhaps predictably, the withdrawal of government support from private industry coincided with major problems in key sectors. The Heath government reversed course in the now-celebrated U-turn of 1972. Industrial policy switched from non-intervention to support; government tried to draw the TUC once more into incomes policy-making. To counter rising unemployment, the government launched a major Keynesian reflationary programme and allowed sterling to float, in the hope of overcoming the balance of payments constraint on growth. The horizons of economic policy shortened as government struggled to control inflationary pressures, but the government's major problems were political. It appeared to have lost control of the economy even before the OPEC oil price rises and the major dispute in coalmining that followed. The government's popular support dwindled, with especially severe criticism coming from the new right.

The Heath government's U-turn and subsequent collapse merely confirmed the conviction of those on the new right that the next Conservative government needed to break trade union power and find an alternative to social democratic Keynesian management. They found much in the work of the US economist Milton Friedman that suited their political project. Friedman

(1956; 1969) suggested that the level of unemployment was set by the real wage and that governments could reduce the rate of unemployment below that set by prevailing real wage levels and institutional factors only at the cost of accelerating inflation. In Friedmanite analysis changes in the inflation rate were directly proportionate to changes in the money stock, and growing interest in his ideas occurred at a time when changes in inflation were preceded by equivalent changes in the most frequently used measure of the money stock, £M3 (Schulze and Woodward 1996). This relationship, which has since evaporated, was noted by leading broadsheet newspapers in the mid-1970s and had a major impact on City opinion.

While monetarist and other new classical ideas were spreading within Conservative circles, the Labour Party was being edged leftwards by its own radicals towards more nationalisation, more interventionist industrial policies and a 'social contract' with the unions to promote long-run wage restraint. Labour began its term in office in 1974 with interventionist industrial policies and substantial new spending commitments in welfare reform, but much of its radicalism was short-lived. The government was pressed from all sides, especially on public spending. The City was highly opposed to the growth of public sector borrowing – note the gap between total public expenditure and public sector receipts in Figure 6.1. Even more significant was the collapse of international confidence, bringing sterling under intense pressure and forcing the government to negotiate the biggest ever support package from the IMF during 1976 (Burk and Cairncross 1992). The Labour Prime Minister, James Callaghan, announced to his party conference in 1976 that the era of social democratic, Keynesian economic management was over and that such policies had failed in increasing stagflation. This speech was almost certainly designed to reassure the money markets rather than indicate the innermost thoughts of leading ministers, but the speech does mark the effective end of the era of full employment and social democratic management. The mid-1970s saw the first significant postwar economic downturn and the effective end of the government promise to maintain high and stable employment (see Woodward 1996, 144–7). For the remainder of its period in office, the government appeared to be blown from one crisis to the next, especially in incomes and industrial policies. The complaint is frequently made that British industrial policy, especially during the 1970s, supported failures and ignored potential successes (see Crafts 1991b), but this is mistaken on two counts. First, governments of the 1970s spent more on the promotion of industrial R&D than on short-run employment protection. Secondly, even successful economies have directed large sums to prop up declining industries: Japan, for example, has a long-established system of compensating the casualties of competitive failure (Calder 1988). Like the Heath government, Labour left office in disarray, but both have had their economic records reappraised and restored; both have been judged to have performed relatively well in enormously difficult international conditions (Cairncross 1996; Artis and Cobham 1991). However, the discussion of Chapter 2 suggested that Britain's relative economic position deteriorated quite noticeably in the 1970s, which implies that other countries coped rather better with this international turbulence. Neither the Heath nor the Wilson/Callaghan governments coped well with floating exchange rates, and Britain's inflation rate came adrift from the OECD average (Schultze and Woodward 1996). In turn, these unstable price signals disturbed industrial relations at a time when British industry had to face more intense competition from its European competitors after joining the EEC. The case for policy failure, albeit in extremely difficult external conditions, has not gone away.

The Conservatives came to power in 1979 with a mandate to embark upon a new direction in economic policy. They were committed to 'roll back' the state, to implement tougher policies on trade unions, welfare benefits and aid to uncompetitive industry, and with the ultimate goal of lowering taxes. At the centre of the programme was the medium-term financial strategy (MTFS), which established clear rules to slow the rate of growth of the money stock (as measured by £M3) and so to reduce inflation on classic Friedmanite lines. There were no targets for the exchange rate, which was allowed to float according to market pressures. At the same time, the government introduced legislation to weaken trade unions and liberalise the labour market. The MTFS failed disastrously. Interest rates rose savagely to curb monetary expansion, but the rate of growth of £M3 remained well above target. High interest rates encouraged sterling's value to rise and severely damaged British competitiveness, which deteriorated by approximately 25 per cent from 1979 to 1981. British firms could not withstand these pressures, and GDP fell by 4 per cent in the second half of 1980 and by a further 1.2 per cent in 1981 (Cairncross 1992, 239). Many manufacturing firms, and not just the least efficient, went into liquidation or became distress borrowers from the banking system. To avoid an economic catastrophe, the banks were obliged to offer these firms lifelines rather than demand closure, with the result that £M3 continued to rise. This was the economics of the madhouse. Despite the rise in the money stock, inflation tumbled in the early 1980s, thanks to the collapse in world commodity prices rather than from any benefits of government policy (Beckerman and Jenkinson 1986). Not surprisingly, unemployment rose rapidly between 1979 and 1983 (Figure 5.2 above).

The government managed to deflect criticisms of its policy by blaming the unions and previous economic policies, but the abject failure of policy in 1979–82 provoked a major reappraisal of 'Thatcherism'. Monetary policy became less blinkered, as the Treasury began to monitor a range of monetary variables and abandoned the effort to guide monetary policy by rules (the MTFS and monetarism). Unfortunately the new, more discretionary macroeconomic policy from the mid-1980s also experienced difficulties. The economy experienced a sustained recovery from the steep recession of 1979–82, but the 'Lawson boom' was mismanaged, and became increasingly speculative, unstable and inflationary, with severe external problems. Consumer spending rose faster than GDP and imports rose as much as total GDP in 1988 (Cairncross 1992, 229). Consumers were encouraged to believe that the economy had entered a new era of prosperity and reduced their savings, borrowed heavily and speculated in assets, notably houses. Property prices rose by 75 per cent in three years (1985–8) and consumer price inflation accelerated in the later 1980s (Figure 5.3 above). The correction to this boom was certain to be difficult following the expansion of corporate and consumer debt in the later 1980s, but it was made much worse by the botched attempt to enter the European ERM in 1990–2 (Chapter 3). The recession was deeper and longer than necessary. Thus, the government that gave priority to macroeconomic stability throughout its term of office presided over the biggest cycle of boom and bust since the inter-war years. In the 1920s and 1930s, instability arose essentially from the international economy, but after 1979 mistakes in domestic economic policy were largely to blame.

When Thatcherism was reinvented in 1982–3, privatisation rather than monetarism became the flagship policy. The policy of selling public sector assets at well below market price (to ensure that the stock was sold) was accompanied by much liberalising rhetoric, but in practice public monopolies became private monopolies and state regulation was replaced by a rather more uncertain system of supervision by semi-autonomous bodies, such as Ofwat, Ofgas, etc. The only privatisation in which the breaking up of a monopoly supplier was a central part of the plan, the railways, was not an outstanding success. Even after more than a decade of privatised utilities, most continued to need external regulation to limit the exploitation of the consumer, and utility managers had to manage the regulators at least as much as they had been compelled to manage politicians and civil servants in the era of nationalisation. The other main initiative in industrial policy in the 1980s was deregulation, or the ending of government and producer controls, which was applied to activities as diverse as the awarding of degrees and running bus services. The main early focus was the financial sector, where a series of changes began with the lifting of exchange controls in 1979 and most spectacularly embraced the 'big bang', which changed the rules of the UK Stock Exchange to try to increase its international position in the global market for securities (Coakley and Harris 1992). The competitiveness of the City undoubtedly improved as a result, but it made the task of maintaining monetary discipline more difficult. The jury is still out on the overall effects of deregulation, with notable failures (of bus services, which induced chaos in timetables and a steady and substantial decline in the use of buses) and successes (the City and in tendering for local authority contracts). Moreover, the wider strategic goal of rolling back the frontiers of the state was not realised. In current value terms, the share of total public expenditure in GDP was little different in 1995 from 1979 (Figure 6.1), and in constant price terms real government consumption continued its slow, steady rise during the Conservative years (Figure 6.2). Government support to the housing market and industry was reduced substantially, but spending on unemployment and the health and education services increased (Figure 6.4). Support was extended to the City, where privatisation arrangements and proceeds formed a major prop during a period of major institutional change.

These limited successes must be set against the squandered opportunities. There was a persistent undercurrent of dissatisfaction with Britain's economic performance throughout the century, both in the aggregate and at the level of specific industries. Successive British governments addressed the problems of perceived national inefficiency with a bewildering variety of remedies. The focus was, however, intermittent because international complications continually intervened, and this unsteady focus was especially unfortunate since many remedies (institutional reform, raising the stock of managerial, technical and manual skills) needed long time horizons before tangible benefits would flow. In this respect, the governments with the largest policy space were those from the later 1970s on, when flows of North Sea oil and gas should have removed the external constraint for the first time almost since 1914. The full test of economic policy after 1977–8 has yet to be seen, but current evidence suggests that the breathing space was not used to best advantage. Quite clearly, it is far too early to make any judgements on the economic performance of the Labour government elected in 1997, but there is no doubt whatsoever that its most severe test will be to provide a stable macroeconomic environment, which will allow British industry to achieve international competitiveness and at the same time encourage investment in human and physical capital.

Problems: The Welfare State and the Postwar Settlement

There are almost no uncontroversial areas of British economic policy during the twentieth century, but the most heated academic and party-political differences were provoked by disagreements over the impact of welfare spending on economic performance and the 'Thatcherite question' of the longer-run effects of the social democratic consensus established during the 1940s. The controversy over welfare spending embraces three main areas. The first, familiar from Chapter 5, is that the inter-war extension of unemployment insurance adversely affected the working of the labour market. The second is that the state's expanded welfare commitments damaged the competitive performance of the private sector. This argument comes in many guises, some of which are more conveniently considered in Chapter 7 as part of a more general 'cultural critique' of British society. Finally, the most controversial account of British economic policy in the 1970s was the Bacon and Eltis thesis (1976), which broadly argued that the expansion of public sector services after 1965 starved the manufacturing sector of resources and weakened its competitive power. This chapter concludes by reviewing each in turn.

The case against the inter-war national insurance scheme was made by contemporary economists, particularly Pigou and Clay, who argued that it shifted the responsibility for the employment consequences of wage bargains from unions to the government (for a discussion, see Casson 1983). They suggested that the expansion of both trade unionism and the unemployment insurance scheme from 1906 to 1922 made the labour market more rigid, and wage rates became 'sticky' (evident in Figure 5.3 above). Efforts to force down money wages through collective bargaining became increasingly costly, as the general strike amply demonstrated. After 1926, Clay, Pigou and others tended to support public works as the most likely policy to reduce unemployment, but still believed that the only long-run solution was to cut real wages (Clarke 1998, 80). For a variety of reasons, these analytical differences were not fully explored until the later 1970s in the revival of neo-classical economics. Benjamin and Kochin (1979) claimed that the bulk of inter-war unemployment was voluntary, arguing that the inter-war benefit system was especially generous relative to wages and encouraged workers to remain on benefits rather than compete vigorously in the labour market. This view created enormous controversy and by common consent is unconvincing, whether applied at the national level or to sub-markets defined by region, age or gender (Hatton 1994, 361–7). This part of the case against welfare spending is weak.

The 'non-cultural' case against the postwar welfare state saw the financial and resource costs of social expenditure as a threat to the efficiency of the business sector of the national economy. It is helpful therefore to begin with some broad comparative brush-strokes. Britain's new social security system came into effect in 1948, and even in 1950 Britain's expenditure on social security as a percentage of GDP was less than that of West Germany, Austria and Belgium. In 1952 British commitment was overtaken by France and Denmark, in 1954 by Italy, in 1955 by Sweden, in 1957 by the Netherlands, and in 1970 by Finland and Norway. Between 1960 and 1981, Britain's rate of growth of GDP was below that of other OECD countries, but so too was its expenditure on social services. The general case for the existence of a parasitic welfare state that hobbled the British economy but not that of competitors looks weak in the context of this easily obtainable basic information (Harris 1990). The British welfare state was (and is) distinctive, but in the extent to which it relied upon a means-tested, tax-financed welfare system at a time when most successful competitors were enthusiastically embracing the model of comprehensive, contributory social insurance. Britain's welfare system concentrated upon the relief of poverty rather than servicing the efficient working of the productive sector of the economy, but this is by no means evidence that Britain's social welfare system caused economic problems (for a review, see Johnson 1994, 297–300).

Most OECD countries experienced difficulties from the late 1960s, when social expenditures began to rise as economies began to decelerate in the face of more turbulent international decisions (OECD 1985). Once again, however, the temptation for British social scientists to interpret the manifestation of these problems within the UK as distinctive, unique and singularly damaging was irresistible. Bacon and Eltis (1976) argued that each capitalist economy could be divided into two parts: a 'market sector', which produces output that is sold; and a 'non-market sector', which produces services such as defence, education, law and order that are not supplied through the market. The value of market sector output will usually exceed the value of the goods consumed in production, and from this surplus must come the resources to finance all the economy's export, investment and consumption needs. They argued that between 1960 and 1975 there was a major expansion of the public sector (non-marketed output) particularly in social welfare services, which was too rapid to be matched by any conceivable growth in the surplus of the market sector. Accordingly, the market sector was 'crowded out' and deprived of the labour and capital needed for growth. The case that the private sector was deprived of labour was always weak: if British manufacturers were so short of labour, why did they not use the labour they had more productively in the 1970s (Alford 1988, 50–1)? The case that expansion of the non-market public sector damaged investment in the market sector has also been undermined. Two independent calculations have shown that the growth of consumption by the non-market sector did not affect the proportion invested by the market sector but was at the expense of marketed sector consumption (Middleton 1996, 108; Crafts 1991b, 271). The idea that the investment and hence the performance of the manufacturing sector was crippled by the growth of the state's welfare provision after 1960 is thus unconvincing.

There was, however, more obvious cause for concern at the end of the century. The European Commission (1995) identified three overlapping crises – one acute, one chronic and one impending – for all EU members at the end of the millennium. The acute problem was the failure of unemployment to return to levels that were regarded as normal before 1973. The chronic problem concerned the ever-rising costs of public health care and the inability of increasing provision to satisfy the increasing public appetite for medical services. The impending crisis was demographic, caused by the postwar baby boom generation approaching retirement age while the number of new recruits to the workforce was thinning as a result of decades of falling birth rates. The cost of the welfare state will continue to rise in the twenty-first century unless access rights are limited or more heavily taxed, as for example occurred over a very long period for prescription charges and more recently for tuition in higher education (Hills 1995). However, there were signs that the resistance to taxation had hardened, even to specific, targeted charges like the fee for NHS prescriptions. There is not much doubt that the increased costs will be financed, since there is no obvious escape route from the steady increase in the share of GDP absorbed by health, education and social security throughout the twentieth century (Figure 6.4). There is, however, some doubt about the extent to which these services will continue to be provided through the public sector. Many countries, including the UK, have shifted responsibility from the public to the private sector, a trend upon which Titmuss (1958, 34–74) commented in lectures during the 1950s. In other European countries major ethical decisions had to be taken whenever changes were proposed in the public–private balance, but in Britain the principle that public and private welfare provision should co-exist has long been accepted. The other silver lining for British policy-makers at the beginning of the twenty-first century is that each of the three problems listed above is currently somewhat less serious in Britain than in its European competitors. There are undoubtedly major problems facing the British economy and policy-makers, but they do not afflict Britain alone. Thus, the argument that the expansion of the system of state welfare created particular efficiency problems during the twentieth century appears to have been exaggerated. There were adverse effects but the best estimates suggest that they were and will remain comparatively small in scale, when compared with other influences on aggregate economic efficiency.

As part of their efforts to explain Britain's long-run comparative productivity performance (reviewed in Chapter 4), Broadberry and Crafts (1996; 1998) argued that the postwar settlement of 1945–8, though understandable and in many ways laudable, was misconceived. They argue that government focused too much on short-run support to employment and industry at the cost of reforming the supply side of the economy. The cost of this short-term perspective was the sacrifice of long-run productivity improvements. This argument revisits many of the fundamental issues raised in Chapters 2 and 4, but the impact of policy on economic performance is now such a contentious issue that some repetition of the basic themes of these chapters might be helpful as a foundation before examining the case for policy failure. The starting point must be to distinguish clearly between the performance of the aggregate economy and that of the manufacturing sector. In the aggregate, the French, German and indeed most European economies grew more rapidly than the British during the golden age, but much of this was inevitable and unavoidable and implies no necessary economic failure by the British economy. France and Germany had two enormous advantages over the UK during the first three postwar decades. At the outset, they had more 'springback' potential from the combination of wartime industrial modernisation and the dislocation of their economies in the 1940s. They also had much more to gain from switching resources from low productivity agriculture into higher productivity activities than did the UK. The 'later industrialising' economies of northern, southern and eastern Europe had this latter advantage in spades. However, British manufacturing showed a noticeable, but relatively minor, deterioration in performance when compared with European performance during the same period. This relatively gentle and modest deterioration was, however, dwarfed by the switchback ride taken by the British manufacturing sector after 1970. The Anglo-German comparative productivity data show a substantial additional deterioration in performance from roughly 1970 to 1978/9, followed by an equally substantial improvement thereafter (see Figure 2.3 above). Figures of comparative manufacturing productivity performance are available also for France and the Netherlands, with the latter also showing a very pronounced switchback but beginning in 1968, whereas the Anglo-French comparison appears to show a steady and substantial British relative deterioration throughout the golden age (van Ark 1990, Figure 1). There appear to be two trends to explore: steady deterioration before 1970 and more substantial and cyclical movement thereafter. The critics of the postwar settlement have to show that both parts of the deterioration were related to the policy regime established after 1945 and that the improvements can be directly attributed to the new politics and policies of the Thatcherite period. Furthermore, all the important developments must concern the supply side of the economy, with a relatively minor role attached to demand.

The discussion above in Chapters 4 and 5 attempted to show that the case for a continuing supply-side failure is less convincing than is commonly supposed. In a number of the more important manufacturing industries it was the complex interaction of supply-side, market (demand) characteristics and institutional arrangements that created problems. The case for uniquely British weaknesses in managerial skills, the ability of firms to undertake technological activity, the unwillingness of workers either to work hard or to embrace technical change is weak. Much of the case for supply-side failure has been built upon limited and scrappy evidence. The small number of rigorous, detailed comparative studies tends to be less clear about British failure. There were, of course, some British supply-side weaknesses that contributed to the slow deterioration of Britain's manufacturing productivity when compared with European rivals. It is not easy, however, to see why the policy choices of the later 1940s should have had their most disastrous impact on British manufacturing during the 1970s. The Broadberry/Crafts argument is not helped by the evidence of the substantial innovation in policy goals, agencies and doctrines during the golden age, outlined in the narrative section above. If policy decisions caused the deterioration in British productivity, it is surely more appropriate to search for causes in the 1970s rather than in the 1940s. The international economic and financial environment of the 1970s made policy-making exceptionally difficult, and Britain's problems were complicated by entry into the EC, the collapse of the sterling area system, the very high exposure of the City to the turbulence on the international capital markets and the beginning of Britain's own flows of oil and gas exports. Almost all these disturbing influences had a substantial impact on Britain's exchange rate. Sterling's roller-coaster ride during the 1970s brought exchange rate movements that were so large and so unpredictable that manufacturers must have lost any idea of a 'natural' level for the currency around which to plan their investments to improve efficiency and competitiveness. Policy-makers had particularly difficult decisions to make in the 1970s, and in retrospect they might have done more to promote the stability of sterling. It is not necessary to look beyond the formidable problems of the 1970s for an explanation of the deterioration in British manufacturing. It is far more difficult to find a convincing account that rests upon the policy decisions of the postwar reconstruction period.

The narrative discussion has also hinted that there are good reasons to be sceptical of the claims of a Thatcherite productivity miracle. The claims rest essentially upon two foundations: an improvement in the functioning of the labour market and the extension of competitive pressures on British manufacturers. The discussion in Chapter 5 drew attention to the authoritative survey of the British labour market of the 1990s by Blanchflower and Freeman (1994), which concluded that there is no strong evidence that the British labour market experienced fundamental change in the 1980s. Similar conclusions are almost inescapable when examining Thatcherism, competition and the improvement in manufacturing productivity. As noted above, the main pro-competition policies – privatisation and deregulation – remained in the background until 1982–3, which is rather late to be critical in the improvement of manufacturing productivity. Privatisation, in particular, was less a policy of promoting competition than of changing the regulatory system. The government certainly spoke the rhetoric of competition and made substantial efforts to increase British industry's exposure to market forces, but business responded with a substantial merger boom, just as it had in similar circumstances in the 1950s. Indeed, given the enormous extension of competition in both the 1950s (the ending of restrictive business practices, the abolition of import quotas and the reduction of tariffs on intra-European trade) and the 1960s (the ending of resale price maintenance and the major reduction in tariffs under the GATT system), it helps little to characterise policy after 1979 as pro-competition and that before 1973 as anti-. In this context, the complexion of policy is perhaps less important than business reactions to it. The evidence that the postwar settlement and Thatcherism can directly explain Britain's comparative productivity performance is much less certain than Broadberry and Crafts allow.

There is also a fundamental methodological problem with the Broadberry/Crafts argument, which is based on a counterfactual statement: the long-run benefits from choosing an alternative policy regime in the reconstruction period would have outweighed the costs. Counterfactual history has been an extremely controversial technique, but these controversies raged three decades ago and many of the very sensible lessons learned at the time appear to have been forgotten. From that intense methodological conflict, basic rules were established for the successful application of counterfactual enquiry. It was agreed that the method is most effective when used in relatively 'closed' contexts (where the range of potential variables is limited and where well-tried economic relationships can be examined) and under carefully controlled conditions. The most powerful requirement is to ensure that any results are produced by 'real world' economic interactions rather than by the assumptions of the investigator. Thus the assumptions made in constructing the counterfactual world should normally be biased *against* the case that the investigator is attempting to prove. Unfortunately, these rules are no longer followed. The debate on the impact of the postwar settlement has not met, and indeed cannot meet, these basic requirements. The relationship between economic policy and economic performance is simply too open and subject to multiple outside forces to be suitable for counterfactual argument. The impact of changes in economic policy on productivity performance is indeterminate. Successive governments from the middle 1950s on attempted to expose British manufacturing to the forces of more intensive competition. British firms were almost invariably able to blunt at least some of this pressure by means of mergers and alliances. The impact of tougher competition on industry is itself indeterminate. In some conditions, firms or industries will collapse, in others there will be a more positive response, depending upon a wide range of other influences. The Broadberry/Crafts argument is a classic example of the fallacy of supposing that it is possible to manipulate one variable in an open economic system without changing the ensemble of relations constituting the totality. Their unwillingness to specify their alternative policy regime acknowledges the problem. They refer only to the need for 'a somewhat more Thatcherite policy' (1996, 86), without any real discussion of detail. This is absolutely no basis on which to build a counterfactual enquiry, with carefully controlled assumptions that do not unduly influence the results. Indeed, there is absolutely no prospect of specifying an alternative policy regime whose initial costs and long-term benefits over three decades can be measured and compared with what was achieved in the real world. In short, the question of the long-term impact of alternative policies to those actually adopted in the late 1940s is one for dogmatic assertion rather than for careful academic scrutiny.

Conclusion

There were two central and very obvious characteristics in twentieth-century economic policy. The first was the extraordinary growth of government influence in the economy, though it was slower and much less dangerous than popularly imagined. The second was the inability to resolve the central conundrum of the most effective role for the state in the economy. Clearly, in an economy based on the principles of private ownership, the central role for government is to ensure that the conditions for profitable production, distribution and exchange of goods and services are maintained. There is, however, no obvious lesson from comparative performance about how this should be done. Twentieth-century experience can show that extreme centralisation of decision-taking is economically inefficient, but it cannot indicate what policies might have raised Britain's twentieth-century per capita growth rate from the rate achieved (1.3 per cent per annum between 1899 and 1992) to the rates recorded by France and Germany (2 per cent per annum). Throughout the twentieth century there was a pervasive assumption that the economy could and should have grown more rapidly, but governments were rather better at arousing than fulfilling expectations of improvement. British governments followed very different economic strategies during the course of the century, without satisfying rising materialist aspirations. They tried to integrate the British economy fully into the network of world markets and, when that failed, to shelter the domestic producers from foreign competition. The limitations of this system slowly became apparent and encouraged new ideas on reintegrating British producers into the international economy. Instead of relying on business leaders to restructure and modernise industry, ministers assumed some of the responsibilities for international competitiveness and hoped to reap the electoral rewards of the improved socio-economic conditions for the mass of the population. This managed economy worked reasonably well until turbulent international economic conditions in the 1970s again stimulated demands for fundamental change in economic policy. On this occasion, however, there was no widespread international move into protectionism and no crisis comparable to that of 1929–32 to force policy choices. The debate on the alternative to the managed economy was intense if relatively short, and policy from the early 1980s was concerned once more to ensure that the British economy responded flexibly and effectively to the requirements of international competition. The idea that the British government had scope for an independent economic policy, which was held strongly in the middle quarters of the century, had largely receded by the end. The function of government policy is now widely viewed as essentially that of facilitating economic activity while offering only a base level of support to the victims of market competition.

Over the century as a whole, British governments showed inventiveness and a willingness to experiment in economic policy at both the macro- and microeconomic levels. Unfortunately the impact on economic performance must be regarded as disappointing when measured against the expectation of improvement. It would be naïve, however, to regard the inability to engineer an economic miracle as definitive evidence of policy failure. In addition to the comparatively unfavourable structural conditions facing British governments from 1900 on, it is important to distinguish between government and governance. The former embraces the activity of policy-making, the latter focuses on the interrelationships between those who make policy and those who are governed. The critics of economic policy tend to believe that it is relatively easy for ministers to influence the behaviour of economic actors simply by devising appropriate policies. But twentieth-century experience cautions against such ingenuous expectations. No governments tried harder than those of the 1980s to make the labour market more responsive to market stimuli, but fundamental reform of the labour market cut across the interests of employees in secure employment and of employers in creating a workforce with multiple firm-specific skills. The 'submerged tenth' of the population identified in Chapter 2 was squeezed between governments who insisted that they price themselves into employment and employers who strongly preferred the far more costly but expensively trained workers already in employment. In similar vein, the efforts of governments throughout the century to push manufacturing to higher productivity by intensifying competitive pressures generally failed because of the ease with which firms could frustrate policy by merger, international cartel agreement or by more vigorous management of their markets. The writ of government is much less powerful than conventionally believed and policy failure is one of the less likely complaints of twentieth-century Britain.

7 The Cultural Critique

Two of the most influential books of the 1980s on British economic performance identified a cultural malaise at the heart of contemporary society. Wiener (1981) argued that since the mid-nineteenth century Britain's elite had been ambivalent about the 'industrial spirit'. In his aggressively written polemic, Barnett (1986) insisted that during the Second World War postwar planning was driven by a religious revivalism towards ideas of social consensus and stability and away from the starkly obvious and frankly urgent needs of manufacturing industry. Neither book was exactly in tune with the Thatcher project, but both were seen to support the Thatcherite idea that Britain's fundamental need was cultural regeneration. Both volumes were widely read, even at the highest reaches of government. They received only mixed reviews from professional historians but their emphasis on the power of values, beliefs and culture to shape economic decisions and performance was a valuable counter to the growing tendency of economic historians to explain actions in narrowly economistic terms. Both Barnett and Wiener were described by Edgerton (1996a, 7) as exponents of the 'cultural history of anti-technology', but there are good grounds for separating these terrible twins. Wiener's central focus is best understood as national and elite culture, especially that portrayed by English (rather than British) writers and artists. He detects a preoccupation with the rural, tradition and aristocratic values that appear quite out of place in a modern, urban, industrial nation and can be explained only by the continuing dominance of the aristocracy and the inability of the industrial bourgeoisie to impose its culture and needs on society. His approach is examined in the next section. Barnett, though equally fascinated by elite culture and the public schools through which this culture has been maintained and transmitted, focuses much of his wrath on a smaller target, the culture of policy-making. In this respect, he can be placed within a long tradition of social scientific and historical writing, which has criticised the 'amateurism' of much British economic policy-making and the bias in policy towards the financial services as a result of the socio-cultural affinities between Whitehall and the City. This broad historiography is surveyed in the second section of the chapter. A third, still narrower, strand of the cultural critique has suggested that elite culture damaged Britain's economic performance by imposing the public school model of liberal education upon state secondary education and thereby undervaluing the contribution of technical and vocational subjects. These arguments are considered in the third section of the chapter. The most powerful conclusions to emerge from these first three sections will be the difficulty of establishing precise links between, on the one hand, the culture and values of elite groups and, on the other, the performance of the average worker, firm or industry. It will be suggested that Britain's elite and its policy-making systems are far from unique and are much less monolithic and centralised than the cultural critique implies. The implication, sketched in the final section, is that the culture of employers, workers and those about to enter the workforce might have more impact on national economic performance than the ideas, values and training of elite groups.

Elite Culture and the Decline of the Industrial Spirit

The core of Wiener's argument is that in the middle of the nineteenth century, British society and politics became uncomfortable with the tensions created by industrialisation. Britain was the first country to modernise its economic structure towards industrialism, but it did so relatively slowly and without a major rejection of the old order. Britain did not experience a bourgeois revolution, but the aristocratic order succeeded in absorbing the new wealthy from industry, while at the same time fashioning a backward-looking culture that evoked a rural, rather than an urban, picture of the national character. He notes that many English (rather than British) traditions were invented in the second half of the nineteenth century and evoked a nostalgic picture of a 'green and pleasant land' at a time when the population was flocking to squalid industrial conurbations. A 'myth of

Englishness' was created and continues to hold a powerful grip on the national psyche. It is the England of warm beer, the village green and cricket, as evoked at the end of his period in office by Prime Minister John Major when he tried to convey what England meant to him. This vision did not emerge without a struggle: Wiener describes a conflict between a 'northern' and a 'southern' 'metaphor of Englishness', the former based on prag-matic calculation, enterprise and the pursuit of self-interest through conflict, the latter more romantic, muddled, organic, traditional and orderly. The southern metaphor triumphed dur-ing the mid-nineteenth century and held sway virtually unchal-lenged until the 1950s. Wiener illustrates the conflict between the two metaphors in the novels of Dickens and Hardy, and the triumph of the southern, rural ideal in the works of numerous novelists, poets, architects and artists and in the discourse of leading political figures of the first half of the twentieth century.

These manifestations of national culture were (and remain) extremely remote from the activities of industry, but Wiener argues that elite culture shaped economic performance through the education system. He draws on the long-established argument that the aristocracy absorbed the socio-political chal-lenge of the industrial middle class by opening up the public schools to the sons of northern industrialists. The major public schools did not provide an education suited to the needs of future entrepreneurs, but instead played a central role in the gentrification of the middle classes by detaching them from the single-minded pursuit of production and profit. The education imparted by the major public schools was more suited to a military, professional or administrative career. The influence of the public schools extended far beyond the small proportion of the population (less than 5 per cent of all males) who received an education there. The public school became the model for the grammar school and thereby for the whole system of second-ary education. In this way, the ethos of the public school pene-trated every corner of the nation and sapped 'the industrial spirit'.

This is a challenging hypothesis, and one that has evoked a mixed response from professional historians. The objections have come at many levels. The very idea of a singular 'national culture' is itself problematic, especially when derived from a necessarily partial survey of contemporary literature and artistic work. In a challenging alternative view, Edgerton (1991a) has argued that the infatuation of all levels of twentieth-century British society with the aeroplane suggests a very different picture of national culture (see also Chapter 3). He describes Britain as a 'technological nation'. With its sprawling empire, Britain needed to harness national science, industry and technology to the goal of developing the most cost-effective systems of mobile weaponry and deterrence. Before 1914, the Admiralty and naval shipbuilders were at the centre of what might be termed a 'military-industrial complex' of unprecedented power (Edgerton 1996a, 38–9). It is worth noting that for all the criticism of British entrepreneurs in electrical engineering and metallurgy before 1914, the radio was developed in Britain because the Royal Navy saw in it the answer to its problems of keeping in touch with its ships. Armaments and special steels producers were leading developers of armour plating for warships and the complex systems required for naval gunnery and gun control. From 1914, aviation became the most important military-supported technology, and government departments continued to support the 'commanding heights of British technology' until the 1970s (Edgerton 1991a, 102–5). For Edgerton, state involvement in high technology is much more than the pursuit of narrow self-interest by the chiefs of staff. He argues that aviation was a very public technology. Sections of the press were very vocal supporters of aviation from the turn of the century, and even the anti-militaristic left championed the aeroplane. At the time that the Prussian upper class saw the horse as its primary means of transport, enthusiastic British 'gentlemen' became pioneers of powered flight. The aeroplane in both its military and civil manifestations became an important cultural icon, especially for the aristocracy whose values were revived and transformed by it. Perhaps the idea of a single, pervasive 'national' culture is unduly simplistic.

The assumption of a simple link between socio-cultural and economic factors is equally problematic. British manufacturers may have hankered after a country estate and enhanced social status, but why should these yearnings have diminished their desire for profits or the growth of their firms? Indeed, Britain's rise to industrial supremacy coincided with the high period of

Romanticism and of the Lake poets, and saw the movement of many industrial pioneers into country houses and 'society'. Pollard (1992b) pointed out that in late nineteenth-century Germany the artistic community also romanticised the quiet, rustic ideal, and denigrated urban money-making. Aristocrats dominated 'society' and were at least as antipathetic towards modern technologies as the most trenchantly drawn British examples. As in Britain, successful German industrialists sought to join the landed elite. The prestige schools and universities were dominated by the classics and attempted to exclude more practical subjects such as engineering. And yet Germany experienced comparatively rapid growth before 1913. Cultural factors may be important in constraining economic development in poor countries (as Wiener points out), but it is a huge step to suggest that they can also explain subtle differences in performance among countries that have experienced modern economic growth.

At the heart of many elite culture hypotheses is the public school, but there is growing evidence that its role has been misunderstood, at least in relation to industry. Berghoff (1990) established that even in the period 1870–1914 the public schools educated no more than a small proportion of the leaders of manufacturing industry, but, far from being handicapped by this liberal education, they were likely to increase their family's wealth. In his detailed research on wealth, culture and economic performance, Rubinstein (1993) demonstrated that the sons of the wealthy were almost never seduced away from industry; there is little evidence of sons abandoning family firms in favour of the higher professions. Rubinstein suggests that manufacturing and the wealthy elite co-existed separately; industrial wealth was less grandiose and spectacular than elite wealth, but this did not necessarily imply that industrialists and industrial performance suffered as a consequence. Nor did the public schools turn the able away from science or industry. Britain's record of Nobel prize-winners in scientific fields is better than that of Germany. In the Edwardian years, there were signs of increasing recruitment of graduates (almost inevitably products of the public schools) into industry. The idea that British elite culture contained a strong anti-industrial bias is simply unconvincing at every level.

Elite Culture and Economic Policy

Less ambitious than Wiener's are the arguments that link gentle-manly culture and poor economic performance by means of the culture of policy-makers. Typically, it is suggested that the social background, education and values of leading bureaucrats and politicians gives them no understanding of industry and its policy needs. This argument appeared in different versions throughout the century, but only the three main strands (civil service 'amateurism', the gentlemanly capitalist hypothesis and Barnett's blast against the culture of the 'new Jerusalem') will be considered.

The case against the 'amateurism' of the administrative class (the policy-making elite) of the British civil service is most closely associated with Thomas Balogh (1959). He believed that White-hall recruited too heavily from those who had received a classical education in the ancient universities. Thus, 85 per cent of recruits to the administrative class (the policy-making elite) of the civil service came from Oxbridge in 1957–62 and were over-whelmingly drawn from arts disciplines (Ham 1981, 26–33). Once recruited, the training of British civil servants ensured that those destined for leading positions received experience that promoted sound judgement rather than specific competence and skill. Balogh insisted that this culture of the 'intelligent gen-eralist' may have been appropriate before 1939 but was funda-mentally inappropriate in the face of the postwar expansion of government responsibilities in economic, industrial and social affairs. These arguments were favourably received in the Fulton report on the civil service (Cmnd 3638 1968) but were almost certainly overstated. There is solid evidence that the British civil service is less distinctive than is customarily imagined. The Jap-anese bureaucracy was equally committed to the cult of the gen-eralist and operated according to seniority rules even more strict than those in Britain (Komiya and Yamamoto 1981). Policy-making by generalists is not *inherently* weak: much depends upon the nature of the wider system of interest representation. The defining feature of postwar Japanese economic policy-mak-ing was the interpenetration of manufacturing industry and the bureaucracy, notably in the extremely powerful Ministry of International Trade and Industry (MITI) (Johnson 1982). In the Japanese case, powerful institutional practices ensured that the values of industry were injected into policy-making at the highest levels. There were sharp contrasts with Britain in this respect, but they can be exaggerated. British government increasingly co-opted specialists into policy-making, especially by the creation of advisory bodies and various forms of specialist inquiry. Indeed, the whole thrust of Edgerton's argument turns on the long-established and close relationship between the service departments and the more technologically advanced sections of British manufacturing. Nevertheless, the shallowness of contacts throughout the century between manufacturing and the principal civil economic departments (above all, the Treasury) is undeniable. By contrast, the richness and closeness of the contacts between the City and leading Treasury officials has been much explored, not least for evidence of shared mutual interdependencies and a common culture.

The most powerful argument in this tradition is to be found in Cain and Hopkins's (1993a, 22–9) analysis of 'gentlemanly capitalism', that is, the form of capitalist enterprise suitable for the employment of gentlemen. The term embraces aristocratic landowning, the upper reaches of the law, the church, the administration, politics and the officer class and, above all, leading roles in the City. This form of 'service capitalism' was held together by the gentlemanly ethic and a common view of the world and how it should be ordered. Disagreements certainly occurred within and between the different parts of gentlemanly capitalism, but 'at the top of the gentlemanly order, the barriers between business and government were no more than Chinese walls' (Cain and Hopkins 1993a, 28). Active participation in markets and the production of goods and services were, according to Cain and Hopkins, beyond the boundaries of gentlemanly capitalism. Thus, the central features of the Cain and Hopkins hypothesis, as of most cultural critiques of British economic performance, are the cultural gulf that separates manufacturing from the elite and the subordinate cultural and political role of industry. In contrast to Wiener, Cain and Hopkins point out that Britain was already the most advanced economic power in Europe before the industrial revolution. It possessed a well-developed commercial and financial sector, efficient agriculture and a base of traditional industry. During the late eighteenth and early nineteenth centuries, a gradual fusion occurred between the aristocracy, whose power was in decline, and the financial service sector whose activities and aspirations were expanding. Gentlemanly capitalism did not absorb leaders of industry as the alliance of the aristocracy and the City was formed as a counterweight to the claims for recognition of provincial manufacturing. Service and industrial capitalism did, however, combine in export-led growth and imperialism after 1850. The empire was simultaneously a superb arena for gentlemanly imperial administrators and the source of new markets for British industry. This continuing need for gentlemanly virtues gave renewed purpose to the public schools, the acknowledged experts in producing gentlemen. At key moments in the late nineteenth and twentieth centuries the interests of manufacturing and service capital did not coincide so fortuitously and friction over the direction of economic policy became unavoidable, as has been illustrated in Chapter 3. The recurrent failure of manufacturing to reorient policy in a 'productionist' direction led many, especially on the left, to argue that the City enjoyed privileged access to policy-makers, notably in a 'Treasury–Bank axis'. However, political factors are by themselves insufficient to explain the apparent ease with which the City's interests were protected in economic policy. There were occasionally very public disagreements and open struggles over policy choices. The tariff reform campaign is a notable example. However, the infrequency of conflict is remarkable. It is difficult to resist the conclusion that gentlemanly capitalism possessed unique cultural advantages, in addition to the political leverage that came from its central role in financing government activity. Cain and Hopkins (1993a, 150–9) argued that the City and industry each tried to persuade government in the late nineteenth century that it was the 'sheet anchor' of the British economy. The shared background, education and values of City financiers, leading politicians and Treasury officials made it easy for government to accept the City rather than industry at its own valuation (Cain and Hopkins 1993a, 189). Industrialists, on the other hand, inhabited a different cultural universe.

To argue that leading *financiers* had unrivalled influence in the formation of international *financial* policy is, however, some way short of proving that gentlemanly capitalism played quite the role and had quite the characteristics that Cain and Hopkins have claimed for it. Neither the state nor service capitalism was quite as monolithic or as gentlemanly as has been claimed. Edgerton's nascent 'military–industrial complex' is a real problem for the gentlemanly capitalism hypothesis and for so many versions of the cultural critique. The quintessentially gentlemanly defence chiefs, far from being antipathetic towards production, technology and industry, spawned a system of support for high technology industry, precision engineering and research into fundamental science and frontier technologies. In much the same way, the most dynamic among the merchant banking houses were cosmopolitan, led by those not educated at public school, who did not become fully absorbed into English society, had little time for politics or the leisurely social life of the country house, and were devoted to the non-aristocratic ideal of hard work (Chapman 1986). Daunton (1989) pointed out just how many difficulties lie in the way of an interpretation of British economic development in terms of three cohesive interests – land, City and industry – in which industry remained subordinate. Much of the City's activity, in particular of the commercial and merchanting firms, was complementary to, rather than separate from and ignorant of, industry. The political cohesion of City interests on many big policy questions was far more limited than Cain and Hopkins have implied, and they have also underestimated the extent to which the landed aristocracy developed industrial interests. Finally, the view that financial policy was dictated from on high is a myth that needs to be exploded. Britain was not and is not a centralised state. Financial policy had to be negotiated with the 'ungentlemanly' clearing banks, who were vigorous champions of their major industrial clients throughout the inter-war years (Kynaston 1999). After 1945, the Treasury had immense difficulties in controlling the banking system, and the Governor of the Bank of England spent at least as much time representing the wishes of the bourgeois, provincial clearing banks to the Treasury as in projecting the needs of the Treasury to the wider financial system (Chapter 3 above). In this key area for the gentlemanly capitalism hypothesis, the City at no stage enjoyed a cultural hegemony over policy.

Though it shares some of the features of the gentlemanly capitalism hypothesis, Barnett's (1986) vision of British political culture during the Second World War is utterly distinctive and fully deserves separate treatment. His views on the nature and course of wartime planning and postwar policy and his unreliable use of evidence have already been criticised heavily in previous chapters. It is worth noting, however, that the cultural dimension of his hypothesis (that wartime policy-makers were driven by a new religious revivalism) has attracted comparatively little comment, favourable or adverse. He contends that, at the time of deepest military crisis, the British political establishment fell under the sway of the ideology of the 'new Jerusalem', a conception of society in which Christian community and pursuit of the common good (rather than, say, Victorian individualism and the pursuit of self-interest) were the dominant moral values. As in the gentlemanly capitalism hypothesis, Anglicanism, as refracted through the public school ethos, acts as the moral authority for policy-making. The 'new Jerusalemers' were drawn from the 'enlightened establishment' of 'moralising internationalism', that is from 'the Liberal and Labour parties, ... the small "l" liberal intelligentsia and, garlic in the salad flavouring the whole, from the religious with a social mission' (Barnett 1986, 11). Significantly, in Barnett's story the Treasury, the Bank of England and the Conservative Party were outside this policy loop. It is not difficult to see why 'Correlli's book' should have been so attractive to ministers in the Thatcher government (see Lawson 1993, 607), nor why the prime minister should have jousted so vigorously with senior Anglican bishops in the mid-1980s, when 'religion with a social mission' reasserted itself. Barnett's account of the ability of senior Anglicans to project themselves as the moral conscience of the nation at war is consistent with many surveys of wartime opinion. Both Addison (1977, 186–8) and Calder (1992, 482–7) note the prominent role of William Temple, Archbishop of Canterbury 1942–4, as the leader of progressive Anglicanism and a force in national public opinion. There is no doubt either that some areas of postwar policy, notably reform of education, were profoundly shaped by both the ideology of the 'new Jerusalem' (in the notion of 'equality of opportunity') and more directly by the Church of England's desire to protect its vested interest in the educational system. However, the forces of religious vision and vested church interests pulled in opposite directions and the Education Act of

1944 made only a minor impact on the course of education policy (Thom 1986). The enlightened establishment did not have a single, clear blueprint for the future in education, and Barnett's problems do not end there.

The key element in postwar planning was undoubtedly the Beveridge report. Its plans for a postwar welfare state appear absolutely central to the ideology of the 'new Jerusalem', and Barnett portrays Beveridge as the most influential prophet of the enlightened establishment. However, Beveridge was neither a Christian nor bore any of the other hallmarks that Barnett attempted to attach to wartime reformers (Harris 1990, 184–7). Indeed, Beveridge was a vigorous proponent of technocratic solutions to economic and social problems throughout his long career in public life and shared many of the assumptions of the disciplined and highly organised Prussian model of government to which Barnett is so attached. Barnett was completely wrong to argue that only representatives of conservative opinion, notably the Treasury, sought to pare the cost of the plans for social reform. Beveridge himself was deliberately ambiguous about the adequacy of his proposed benefit levels, which were about one-third below the recognised poverty line. Keynes, another member of the liberal, progressive establishment who had no Christian affiliations, mediated between Beveridge and the Treasury, and both men fought to obtain the *cheapest* proposals that might be acceptable to public opinion. Thus, there may be some persuasive elements in the 'new Jerusalem' hypothesis, but it fails as an analysis of the mentality of postwar planners. Indeed, the whole idea of a major wartime discontinuity in policy-making, which reflected the enhanced influence of the liberal establishment, sits uneasily with detailed evidence of substantial continuities from the 1930s in many aspects of social policy, notably in health and education policies but also in land use planning (see the essays collected in Smith 1986).

Elite Culture and Education Policy: The Public Schools and Technical Education

At the core of the arguments considered in the two previous sections has been the malign influence of the public school. If it is asking too much to believe that public school education either weakened the 'industrial spirit' (whatever that term might mean) or moulded economic and social policy in ways which handicapped postwar industrial performance, there is more obvious leverage for cultural explanations to account for deficiencies in the British education system. Sanderson (1994) pointed to the 'missing stratum' of formal technical education in Britain. Periodically after 1850 there was significant interest for British policy-makers in the systems of technical and vocational education adopted by other countries, but the impact on British education was small. The most notable burst of interest and activity occurred between 1890 and 1914, when technical education developed rapidly. In London, the creation of the City and Guilds of London Institute in 1880 channelled the wealth of City companies into support for two major technical colleges and a national system of examinations in technical and vocational subjects. In the provinces, the Technical Instruction Act of 1889 empowered local authorities to establish technical colleges, which spread rapidly in the 1890s. Technical college buildings were also used by post-elementary (for those aged 13 years and upwards) higher grade schools in which a technical and vocational curriculum was offered to meet the distinctive needs of children drawn overwhelmingly from lower-middle and skilled and semi-skilled working classes in the industrial districts (Sanderson 1990; Vlaeminke 1990). The education offered by the higher grade schools was extremely popular with teachers and pupils, but also with parents and some employers. This stratum of education nevertheless made only very limited impact on the English education system (Wales and Scotland had separate arrangements and to some extent deliberately steered a different course from that in England).

The reasons for such a limited impact are diverse, but from a cultural perspective, the most interesting focuses on the role of the Board of Education. The board, uniquely among Whitehall departments in the late nineteenth century, recruited on the basis of patronage, rather than through competitive examination. From 1895, the board's leading civil servant was Sir Robert Morant, who has variously been described as 'one of the greatest of all civil servants', but also as 'not quite sane' and 'overweeningly ambitious, tortuous and indifferent to common standards of honour' (Vlaeminke 1990, 64). Educated at Winchester and Oxford, he could see little fault in the British public school system, and used the powers of patronage to recruit likeminded souls to the board. He was antipathetic to technical education and had no scruples about forcing out those who disagreed with his priorities. The experiments in educational provision in the 1890s and early 1900s had produced a wide range of teaching styles and approaches, which Morant saw as chaotic and sought to narrow. His model was the public school, and he chose the grammar school to carry its ethos into the wider educational system. The board's power to inspect and provide financial support was used to attack provision of scientific and technical subjects (the real successes of the experiments around the turn of the century) and encourage greater provision of classics and the humanities. At the same time, the very obvious faults of the grammar schools were overlooked because they provided the style of education that Morant and his officials favoured.

This is perhaps the strongest argument that links culture and policy, but even so there are difficulties. For all the powers of the Board of Education over finance and inspection, education policy was very decentralised, with central government providing funding and a framework within which, at least until the 1980s, local government held the responsibility for arranging the details of schooling. Despite the Board of Education's strong preference for liberal education, many inter-war local authorities, notably in London, ensured that commercial subjects were taught in their schools to meet local demand (King 1990). Coventry developed an excellent system of technical education that helped overcome potential skill shortages in what was an extremely dynamic local economy; engineering employers responded equally favourably to similar developments in other parts of the Midlands (Thoms 1990; Sanderson 1990). There were indeed signs in the 1930s that the Board of Education was beginning to recognise the positive role that technical and vocational education could play in improving economic performance. The minister, Lord Eustace Percy, deplored the liberal bias in English education and publicly recognised the value of hard-edged technical training. Despite the antipathy of its officials, the inter-war board issued reports critical of failure to develop technical schools more fully. Wartime reports were still more favourable, calling for more junior technical schools and technical colleges (Lowe 1993, 228–32). The case for technical education seemed to be gathering strength within central government.

But just as the inter-war Board of Education failed to prevent localised experiments in technical education, so the postwar ministry failed to promote technical schools as desired. The number of technical schools did increase, but expansion was short-lived and separate technical schools were swallowed up by comprehensive reorganisation. The technical colleges also had a rather ambiguous position within the educational system until the 1950s, when the Conservative government embarked upon a vigorous programme not only of expansion but also of the development of a hierarchy of technical colleges outside the formal university system (Cmd 9703 1956). From this latter initiative sprang the technological universities and the new universities of the 1980s via the colleges of advanced technology and the polytechnics of the 1960s. As far as schooling is concerned, technical subjects had a relatively inferior position in the secondary school curriculum throughout the postwar period until a new attempt to restructure the education system began in the 1980s. The main outlines of this programme have already been given in Chapter 6, with the increasing centralisation of control over the school curriculum and the introduction of a more obvious and substantial vocational element to mainstream secondary schooling. Perhaps the most significant change was the steady transfer of responsibilities for organising aspects of secondary education from the Department for Education to the Department of Employment and its offshoots. The ultimate step was the merger of the two departments in 1997, but before that the dividing line between education and training had become much less distinct. The Thatcher government and its successors attempted to change the culture of the English educational system away from the liberal ethos drawn from the public school towards a more vocational and technological orientation geared to the needs of employers. Government tried to draw employers into the organisation of post-compulsory education, through the Training and Enterprise Councils and the more recent 'New Deal', though with mixed results (King 1997). Sanderson (1990, 253–6) pointed out that before the 1980s, many employers had had a very ambivalent attitude to formal technical and vocational education. The majority of employers were reluctant to recruit from the technical schools and many employers who provided training to their juvenile workers were reluctant to allow trainees to spend time in technical colleges to pursue formal vocational qualifications. Employer attitudes to technical education can justifiably be described as negative, but the positions of the teaching profession, parents and even students were little better for much of the period after 1945.

The extent of this ambivalence towards technical education illustrates both the strengths and the weaknesses of cultural explanation. It is very clear that the development of a separate strand of technical education was held back throughout the century because of a general perception that grammar schools, themselves watered-down versions of the public school, were better. This general preference for liberal, non-vocational education did not, however, prevent outstanding and vigorous development of technical education at the local level, especially where the engineering and building industries were major employers. Nor did the general indifference to technical *schools* mean that technical *subjects* were excluded entirely from the curriculum of state schools, in either the inter-war or the postwar periods. It is important also to recall that the apprenticeship was viewed by both employers and new recruits to industry as the most appropriate method of acquiring technical competence (Chapter 6 above). The system of apprenticeship may have been the arena of intense industrial bargaining, but apprentices were produced in what must be construed as comparatively adequate numbers at least until 1939, if not later. It is difficult to see therefore precisely where cultural explanations bite. Training for industry proceeded at a pace set by industrial employers. At the same time, liberal education produced a steady stream of new recruits into the service class (Halsey et al. 1986), where Britain's comparative performance was somewhat better than in manufacturing, albeit with a tendency to deteriorate slowly during the century (Chapter 4). In this respect the public schools, liberal education and elite culture were sources of economic strength as much as causes of comparative failure.

In truth, the attempt to identify cultural determinants of economic performance 'from the top down' has shown clearly neither an unequivocal link between culture and economic performance nor even that elite culture is the most appropriate place to search for such a link. This discussion of culture, education and industry has, on the other hand, offered substantial hints that study of employers, workers and training at the local level might be a more appropriate place to begin.

Business and Working-class Culture, Education and Training

With these last observations in mind, this final section attempts a different perspective on the link between culture, education and economic performance. Attention has already been drawn to the NIESR project on the relationship between educational standards and comparative productivity (see Chapter 5). Given the disappointing results from the 'top-down, culture-first' agenda, there is a strong case for probing the place of cultural forces in the 'bottom-up, productivity-first' research project of the NIESR. It was at least able to identify a measurable impact of educational and training qualifications on worker output and productivity at the level of the firm. This research was based on a number of carefully constructed, matched comparisons of factories in Britain and in other countries. Productivity levels were linked to differences in the proportion of the workforce with recognised vocational training qualifications and to differences in the level of school attainment in mathematics in Britain and the different countries with which it is compared. Although the cultural dimension plays an uncertain part in the research, these conclusions have very obvious implications for the cultural critique. These ramifications can be teased out most easily by beginning with teaching and learning in mathematics and science subjects for and by less able British pupils.

The relationships between culture, schooling for children of average ability and productivity are complex. In a series of tests carried out by the International Association for the Evaluation of Educational Achievement in the 1960s and 1970s and the NIESR's own survey in the 1980s, British schoolchildren of average and below-average academic ability tended to be approximately two years behind their German peers in terms of mathematical ability (Prais and Wagner 1985). In the top third of the ability range British children were ahead of comparable

German children, but on average British standards were lower. In the 1980s, similar results were found in tests of science teaching and learning. Prais's conclusions are perhaps more interesting than the evidence itself. He identified the supply side – the organisation of British education and standards of teaching – as the area of primary concern. Many of his proposals for reform seem designed to reverse the innovations in British education of the last four decades of the century. He advocates the reintroduction of streaming, a reversion to whole-class teaching and a return to smaller schools. In every case, the proposals were taken from prevailing German practice (Prais 1995, 80–101). However, many of the post-1960 reforms to British secondary education were adopted because of the acknowledged failure of the prevailing system to meet the needs of working-class children (a system in which streaming, whole-class teaching and small scale were common characteristics). Official reports of the 1950s and early 1960s pointed to severe weaknesses in educational provision for teenagers, especially for those of average and below-average ability. Among the more powerful explanations of the inability of the education system to engage working-class children was the cultural alienation felt by such children and their parents (Bantock 1968; 1973). The language, customs and procedures of schools were not those with which working-class families were comfortable, implying that changes in structure and style of teaching might have only limited impact. This is, however, a difficult relationship to investigate empirically, and even the most sophisticated examination of the impact of schools and educational attainment can find only the most rudimentary method of modelling culture (Halsey et al. 1986).

Prais appears to imagine a mechanical relationship between types of policy and educational and, for that matter, economic outcomes, but this is optimistic. It is much more difficult than commonly imagined to apply lessons in education policy from experience in other countries, not least because of profound cultural and institutional differences (Bliss and Garbett 1990). It is equally difficult to draw on Britain's past experiences in educational policy, but nonetheless worth recalling the full engagement of working-class parents and their children in the syllabus and structures of higher grade schools around the turn of the century (Vlaeminke 1990). The sense that these 'consumers' of education were outside the formal system yet able to contribute fully to its design and organisation appears to have been an important aspect of working-class involvement. But in contrast to the wealth of research on elite values and preferences, comparatively little is known about working-class culture and education. With luck, cultural theorists and historians will begin to probe those aspects of youth culture concerned with education, employment and qualifications with as much enthusiasm as they have demonstrated for sex, drugs and rock-and-roll.

The possibility of a non-elite cultural influence on the acquisition of technical qualifications is also intriguing. The NIESR matched-firm studies tended to find that British firms suffered a very big productivity gap relative to their French and German rivals because of the greater use of apprentice-trained personnel by European firms. The apprenticeship is, of course, only one type of 'intermediate' technical qualification (that is, those appropriate to craft and technical workers and below the level equivalent to a university degree). As was seen in Chapter 5, Britain lagged behind Germany in the proportion of the workforce with formal apprenticeship training, and the gap in terms of intermediate qualifications was even more substantial, as can be seen in Figure 7.1. It is impossible to define the categories in exactly comparable ways for different countries but Prais (1995, 15–41) seems reasonably happy with the results. Figure 7.1 also shows (in parentheses along the horizontal axis) Maddison's estimate of the 1992 level of labour productivity in each country, as measured by GDP per hour worked in 1990 international US\$. These national figures show a less clear picture than did the matched-firm comparisons. The most productive workers are the French, and the least are the British. However, the levels of French workforce qualifications appear to be closer to those of Britain than to any other country in the sample. The best-qualified workforce is the Swiss, but productivity levels are only marginally above those in Britain. In fact, these figures only serve to emphasise the perennial difficulty of establishing a statistical relationship between productivity and *direct* measures of human capital. The data in Figure 7.1 do not measure the proportions of *trained* workers in each country, only those with formal qualifications. Formal qualifications signify levels of general skills and competence. However, firms also train their workers in firm-specific

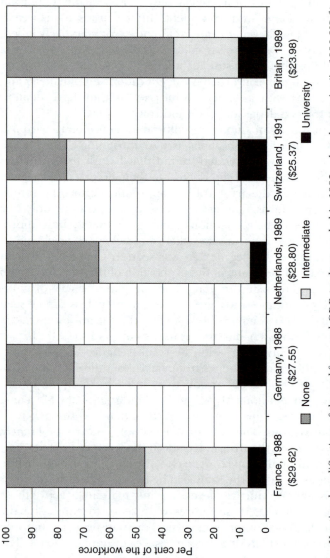

Figure 7.1 *Vocational qualifications of the workforce and GDP per hour worked in 1992, selected countries (in 1990 US $)*
Sources: Prais 1995, Table 2.5; Maddison 1995, Table J-5.

skills for which formal systems of qualification may be inappropriate, as such skills are of limited relevance and use to other employers. Statistics of those with formal, general qualifications are not easy to find, but data on firm-specific skills are virtually impossible to uncover. There seems to be little doubt that at the end of the twentieth century Britain did suffer a 'skills gap', but it was unlikely to be as broad as a casual glance at Figure 7.1 might suggest. It is also clear that the balance between general and firm-specific training across countries was at least in part determined by interconnected historical, cultural and institutional factors.

Almost from its creation as a separate state, German society has placed enormous emphasis on the linking of school and employment through systems of formal vocational training in the effort to overcome its initial relative economic backwardness. The German example was noted with approval on many occasions in the later nineteenth and twentieth centuries as concerns were raised in Britain about the competitive power of its manufacturing industries. However, the culture of voluntarism, which coloured so many aspects of Britain's employer–worker relations, encouraged British employers to favour firm-specific to general training (King 1997). German industry also benefited from the heritage of cartels and the continuing strong central regulation of industry in establishing national training standards. By contrast, none of the advanced capitalist countries with weak collective organisation of industry, such as Britain, developed an effective system of technical and vocational training for those about to enter the workforce (King 1997). Clearly the differences between the British and German systems of technical education contributed to Britain's productivity shortfall, and differences between German and British employer cultures shaped their respective training regimes, but these cultural influences need to be set within a framework of substantial differences in Anglo-German institutional and market structures.

It is possible, therefore, to suggest cultural influences that operate on business and worker attitudes to skill, education and training and may affect national economic performance. The conclusions are necessarily very tentative because of the absence of interest in this level from cultural historians and the equal lack of attention to the cultural variable from those most heavily

engaged in research on education, skill and economic performance. These are, therefore, hesitant suggestions rather than
conclusions and prompts for new work rather than summaries
of work that has already been undertaken.

Conclusion

Like so many interpreters of twentieth-century Britain, the cultural historians who have so far ventured into the choppy seas of
economic performance have been obsessed with the theme of
decline. They have undoubtedly made a substantial contribution
and have underlined the significance of the mobilisation and
accumulation of physical and human capital in the study of
national economic performance. Cultural historians have high-
lighted aspects of the British education system and the mobilisation of capital for industry that would have remained closed to
narrow economic history. However, it would be misleading to
suggest that the cultural critique has been entirely successful in
its contribution to the understanding of national economic performance. Too many reservations have been raised about the
core methodology and too little effort has been made, with the
honourable exceptions of Cain and Hopkins (1993a, 1–104), to
try to explore how cultural and economic explanations interact.
Hard analysis of the relationship between culture and economic
performance has been extremely thin on the ground. The most
obvious criticism of the cultural critique is its predilection for
monoliths and stereotypes. The elite is drawn much more widely
than is customary in political science, both liberal and radical,
but its culture remains singular and homogeneous. The Cain/
Hopkins and Barnett analyses rest on rather brazen oversimpli-
fication of the cultural values of their targets, as indicated above.
More generally, the cultural critique rests on distinctions
(between industry and finance; metropolitan and provincial;
gentleman and trader) that are undoubtedly convenient but
may actively mislead. Many elite families retained immense economic, political and social power in the localities from which they
sprang. They may have transferred wealth into financial instruments, but this does not imply that they became disengaged from
industry, far from it. There are very clear indications that the

wealthy shifted the balance of their portfolios significantly out of government bonds into industrial equities as the share booms of the 1920s and 1930s gathered momentum (Solomou and Weale 1997, Table 6). The alleged cultural antipathy of the wealthy to all things industrial may thus have been little more than skin deep. It certainly did not survive the expansion of the market for industrial shares after 1918 and the growing awareness that balance of advantages had shifted away from holdings in government bonds and overseas assets. The most serious weakness of the cultural critique is its unwillingness to essay any estimate of the relative importance of economic and cultural explanations. Wiener (1981, 168–9), for example, follows the perfectly reasonable point that econometric analysis cannot explain in fine detail national differences in growth rates, with the extravagant claim that it is therefore an unsuitable tool for analysing national economic performance. Too often proponents of the cultural critique allow themselves to be carried away by apocalyptic pessimism. The role of industry and the extent of decline are customarily exaggerated (Allen 1979, 16, 78; Barnett 1986, 7–8), and that of services has been virtually ignored by every commentator except Cain and Hopkins. If the undoubted potential of cultural analysis is to be realised, much more effort is needed to devise a way of both measuring the relative weight of economic and cultural explanations and embracing a more variegated pattern of influences.

Guide to Further Reading

Although this volume has been conceived for students who come to the subject at an introductory level, it might be helpful to give some indication of the primary sources available. The most obvious locations are the Public Records Office at Kew (PRO), the Modern Records Centre at the University of Warwick (MRC) and the Guildhall Library in the City of London. The PRO contains the declassified papers of government departments. In very broad terms, PRO files are the working files of civil servants and administrative bodies (the cabinet, government departments, royal commissions, etc.) and are opened to public scrutiny 30 years after the closure of the file. Thus, at the time of writing (September 2000) historians can consult those files covering the period up to 1969. For those interested in major economic and social policies, the records of the cabinet and the Treasury are almost essential and contain many examples of what might be called researchable dissertations. I have had students looking at budgetary strategies of the early 1960s and the introduction of premium bonds, for example. The papers of the Board of Trade contain much on industrial performance and structure and aspects of overseas trade, as well as on industrial policy more narrowly defined. Likewise, the papers of the Ministry of Labour contain much on wages, conditions and the management of labour by British companies as well as the more obvious industrial relations policy. Indeed, for a lengthy period after the Second World War, each British industry had a 'sponsoring department' in Whitehall and much information on industry lies within the PRO. For the years before 1939, there is less material, but Board of Trade files concerned with protection offer some possibilities. Finding this material has become much easier with the creation of the PRO's online catalogue (www.pro.gov.uk), which allows a search for up to three key words through the entire catalogue of several million files. The PRO has become one of the least stuffy, most user-friendly and accessible archives in the UK. The MRC is the main archive for those interested in twentieth-century British industry. It contains records of many British unions and employers' organisations, which tend not to be subject to the same 30-year rule as government papers. It is particularly rich in records of the manufacturing industries of the West Midlands, with notable collections on some of the major car producers. The Guildhall Library is, in effect, the library of the Stock Exchange and holds the company reports and prospectuses of companies listed on the exchange. It is clearly an excellent resource for those interested in some aspects of the business history of larger British companies. For smaller concerns, the best resources are almost certainly local record offices, the trade press and local newspapers. The most frequently used statistical sources are undoubtedly the publications of the Office for National Statistics, *The Annual Abstract of Statistics*, *Economic Trends* (especially its annual supplement) and the National Income *Blue Books*, which again appear annually. There are sufficient health warnings about changes of definition and subsequent re-evaluation of figures in the text above to indicate the need for care and precision in using these materials. These government publications cover the period after 1945, and the best source for the first half of the century remains C. H. Feinstein, *National Income, Expenditure and Output of the UK, 1855–1965* (Cambridge, 1972).

If we now turn to published sources, the number of books and articles published on British economic performance increases rapidly year by year. There are reasonable bibliographies in Roger Middleton, *Government Versus the Market* (Cheltenham, 1996) and in Sean Glynn and Alan Booth, *Modern Britain* (1996), but both are now a little dated and should be supplemented by reference to the annual list of publications provided by the *Economic History Review* each November for items published in the previous calendar year. This is an extremely valuable resource.

There are many texts suitable for first-year undergraduates. In addition to the two mentioned in the previous paragraph, B. W. E. Alford, *Britain in the World Economy since 1880* (1996), Sidney Pollard, *The Development of the British Economy, 1914–1990* (1992) and Paul Johnson, ed., *Twentieth Century Britain* (1994) cover almost the whole of the period. Bernard Elbaum and William Lazonick, eds, *The Decline of the British Economy* (Oxford, 1986) contains essays of variable quality and deals with the period from the mid-nineteenth to the late twentieth centuries, but in a stimulating and immensely readable manner. There are also a number of very solid textbooks on the postwar years, among which Roger Middleton's *The British Economy since 1945* (2000) is the most recent addition and B. W. E. Alford's *British Economic Performance, 1945–75* (1988) continues to have valuable insights into performance during the golden age. More advanced treatments are available from R. Floud and D. N. McCloskey, eds, *The Economic History of Britain since 1700* (2nd edn, Cambridge, 1994), vols 2 and 3, for the whole period, and from N. F. R. Crafts and N. C. Woodward, eds, *The British Economy since 1945* (Oxford, 1991, though a new edition is expected in the very near future). Alec Cairncross, *The British Economy since 1945* (Oxford, 1992) has the insights that might be expected from a former government economic adviser.

The theme of decline has absorbed attention and two good introductions to it are Michael Dintenfass, *The Decline of Industrial Britain* (1992) and, from a political science perspective, Andrew Gamble, *Britain in Decline* (4th edn, 1994). A recent stimulating contribution on the performance of British manufacturing since 1945 is available in Geoffrey

Owen, *From Empire to Europe* (1999). As might be expected from this author, who was editor of the *Financial Times*, the book reads exceptionally well and its knowledge of the boardrooms of British firms is unrivalled. It does, however, over-egg the pudding of manufacturing decline and revival, and, indeed, it is the opinion of this author that the theme of decline has been overdrawn in all the titles listed thus far. A useful corrective can be found in the work of David Edgerton, whose *Science, Technology and the British Industrial 'Decline', 1870–1970* (1996) is a stimulating review of both the theme of decline and the underestimated role of technology in British industry. Useful collections of political speeches and other key contributions can be found in the three volumes edited by David Coates and John Hilliard: *The Economic Decline of Modern Britain: The Debate between Left and Right* (Brighton, 1986); *The Economic Revival of Modern Britain: The Debate between Left and Right* (Aldershot, 1987); and *UK Economic Decline: Key Texts* (1995).

The discussion of the labour market in Chapter 5 concentrates on institutional questions and misses much of the historical fabric of industrial politics. Fortunately, there are some very solid histories of trade unions and industrial relations from which to broaden the approach. The obvious starting points are H. A. Clegg's three-volume *A History of British Trade Unions since 1889* (Oxford, 1964–94) (the first volume having been jointly written with Fox and Thompson) and Chris Wrigley's three-volume *History of British Industrial Relations* (Brighton, 1982–7). There are some excellent essays on the miners' union in *Miners, Unions and Politics, 1910–47*, edited by Alan Campbell, Nina Fishman and David Howell (Aldershot, 1996). Finally on this theme, John McIlroy, Nina Fishman and Alan Campbell have edited a two-volume history of *British Trade Unions and Industrial Politics* (Aldershot, 1999) which contains a good range of material and approaches.

Economists and economic historians have tended to look to the state to resolve problems in British industrial efficiency and competitiveness, so surveys of economic policy figure heavily on reading lists. By far the best starting points are the two volumes written by Jim Tomlinson on macroeconomic and microeconomic policy respectively: *Public Policy and the Economy since 1900* (Oxford, 1990) and *Government and the Enterprise since 1900* (Oxford, 1994). There is also much discussion of policy in the volumes edited by Floud and McCloskey and Crafts and Woodward. Major volumes on social policy are also obviously of interest to economic historians. Rodney Lowe, *The Welfare State in Britain since 1945* (2nd edn, 1999), Nicholas Timmins, *The Five Giants: A Biography of the Welfare State* (1995) and Charles Webster, *The National Health Service: A Political History* (Oxford, 1998) provide not only authoritative surveys of the field, but also much that is of potential use in grappling with the cultural critique of British economic performance. Industry, on the other hand, is less well served than government by good academic studies, but mention must be made of three excellent recent contributions: S. N. Broadberry, *The Productivity Race* (Cambridge, 1997), David Jeremy, *A Business History of Britain, 1900–1990s* (Oxford, 1998) and Geoffrey Owen's volume noted above. The first utilises a comparative framework to good effect. The second is simply excellent. The third is excellent in its areas of strength, but ventures a somewhat problematic general thesis. The cultural critique can be approached directly through Correlli Barnett, *The Audit of War* (1986) and Martin Wiener, *English Culture and the Decline of the Industrial Spirit* (Cambridge, 1981). Both are stimulating and irritating in equal measure.

Finally, I list two books that I hope all students will read as examples of individual brilliance and courageous argument: David Edgerton, *England and the Aeroplane* (1991) and Theo Nichols, *The British Worker Question* (1986). Both are immensely powerful attacks on the received wisdom and are extremely persuasive. They are very highly recommended.

Bibliography

(The place of publication is London, except where indicated.)

Journal Abbreviations used in the Bibliography

BH	*Business History*
BHR	*Business History Review*
BJIR	*British Journal of Industrial Relations*
EcHR	*Economic History Review*
EEH	*Explorations in Economic History*
EJ	*Economic Journal*
JEH	*Journal of Economic History*
JPE	*Journal of Political Economy*
NIER	*National Institute Economic Review*
OBES	*Oxford Bulletin of Economics and Statistics*
OREP	*Oxford Review of Economic Policy*
PP	*Past and Present*
QJE	*Quarterly Journal of Economics*
TCBH	*Twentieth Century British History*

Abelshauser, W. 1995. 'Two Kinds of Fordism: On the Differing Roles of the Automobile Industry in the Development of the two German States'. In *Fordism Transformed: The Development of Production Methods in the Automobile Industry*, ed. H. Shiomi and K. Wada: 269–96. Oxford: OUP.

Abramovitz, M. 1986. 'Catching Up, Forging Ahead, and Falling Behind'. *JEH*, 46: 385–406.

Abramovitz, M. 1994. 'Catch-up and Convergence in the Postwar Growth Boom and After'. In *Convergence of Productivity: Cross-national Studies and Historical Evidence*, ed. W. J. Baumol, R. R. Nelson and E. N. Wolff: 86–125. Oxford: OUP.

Ackers, P., Smith, C. and Smith, P. 1996. 'Against All Odds? British Trade Unions in the New Workplace'. In *The New Workplace and Trade Unionism: Critical Perspectives on Work and Organisation*, ed. P. Ackers, C. Smith and P. Smith: 1–40. Routledge.

Ackrill, M. 1988. 'Britain's Managers and the British Economy: 1870s to the 1980s'. *OREP*, 4: 59–73.

Addison, P. 1977. *The Road to 1945: British Politics and the Second World War*. Quartet.

Aldcroft, D. H. and Richardson, H. W. 1969. *The British Economy, 1870–1939*. Macmillan – now Palgrave.

Alford, B. W. E. 1988. *British Economic Performance, 1945–75*. Macmillan – now Palgrave.

Alford, B. W. E. 1996. *Britain in the World Economy since 1880*. Longman.

Allen, G. C. 1979. *The British Disease: A Short Essay on the Nature and Causes of the Nation's Lagging Wealth*. IEA.

Alt, J. and Chrystal, A. 1983. *Political Economics*. Brighton: Wheatsheaf.

Ark, B. van. 1990. 'Comparative Levels of Manufacturing Productivity in Postwar Europe: Measurement and Comparisons', *OBES*, 52: 343–73.

Ark, B. van. 1993. *International Comparisons of Output and Productivity: Manufacturing Productivity Performance of Ten Countries from 1950 to 1990*. Groningen: Groningen Growth and Development Centre.

Armstrong, P., Glyn, A. and Harrison, J. 1991. *Capitalism since 1945*. Oxford: Blackwell.

Artis, M. and Cobham, D. 1991. 'Summary and Appraisal'. In *Labour's Economic Policies, 1974–9*, ed. M. Artis and D. Cobham: 266–77. Manchester: MUP.

Atkinson, A. B., Gordon, J. P. F. and Harrison, A. J. 1989. 'Trends in the Shares of Top Wealth Holders, 1923–81'. *OBES*, 51: 315–32.

Bacon, R. and Eltis, W. A. 1976. *Britain's Economic Problem: Too Few Producers*. Macmillan – now Palgrave.

Bairoch, P. 1982. 'International Industrialisation Levels from 1750 to 1980'. *Journal of European Economic History*, 11: 269–310.

Balogh, T. 1959. 'The Apotheosis of the Dilettante'. In *The Establishment*, ed. H. Thomas: 83–126. Anthony Blond.

Bantock, G. H. 1968. *Culture, Industrialisation and Education*. Routledge.

Bantock, G. H. 1973. *Education in an Industrial Society*. Faber. 2nd edn.

Barnett, C. 1986. *The Audit of War: The Illusion and Reality of Britain as a Great Nation*. Macmillan – now Palgrave.

Barnett, C. 1999. 'Audit of the Great War'. In *The British Industrial Decline*, ed. J-P. Dormois and M. Dintenfass: 103–13. Routledge.

Barro, R. J. 1991. 'Economic Growth in a Cross Section of Countries'. *QJE*, 106: 407–43.

Batstone, E. 1986. 'Labour and Productivity'. *OREP*, 2: 32–43.

Baumol, W. J. 1994. 'Multivariate Growth Patterns: Contagion and Common Forces as Possible Sources of Convergence'. In *Convergence of Productivity: Cross-national Studies and Historical Evidence*, ed. W. J. Baumol, R. R. Nelson and E. N. Wolff: 62–85. Oxford: OUP.

Bean, C. and Crafts, N. F. R. 1996. 'British Economic Growth since 1945: Relative Economic Decline . . . and Renaissance?' In *Economic Growth in Europe since 1945*, ed. N. Crafts and G. Toniolo: 131–72. Cambridge: CUP.

Beckerman, W. and Jenkinson, T. 1986. 'What Stopped Inflation: Unemployment or Commodity Prices?' *EJ*, 96: 39–54.

Beenstock, M. F., Capie, F. and Griffiths, B. 1984. 'Economic Recovery in the UK in the 1930s'. In *The UK Economic Recovery in the 1930s*, Bank of England's Panel of Academic Consultants, Panel Paper 23.

Begg, I., Blake, A. and Deakin, M. 1991. 'YTS and the Labour Market'. *BJIR*, 29: 223–36.

Benjamin, D. K. and Kochin, L. A. 1979. 'Searching for an Explanation of Unemployment in Interwar Britain'. *JPE*, 87: 441–78.

Berghoff, H. 1990. 'Public Schools and the Decline of the British Economy, 1870–1914'. *PP*, 129: 148–67.

Black, J. 1962. 'The Volume and Prices of British Exports'. In *The British Economy in the Nineteen-fifties*, ed. G. D. N. Worswick and P. H. Ady: 114–30. Oxford: OUP.

Blackaby, F. 1978. *De-industrialisation*. Heinemann.

Blanchflower, D. and Freeman, R. 1994. 'Did the Thatcher Reforms Change British Labour Market Performance?' In *The UK Labour Market: Comparative Aspects and Institutional Developments*, ed. R. Barrell: 51–92. Cambridge: CUP.

Blank, S. 1973. *Industry and Government in Britain: The Federation of British Industries in Politics, 1945–65*. Farnborough: Saxon House.

Bliss, I. and Garbett, J. 1990. 'Learning Lessons from Abroad'. In *Technical Education and the State since 1850: Historical and Contemporary Perspectives*, ed. P. Summerfield and E. J. Evans: 189–216. Manchester: MUP.

Boltho, A. and Holtham, G. 1992. 'New Approaches to Economic Growth'. *OREP*, 8: 1–14.

Booth, A. 1987. 'Britain in the 1930s: A Managed Economy'. *EcHR*, 40: 499–522.

Booth, A. 2000. 'Inflation, Expectations, and the Political Economy of Conservative Britain, 1951–64'. *Historical Journal*, 43: 827–47.

Booth, A. and Bufton, M. 2000. 'Macro-myths and Micro-realities: Automation in the UK in the 1950s'. Paper given to the Department of Economic History, University of Glasgow, January 2000.

Booth, A., Melling, J. and Dartmann, C. 1997. 'Institutions and Economic Growth: The Politics of Productivity Growth in West Germany, Sweden and the UK, 1945–55'. *JEH*, 57: 416–44.

Booth, C. 1889–1903. *Life and Labour of the People in London*. Williams and Norgate.

Bowden, S. and Offer, A. 1994. 'Household Appliances and the Use of Time: The United States and Britain since the 1920s'. *EcHR*, 47: 725–48.

Braverman, H. 1974. *Labour and Monopoly Capital*. New York: Monthly Review Press.

Brittan, S. 1971. *Steering the Economy: The Role of the Treasury*. Harmondsworth: Penguin.

Brittan, S. and Lilley, P. 1977. *The Delusion of Incomes Policy*. Temple Smith.

Broadberry, S. N. 1990. 'The Emergence of Mass Unemployment: Explaining Macroeconomic Trends in Britain during the Trans-World War 1 Period'. *EcHR*, 43: 71–82.

Broadberry, S. N. 1993. 'Manufacturing and the Convergence Hypothesis: What the Long-run Data Show'. *JEH*, 53: 772–95.

Broadberry, S. N. 1997. *The Productivity Race: British Manufacturing in International Perspective, 1850–1990*. Cambridge: CUP.

Broadberry, S. N. 1998. 'How Did the United States and Germany Overtake Britain? A Sectoral Analysis of Comparative Productivity Levels, 1870–1990'. *JEH*, 58: 375–407.

Broadberry, S. N. and Crafts, N. F. R. 1990. 'Explaining Anglo-American Productivity Differentials in the Mid-twentieth Century'. *OBES*, 52: 375–402.

Broadberry, S. N. and Crafts, N. F. R. 1992. 'Britain's Productivity Gap in the 1930s: Some Neglected Factors'. *JEH*, 52: 531–58.

Broadberry, S. N. and Crafts, N. F. R. 1996. 'British Economic Performance in the Early Postwar Period'. *BH*, 38: 65–91.

Broadberry, S. N. and Crafts, N. F. R. 1998. 'The Postwar Settlement: Not such a Good Bargain after all'. *BH*, 40: 73–9.

Broadberry, S. N. and Wagner, K. 1996. 'Human Capital and Productivity in Manufacturing during the Twentieth Century: Britain, Germany and the United States'. In *Quantitative Aspects of Postwar European Economic Growth*, ed. B. van Ark and N. F. R. Crafts: 244–70. Cambridge: CUP.

Brown, W. and Nolan, P. 1988. 'Wages and Productivity: The Contribution of Industrial Relations Research to the Understanding of Pay Determination'. *BJIR*, 26: 339–61.

Brown, W. and Walsh, J. 1991. 'Pay Determination in Britain in the 1980s: The Anatomy of Decentralisation'. *OREP*, 7: 44–59.

Buchanan, J. M. and Wagner, R. E. 1977. *Democracy in Deficit: The Political Legacy of Lord Keynes*. New York: Academic Press.

Burk, K. 1988. *The First Privatisation: Politicians, the City, and the Denationalisation of Steel*. Historians' Press.

Burk, K. and Cairncross, A. 1992. *Goodbye, Great Britain: The 1976 IMF Crisis*. New Haven, Conn.: Yale University Press.

Buxton, N. K. 1977. 'The Role of the "New" Industries in Britain during the 1930s: A Reinterpretation'. *BHR*, 49: 205–22.

Cain, P. J. and Hopkins, A. G. 1993a. *British Imperialism: Innovation and Expansion, 1688–1914*. Longman.

Cain, P. J. and Hopkins, A. G. 1993b. *British Imperialism: Crisis and Deconstruction, 1914–1990*. Longman.

Cairncross, A. 1985. *Years of Recovery: British Economic Policy, 1945–51*. Methuen.

Cairncross, A. 1992. *The British Economy since 1945*. Oxford: Blackwell.

Cairncross, A. 1996. 'The Heath Government and the British Economy'. In *The Heath Government, 1970–4*, ed. S. Ball and A. Seldon: 107–38. Longman.

Cairncross, A. and Eichengreen, B. 1983. *Sterling in Decline: The Devaluations of 1931, 1949 and 1967*. Oxford: Blackwell.

Calder, A. 1992. *The People's War: Britain, 1939–45*. Pimlico.

Calder, K. 1988. *Crisis and Compensation: Public Policy and Political Stability in Japan, 1949–86.* Princeton, NJ: Princeton UP.

Cannadine, D. 1997. 'Apocalypse When? British Politicians and "Decline" in the Twentieth Century'. In *Understanding Decline: Perceptions and Realities of British Economic Performance*, ed. P. Clarke and C. Trebilcock: 261–84. Cambridge: CUP.

Casson, M. 1983. *The Economics of Unemployment: An Historical Perspective.* Oxford: Martin Robertson.

Caves, R. E. 1980. 'Productivity Differentials among Industries'. In *Britain's Economic Performance*, ed. R. E. Caves and L. B. Krause: 135–92. Washington DC: Brookings Institution.

Chandler, A. D. 1977. *The Visible Hand: The Managerial Revolution in American Business.* Cambridge, Mass.: Belknap Press.

Chandler, A. D. 1990. *Scale and Scope: The Dynamics of Industrial Capitalism.* Cambridge, Mass: Harvard UP.

Channon, D. 1973. *The Strategy and Structure of British Enterprise.* Macmillan – now Palgrave.

Chapman, S. J. 1986. 'Aristocracy and Meritocracy in Merchant Banking'. *British Journal of Sociology*, 37: 180–97.

Chick, M. 1998. *Industrial Policy in Britain, 1945–51.* Cambridge: CUP.

Clark, C. 1937. *National Income and Outlay.* Macmillan – now Palgrave.

Clarke, P. 1998. *The Keynesian Revolution and Its Consequences: Selected Essays by Peter Clarke.* Cheltenham: Edward Elgar.

Clegg, H. A. 1979. *The Changing System of Industrial Relations in Great Britain.* Oxford: Blackwell.

Clegg, H. A. 1985. *A History of British Trade Unions since 1889: Volume II, 1911–33.* Oxford: Clarendon Press.

Clegg, H. A., Fox, A. and Thompson, A. F. 1964. *A History of British Trade Unions since 1889, Volume I, 1889–1910.* Oxford: Clarendon Press.

Cline, P. 1982. 'Winding Down the War Economy: British Plans for Peacetime Recovery, 1916–19'. In *War and the State: The Transformation of British Government, 1914–19*, ed. K. Burk: 157–81. Allen and Unwin.

Cmd 9703. 1956. *Technical Education.* HMSO.

Cmd 2563. 1994. *Competitiveness: Helping Business to Win.* HMSO.

Cmnd 827. 1959. *Committee on the Working of the Monetary System: Report* (the Radcliffe report). HMSO.

Cmnd 2764. 1965. *The National Plan.* HMSO.

Cmnd 3623. 1968. *Royal Commission on Trade Unions and Employers' Associations: Report* (the Donovan report). HMSO.

Cmnd 3638. 1968. *Royal Commission on the Civil Service: Report* (the Fulton report). HMSO.

Coakley, J. and Harris, L. 1992. 'Financial Globalisation and Deregulation'. In *The Economic Legacy, 1979–92*, ed. J. Michie: 37–57. Academic Press.

Coleman, D. C. 1987. 'Failings and Achievements: Some British Businesses, 1910–80'. *BH*, 29: 1–17.

Coleman, D. C. and MacLeod, C. 1986. 'Attitudes to New Techniques: British Businessmen, 1800–1950'. *EcHR*, 39: 588–611.

Cook, P. L. 1958. 'The Cement Industry'. In *The Effects of Mergers: Six Studies*, ed. P. L. Cook: 19–130. Allen and Unwin.

CPRS. 1975. Central Policy Review Staff: *The Future of the British Car Industry*. HMSO.

Crafts, N. F. R. 1991a. 'Reversing Economic Decline?' *OREP*, 7: 81–98.

Crafts, N. F. R. 1991b. 'Economic Growth'. In *The British Economy since 1945*, ed. N. F. R. Crafts and N. C. Woodward: 261–90. Oxford, OUP.

Crafts, N. F. R. 1996. 'Economic Growth in the 1970s'. In *Britain in the 1970s: The Troubled Economy*, ed. R. Coopey and N. C. Woodward: 81–105. UCL Press.

Crafts, N. F. R. 1997. *Britain's Relative Economic Decline, 1870–1995*. Social Market Foundation.

Crafts, N. F. R. and Thomas, M. 1986. 'Comparative Advantage in UK Manufacturing Trade, 1910–35'. *EJ*, 96: 629–45.

Crafts, N. F. R., Leybourne, S. J. and Mills, T. C. 1989. 'The Climacteric in Late Victorian Britain and France: A Reappraisal of the Evidence'. *Journal of Applied Econometrics*, 4: 237–50.

Cronin, J. E. 1979. *Industrial Conflict in Modern Britain*. Croom Helm.

CSO. 1991. *Annual Abstract of Statistics, 1990*. HMSO.

Cutler, A., Haslam, C., Williams, K. and Williams, J. 1989. *1992 – The Struggle for Europe: A Critical Evaluation of the European Community*. Oxford: Berg.

Daly, A., Hitchens, D. M. W. N. and Wagner, K. 1985. 'Productivity, Machinery and Skills in a Sample of British and German Manufacturing Plants: Results of a Pilot Enquiry'. *NIER*, 111: 48–61.

Dangerfield, G. 1935. *The Strange Death of Liberal England*. New York: Smith and Haas.

Daniel, W. W. 1987. *Workplace Industrial Relations and Technical Change*. Pinter.

Daunton, M. J. 1989. 'Gentlemanly Capitalism and British Industry, 1820–1914'. *PP*, 122: 119–58.

Davis Smith, J. 1990. *The Attlee and Churchill Administrations and Industrial Unrest, 1945–55*. Pinter.

Deacon, A. 1987. 'Systems of Inter-war Unemployment Relief'. In *The Road to Full Employment*, ed. S. Glynn and A. Booth: 31–42. Allen and Unwin.

DEE. 1998. *Labour Market Trends*, July 1998.

Denison, E. F. 1967. *Why Growth Rates Differ: Postwar Experience in Nine Western Countries*. Washington DC: Brookings Institution.

DEP. 1971. *British Labour Statistics: Historical Abstract, 1886–1968*. HMSO.

Dex, S. 1985. *The Sexual Division of Work*. Brighton: Wheatsheaf.

Dimsdale, N. H. 1984. 'Employment and Real Wages in the Interwar Period'. *NIER*, 110: 94–103.

DoE. 1976. 'Distribution and Concentration of Industrial Stoppages in Great Britain'. *Department of Employment Gazette*, Nov. 1976: 1219–24.

Dormael, A. van. 1978. *Bretton Woods: Birth of a Monetary System*. Macmillan – now Palgrave.

Dowie, J. A. 1975. '1919–20 is in Need of Attention'. *EcHR*, 28: 94–103.

Dumke, R. H. 1990. 'Reassessing the *Wirtschaftswunder*: Reconstruction and Postwar Growth in West Germany in an International Context'. *OBES*, 52: 451–91.

Dunning, J. H. 1958. *American Investment in British Manufacturing Industry*. Allen and Unwin.

Dunning, J. H. 1998. 'US-owned Manufacturing Affiliates and the Transfer of Managerial Techniques: The British Case'. In *The Americanisation of European Business: The Marshall Plan and the Transfer of US Management Models*, ed. M. Kipping and O. Bjarnar: 74–90. Routledge.

Durcan, J. W., McCarthy, W. E. J. and Redman, G. P. 1983. *Strikes in Postwar Britain: A Study of Stoppages of Work due to Industrial Disputes, 1946–73*. Allen and Unwin.

Edelstein, M. 1982. *Overseas Investment in the Age of High Imperialism: The United Kingdom, 1850–1914*. Methuen.

Edelstein, M. 1994. 'Foreign Investment and Accumulation'. In *The Economic History of Britain since 1700*, vol. 2, 1860–1939, ed. R. Floud and D. McCloskey: 173–96. Cambridge: CUP, 2nd edn.

Edgerton, D. 1991a. *England and the Aeroplane: An Essay on a Militant and Technological Nation*. Macmillan – now Palgrave.

Edgerton, D. 1991b. 'The Prophet Militant and Industrial: The Peculiarities of Correlli Barnett'. *TCBH*, 2: 359–79.

Edgerton, D. 1996a. *Science, Technology and the British Industrial 'Decline', 1870–1970*. Cambridge: CUP.

Edgerton, D. 1996b. 'The "White Heat" Revisited: The British Government and Technology Policy in the 1960s'. *TCBH*, 7: 53–82.

Edgerton, D. and Horrocks, S. 1994. 'British Industrial R&D before 1945'. *EcHR*, 47: 213–38.

Edwards, P. and Whitston, C. 1991. 'Workers are Working Harder: Effort and Shop-floor Relations in the 1980s'. *BJIR*, 29: 593–9.

Egan, D. 1996. '"A Cult of Their Own": Syndicalism and *The Miners' Next Step*'. In *Miners, Unions and Politics, 1910–47*, ed. A. Campbell, N. Fishman and D. Howell: 13–34. Aldershot: Scolar.

Eichengreen, B. 1990. *Elusive Stability: Essays in the History of International Finance, 1919–1939*. Cambridge: CUP.

Eichengreen, B. 1992. 'The Origins and Nature of the Great Slump Revisited'. *EcHR*, 45: 213–39.

Eichengreen, B. 1996. 'Institutions and Economic Growth: Europe after World War II'. In *Economic Growth in Europe since 1945*, ed. N. Crafts and G. Toniolo: 38–72. Cambridge: CUP.

Elbaum, B. 1986. 'The Steel Industry before World War I'. In *The Decline of the British Economy*, ed. B. Elbaum and W. Lazonick: 51–81. Oxford: OUP.

Elbaum, B. and Lazonick, W. 1986. *The Decline of the British Economy*. Oxford: OUP.

European Commission. 1995. *Social Protection in the Member States of the Community*. Brussels: European Commission.

Feinstein, C. H. 1972. *National Income, Expenditure and Output of the UK, 1855–1965*. Cambridge: CUP.

Feinstein, C. H. 1990a. 'Benefits of Backwardness and Costs of Continuity'. In *Government and Economies in the Postwar World: Economic Policies and Comparative Performance, 1945–85*, ed. A. Graham and A. Seldon: 284–93. Routledge.

Feinstein, C. H. 1990b. 'Britain's Overseas Investments in 1913'. *EcHR*, 43: 288–95.

Feinstein, C. H. 1990c. 'What Really Happened to Real Wages? Trends in Wages, Prices and Productivity in the United Kingdom, 1880–1913'. *EcHR*, 43: 329–55.

Feinstein, C. H. 1990d. 'New Estimates of Average Earnings in the UK, 1880–1913'. *EcHR*, 43: 595–632.

Feinstein, C. H., Matthews, R. C. O. and Odling-Smee, J. C. 1982. 'The Timing of the Climacteric and its Sectoral Incidence in the UK'. In *Economics in the Long View: Essays in Honour of W. W. Rostow*, vol. 2, ed. C. P. Kindleberger and G. di Tella: 168–85. Macmillan – now Palgrave.

Feinstein, C. H., Temin, P. and Toniolo, G. 1997. *The European Economy between the Wars*. Oxford: OUP.

Finegold, D. and Soskice, D. 1988. 'The Failure of Training in Britain: Analysis and Prescription'. *OREP*, 4: 21–53.

Flora, P., Kraus, F. and Pfenning, W. 1987. *State, Economy and Society in Western Europe, 1815–1975: A Data Handbook. Volume 2: The Growth of Industrial Societies and Capitalist Economies*. Macmillan – now Palgrave.

Foreman-Peck, J. 1983. *A History of the World Economy: International Economic Relations since 1850*. Brighton: Wheatsheaf.

Foreman-Peck, J. 1994. 'Industry and Industrial Organisation between the Wars'. In *The Economic History of Britain since 1700: Volume 2, 1860–1939*, ed. R. C. Floud and D. N. McCloskey: 386–414. Cambridge: CUP, 2nd edn.

Foreman-Peck, J. 1999. 'The Balance of Technological Transfers, 1870–1914'. In *The British Industrial Decline*, ed. J-P. Dormois and M. Dintenfass: 114–38. Routledge.

Foreman-Peck, J., Bowden, S. and McKinlay, A. 1995. *The British Motor Industry*. Manchester: MUP.

Fox, A. 1985. *History and Heritage: The Social Origins of the British Industrial Relations System*. Allen and Unwin.

Friedman, M. 1956. *Studies in the Quantity Theory of Money*. Chicago: Harper and Row.

Friedman, M. 1969. *The Optimum Quantity of Money and Other Essays*. Macmillan – now Palgrave.

Gallie, D. 1996. 'Skill, Gender and the Quality of Employment'. In *Changing Forms of Employment: Organisations, Skills and Gender*, ed. R. Crompton, D. Gallie and K. Purcell: 133–59. Routledge.

Gamble, A. 1974. *The Conservative Nation*. Routledge.

Gamble, A. 1994. *Britain in Decline: Economic Policy, Political Strategy and the British State*. Macmillan – now Palgrave.

Garside, W. 1990. *British Unemployment, 1919–39: A Study in Public Policy*. Cambridge: CUP.

Gilbert, D. 1996. 'Strikes in Postwar Britain'. In *A History of British Industrial Relations, 1939–79: Industrial Relations in a Declining Economy*, ed. C. Wrigley: 128–61. Cheltenham: Edward Elgar.

Glynn, S. 1991. *No Alternative: Unemployment in Britain*. Faber.

Glynn, S. and Booth, A. 1983. 'Unemployment in Interwar Britain: A Case for Re-learning the Lessons of the 1930s?' *EcHR*, 36: 329–48.

Glynn, S. and Booth, A. 1996. *Modern Britain: An Economic and Social History*. Routledge.

Goodman, A. and Webb, S. 1994. *For Richer or Poorer: The Changing Distribution of Income in the UK*. Institute of Fiscal Studies.

Gospel, H. F. 1992. *Markets, Firms and the Management of Labour in Modern Britain*. Cambridge: CUP.

Gospel, H. F. 1994. 'The Survival of Apprenticeship Training: A British, American and Australian Comparison'. *BJIR*, 32: 505–22.

Gourvish, T. R. 1979. 'Mechanical Engineering'. In *British Industry between the Wars: Instability and Industrial Development, 1919–39*, ed. N. K. Buxton and D. H. Aldcroft: 129–55. Scolar Press.

Gourvish, T. R. 1987. 'British Business and the Transition to a Corporate Economy: Entrepreneurship and Management Structures'. *BH*, 29: 18–45.

Greasley, D. and Oxley, L. 1995. 'Balanced Versus Compromise Estimates of UK GDP, 1870–1913'. *EEH*, 32: 262–72.

Greasley, D. and Oxley, L. 1996. 'Discontinuities in Competitiveness: The Impact of the First World War on British Industry'. *EcHR*, 49: 82–100.

Greasley, D. and Oxley, L. 1999. 'Competitiveness and Growth: New Perspectives on the Late Victorian and Edwardian Economy'. In *The British Industrial Decline*, ed. J.-P. Dormois and M. Dintenfass: 65–84. Routledge.

Gregg, P., Machin, S. and Metcalf, D. 1993. 'Signals and Cycles? Productivity Growth and Changes in Union Status in British Companies, 1984–9'. *EJ*, 103: 894–907.

Guardian. 2000. 'Tories' Legacy of Poverty', 12 Jan 2000.

Halsey, A. H. 1972. *Trends in British Society since 1900: A Guide to the Changing Social Structure of Britain*. Macmillan – now Palgrave.

Halsey, A. H., Heath, A. F. and Ridge, J. M. 1986. *Origins and Destinations: Family, Class and Education in Modern Britain*. Oxford: OUP.

Ham, A. 1981. *Treasury Rules: Recurrent Themes in British Economic Policy*. Quartet.

Hannah, L. 1976. *The Rise of the Corporate Economy*. Methuen, 2nd edn.

Hannah, L. 1986. *Inventing Retirement: The Development of Occupational Benefits in Britain*. Cambridge: CUP.

Harris, J. 1972. *Unemployment and Politics: A Study in English Social Policy, 1886–1914*. Oxford: Clarendon Press.

Harris, J. 1990. 'Enterprise and Welfare States: A Comparative Perspective'. *Transactions of the Royal Historical Society*, 5th series, 40: 175–95.

Harris, L. 1984. 'State and Economy in the Second World War'. In *State and Society in Contemporary Britain: A Critical Introduction*, ed. G. McLennan, D. Held and S. Hall: 50–76. Cambridge: Polity Press.

Hart, P. E. 1965. *Studies in Profit, Business Saving and Investment in the UK, 1920–62*. Allen and Unwin.

Hatton, T. J. 1994. 'Unemployment and the Labour Market in Interwar Britain'. In *The Economic History of Britain since 1700: Volume 2, 1860–1939*, ed. R. C. Floud and D. N. McCloskey: 359–85. Cambridge: CUP, 2nd edn.

Hatton, T. J. and Chrystal, A. 1991. 'The Budget and Fiscal Policy'. In *The British Economy since 1945*, ed. N. F. R. Crafts and N. C. Woodward: 52–88. Oxford: OUP.

Hay, J. R. 1975. *The Origin of the Liberal Welfare Reforms, 1906–14*. Macmillan – now Palgrave.

Heller, F. and Porter, L. 1977. 'Two Research Projects on American and British Managers'. In *Culture and Management*, ed. T. Weinshall. Harmondsworth: Penguin.

Hills, J. 1995. 'Funding the Welfare State'. *OREP*, 11: 27–43.

Hinton, J. 1973. *The First Shop Stewards' Movement*. Allen and Unwin.

Hinton, J. 1994. *Shop Floor Citizens: Engineering Democracy in 1940s Britain*. Aldershot: Edward Elgar.

Holton, B. 1976. *British Syndicalism, 1900–14: Myths and Realities*. Pluto Press.

Hopkins, A. 1997. 'Macmillan's Audit of Empire, 1957'. In *Understanding Decline: Perceptions and Realities of British Economic Performance*, ed. P. Clarke and C. Trebilcock: 234–60. Cambridge: CUP.

Howlett, P. 1994. 'The Wartime Economy, 1939–45'. In *The Economic History of Britain since 1700: Volume 3, 1939–92*, ed. R. C. Floud and D. N. McCloskey: 1–31. Cambridge: CUP, 2nd edn.

Howson, S. 1976. *Domestic Monetary Management in Britain, 1919–38*. Cambridge: CUP.

Howson, S. 1980. *Sterling's Managed Float: The Operation of the Exchange Equalisation Account, 1932–9*. Princeton Studies in International Finance, 46. Princeton, NJ: Princeton UP.

Howson, S. 1993. *British Monetary Policy, 1945–51*. Oxford: Clarendon Press.

Hyman, R. 1987. 'Rank-and-file Movements and Workplace Organisation, 1914–39'. In *A History of British Industrial Relations*, vol. 2, 1914–1939, ed. C. Wrigley: 129–58. Brighton: Harvester.

Irwin, D. 1995. 'The GATT's Contribution to Economic Recovery in Postwar Western Europe'. In *Europe's Postwar Recovery*, ed. B. Eichengreen: 127–50. Cambridge: CUP.

Jeremy, D. J. 1998. *A Business History of Britain, 1900–1990s*. Oxford: OUP.

Johnson, C. 1982. *MITI and the Japanese Miracle: The Growth of Industrial Policy, 1925–75*. Stanford, Calif.: Stanford UP.

Johnson, C. 1991. *The Economy under Mrs. Thatcher, 1979–90*. Harmondsworth: Penguin.

Johnson, P. 1984. 'Self-help Versus State Help: Old Age Pensions and Personal Savings in Great Britain, 1906–37'. *EEH*, 21: 329–50.

Johnson, P. 1994. 'The Welfare State'. In *The Economic History of Britain since 1700, Volume 3: 1939–1992*, ed. R. C. Floud and D. N. McCloskey: 284–317. Cambridge: CUP.

Jones, G. 1988. 'Foreign Multinationals in British Industry before 1945'. *EcHR*, 41: 429–53.

Jones, R. 1987. *Wages and Employment Policy, 1936–85*. Allen and Unwin.

Kaldor, N. 1961. 'Capital Accumulation and Economic Growth'. In *The Theory of Capital*, ed. F. Lutz and D. Hague: 177–222. Macmillan – now Palgrave.

Kaldor, N. 1966. *Causes of the Slow Rate of Economic Growth in the UK*. Cambridge: CUP.

Kaldor, N. 1971. 'Conflicts in National Economic Objectives'. *EJ*, 81: 1–16.

Katz, R. 1998. *Japan: The System that Soured*. Armonck, NY: M.E. Sharpe.

Keeble, S. P. 1992. *The Ability to Manage: A Study of British Management, 1890–1990*. Manchester: MUP.

Keep, E. and Mayhew, K. 1988. 'The Assessment: Education, Training and Economic Performance'. *OREP*, 4: i–xv.

Kennedy, W. P. 1976. 'Institutional Response to Economic Growth: Capital Markets in Britain to 1914'. In *Management Strategy and Business Development: A Historical and Comparative Study*, ed. L. Hannah: 151–83. Macmillan – now Palgrave.

Kennedy, W. P. 1987. *Industrial Structure, Capital Markets and the Origins of British Economic Decline*. Cambridge: CUP.

Kilpatrick, A. and Lawson, T. 1980. 'On the Nature of Industrial Decline in the UK'. *Cambridge Journal of Economics*, 4: 85–102.

King, D. 1997. 'Employers, Training Policy and the Tenacity of Voluntarism in Britain'. *TCBH*, 8: 383–411.

King, S. 1990. 'Technical and Vocational Education for Girls: A Study of the Central Schools of London, 1918–39'. In *Technical Education and the State since 1850: Historical and Comparative Perspectives*, ed. P. Summerfield and E. J. Evans: 77–96. Manchester: MUP.

Kirby, M. W. 1992. 'Institutional Rigidities and Economic Decline: Reflections on the British Experience'. *EcHR*, 45: 637–60.

Kitson, M. and Solomou, S. 1990. *Protectionism and Economic Revival: The British Interwar Economy*. Cambridge: CUP.

Klundert, T. van de and Schaik, A. van. 1996. 'On the Historical Continuity of the Process of Economic Growth'. In *Quantitative Aspects of Postwar European Economic Growth*, ed. B. van Ark and N. Crafts: 388–414. Cambridge: CUP.

Komiya, R. and Yamamoto, K. 1981. 'Japan: The Officer in Charge of Economic Affairs'. In *Economists in Government: An International Comparative Study*, ed. A. W. Coats: 262–90. Durham, NC: Duke UP.

Kuznets, S. 1966. *Modern Economic Growth: Rate, Structure and Spread*. New Haven, Conn.: Yale UP.

Kynaston, D. 1999. *The City of London*, vol. 3: *Illusions of Gold, 1914–1945*. Chatto and Windus.

Lawson, N. 1993. *The View from No. 11: Memoirs of a Tory Radical*. Corgi.

Lazonick, W. 1986. 'The Cotton Industry'. In *The Decline of the British Economy*, ed. B. Elbaum and W. Lazonick: 18–50. Oxford: Clarendon Press.

Lazonick, W. 1994. 'Social Organization and Technological Leadership'. In *Convergence of Productivity: Cross-national Studies and Historical Evidence*, ed. W. J. Baumol, R. R. Nelson and E. N. Wolff: 164–93. Oxford: OUP.

LCES. 1967. *The British Economy: Key Statistics, 1900–66*. London and Cambridge Economic Service.

Lee, C. 1994. 'The Service Industries'. In *The Economic History of Britain since 1700*, vol. 2, ed. R. C. Floud and D. N. McCloskey: 117–44. Cambridge: CUP, 2nd edn.

Lewchuk, W. 1986. 'The Motor Vehicle Industry'. In *The Decline of the British Economy*, ed. B. Elbaum and W. Lazonick: 135–61. Oxford: Clarendon Press.

Lewchuk, W. 1987. *American Technology and the British Vehicle Industry*. Cambridge: CUP.

Louis, W. 1985. 'American Anti-colonialism and the Dissolution of the British Empire'. *International Affairs*, 61: 395–420.

Lowe, R. 1978. 'The Erosion of State Intervention in Britain, 1917–24'. *EcHR*, 31: 270–86.

Lowe, R. 1987. 'The Government and Industrial Relations, 1919–39'. In *A History of British Industrial Relations, Volume 2: 1914–39*, ed. C. Wrigley: 185–210. Brighton: Harvester.

Lowe, R. 1993. *The Welfare State in Britain since 1945*. Macmillan – now Palgrave.

Lowe, R. and Rollings, N. 2000. 'Modernising Britain, 1957–64: A Classic Case of Centralisation and Fragmentation?' In *Transforming British Government, Volume 1*, ed. R. Rhodes. Macmillan – now Palgrave.

Lyddon, D. 1996. 'The Car Industry, 1945–79: Shop Stewards and Workplace Unionism'. In *A History of British Industrial Relations, 1939–79: Industrial Relations in a Declining Economy*, ed. C. Wrigley: 186–211. Cheltenham: Elgar.

Lyddon, D. 1999. 'Glorious Summer, 1972: The High Tide of Rank and File Militancy'. In *British Trade Unions and Industrial Politics: The High Tide of Trade Unionism, 1964–79*, ed. J. McIlroy, N. Fishman and A. Campbell: 326–52. Aldershot: Ashgate.

MacKinnon, M. 1994. 'Living Standards, 1870–1914'. In *The Economic History of Britain since 1700*, vol. 2, ed. R. C. Floud and D. N. McCloskey: 265–90. Cambridge: CUP.

Maddison, A. 1982. *Phases of Capitalist Development*. Oxford: OUP.

Maddison, A. 1989. *The World Economy in the Twentieth Century*. Paris: OECD.

Maddison, A. 1991. *Dynamic Forces in Capitalist Development: A Long-run Comparative View*. Oxford: OUP.

Maddison, A. 1995. *Monitoring the World Economy, 1820–1992*. Paris: OECD.

Maizels, A. 1963. *Industrial Growth and World Trade: An Empirical Study of Trends in Production, Consumption and Trade in Manufactures from 1899 to 1955 with a Discussion of Probable Future Trends*. Cambridge: CUP.

Marquand, D. 1988. *The Unprincipled Society: New Developments and Old Politics*. Fontana.

Marrison, A. 1996. *British Industry and Protection, 1903–1932*. Oxford: Clarendon Press.

Matthews, R. C. O., Feinstein, C. H. and Odling-Smee, J. C. 1982. *British Economic Growth, 1856–1973*. Oxford: Clarendon Press.

McCloskey, D. N. 1970. 'Did Victorian Britain Fail?' *EcHR*, 23: 446–59.

McCloskey, D. N. 1973. *Economic Maturity and Entrepreneurial Decline*. Cambridge, Mass.: Harvard UP.

McCloskey, D. N. 1990. *If You're So Smart: The Narrative of Economic Expertise*. Chicago: University of Chicago Press.

McCombie, J. S. L. and Thirlwall, A. P. 1994. *Economic Growth and the Balance of Payments Constraint*. Macmillan – now Palgrave.

McCormick, B. J. 1979. *Industrial Relations in the Coal Industry*. Macmillan – now Palgrave.

McIvor, A. J. 1996. *Organised Capital: Employers' Associations and Industrial Relations in Northern England, 1880–1939*. Cambridge: CUP.

McKinlay, A. 1991. '"A Certain Short-sightedness": Metal-working, Innovation and Apprenticeship, 1897–1939'. In *Industrial Training and Technological Innovation: A Comparative and Historical Study*, ed. H. F. Gospel: 93–111. Routledge.

Melling, J. and Johansson, A. 1994. 'Employers, Craft Workers and the Effort Bargain: The Institutional Context of Engineering Firms' Labour Policies in Britain and Sweden, c. 1920–40'. *Scandinavian Economic History Review*, 43: 200–19.

Mercer, H. 1995. *Constructing a Competitive Order: The Hidden History of British Antitrust Policies*. Cambridge: CUP.

Metcalf, D. 1991. 'British Unions: Dissolution or Resurgence?' *OREP*, 7: 19–32.

Metcalf, D., Nickell, S. J. and Floros, N. 1982. 'Still Searching for a Solution to Unemployment in Interwar Britain'. *JPE*, 90: 386–99.

Middlemas, K. 1979. *Politics in Industrial Society: The Experience of the British System since 1911*. Andre Deutsch.

Middleton, R. 1996. *Government Versus the Market: The Growth of the Public Sector, Economic Management and British Economic Performance, c. 1890–1979*. Cheltenham: Edward Elgar.

Milward, A. S. 1984. *The Reconstruction of Western Europe, 1945–51*. Methuen.

Milward, A. S. and Saul, S. B. 1977. *The Development of the Economies of Continental Europe, 1850–1914*. Allen and Unwin.

Mitchell, B. R. 1980. *European Historical Statistics, 1750–1975*. Macmillan – now Palgrave.

Mitchell, B. R. 1992. *International Historical Statistics: Europe, 1750–1988*. Macmillan – now Palgrave.

Mitchell, B. R. 1993. *International Historical Statistics: Africa, Asia and Oceania, 1750–1988*. Macmillan – now Palgrave.

Mitchell, B. R. 1995. *International Historical Statistics: The Americas, 1750–1988*. Macmillan – now Palgrave.

Mitchell, B. R. and Deane, P. 1962. *Abstract of British Historical Statistics*. Cambridge: CUP.

Moggridge, D. E. 1972. *British Monetary Policy, 1924–31: The Norman Conquest of $4.86*. Cambridge: CUP.

Morgan, K. O. 1984. *Labour in Power, 1945–51*. Oxford: Clarendon Press.

Nichols, T. 1986. *The British Worker Question: A New Look at Workers and Productivity in Manufacturing*. Routledge.

North, D. 1990. *Institutions, Institutional Change and Economic Performance*. Cambridge: CUP.

O'Brien, P. K. 1983. 'The Analysis and Measurement of the Service Sector Economy in European Economic History'. In *Productivity in the Economies of Europe*, ed. R. Fremdling and P. K. O'Brien: 79–88. Stuttgart: Klett-Cotta.

O'Brien, P. K. 1994. 'Central Government and the Economy, 1688–1815'. In *The Economic History of Britain since 1700, Vol. I: 1700–1860*, ed. R. C. Floud and D. N. McCloskey: 205–41. Cambridge: CUP.

O'Brien, P. 1997. 'The Security of the Realm and the Growth of the Economy, 1688–1914'. In *Understanding Decline: Perceptions and Realities of British Economic Performance*, ed. P. Clarke and C. Trebilcock: 49–72. Cambridge: CUP.

OECD. 1985. *Social Expenditure, 1960–90: Problems of Growth and Control*. Paris: OECD.

OECD. 1995. *OECD Historical Statistics, 1960–93*. Paris: OECD.

OECD. 1999. *Main Economic Indicators*, Dec. 1999.

Oliver, N. and Wilkinson, B. 1992. *The Japanisation of British Industry: New Developments in the 1990s*. Oxford: Blackwell.

Olson, M. 1982. *The Rise and Decline of Nations: Economic Growth, Stagflation and Social Rigidities*. New Haven, Conn.: Yale UP.

ONS. 1997. *Economic Trends: Annual Supplement, 1996–7*. HMSO.

ONS. 1999a. *Annual Abstract of Statistics, 1999*. HMSO.

ONS. 1999b. *UK National Accounts: The Blue Book, 1999 edition*. HMSO.

ONS. 2000. *Economic Trends: Annual Supplement, 1999*. HMSO.

Ormerod, P. 1994. *The Death of Economics*. Faber.

Overy, R. 1984. *Goering: The 'Iron Man'*. Routledge.

Owen, G. 1999. *From Empire to Europe: The Decline and Revival of British Industry since the Second World War*. Harper Collins.

Pacqué, K-H. 1996. 'Why the 1950s and not the 1920s? Olsonian and non-Olsonian Interpretations of Two Decades of German History'. In *Economic Growth in Europe since 1945*, ed. N. Crafts and G. Toniolo: 95–106. Cambridge: CUP.

Panitch, L. 1976. *Social Democracy and Industrial Militancy: The Labour Party, the Trade Unions and Incomes Policy, 1945–74*. Cambridge: CUP.

Parker, H. M. D. 1957. *Manpower in War*. HMSO and Longman: UK Official History of the Second World War.

Parsley, C. 1980. 'Labor Union Effects on Wage Gains: A Survey of Recent Literature'. *Journal of Economic Literature*, 18: 1–31.

Patel, P. and Pavitt, K. 1987. 'The Elements of British Technological Competitiveness'. *NIER*, 122: 72–83.

Paxman, J. 1999. *The English: A Portrait of a People*. Harmondsworth: Penguin.

Payne, P. 1974. *British Entrepreneurship in the Nineteenth Century*. Macmillan – now Palgrave.

Peacock, A. and Wiseman, J. 1961. *The Growth of Public Expenditure in the UK*. Princeton, NJ: Princeton UP.

Phelps Brown, H. 1959. *The Growth of British Industrial Relations: A Study from the Standpoint of 1906–14*. Methuen.

Phelps Brown, H. 1977. 'What is the British Predicament?' *Three Banks Review*, 116: 3–29.

Phillips, J. 1996. 'Decasualisation and Disruption: Industrial Relations in the Docks, 1945–79'. In *A History of British Industrial Relations, 1939–79: Industrial Relations in a Declining Economy*, ed. C. Wrigley: 165–85. Cheltenham: Elgar.

Piachaud, D. 1988. 'Poverty in Britain, 1899–1883'. *Journal of Social Policy*, 17: 335–49.

Piore, M. and Sabel, C. 1984. *The Second Industrial Divide: Possibilities for Prosperity*. New York: Basic Books.

Pollard, S. 1981. *Peaceful Conquest: The Industrialisation of Europe, 1760–1970*. Oxford: OUP.

Pollard, S. 1989. *Britain's Prime and Britain's Decline: The British Economy, 1870–1914*. Arnold.

Pollard, S. 1992a. *The Development of the British Economy, 1914–90*. Arnold, 4th edn.

Pollard, S. 1992b. 'Cultural Influences on Economic Action'. In *Culture in History: Production, Consumption and Values in Historical Perspective*, ed. J. Barry and J. Melling: 3–27. Exeter: University of Exeter Press.

Pollard, S. 1994. 'Entrepreneurship, 1870–1914'. In *The Economic History of Britain since 1700*, vol. 2, ed. R. C. Floud and D. N. McCloskey: 62–89. Cambridge: CUP, 2nd edn.

Porter, M. 1985. *Competitive Advantage: Creating and Sustaining Superior Performance*. New York: Free Press.

Prais, S. J. 1981. *Productivity and Industrial Structure: A Statistical Study of Manufacturing Industry in Britain, Germany and the United States*. Cambridge: CUP.

Prais, S. J. 1995. *Productivity, Education and Training: An International Perspective*. Cambridge: CUP.

Prais, S. J. and Wagner, K. 1985. 'Schooling Standards in England and Germany: Some Summary Comparisons Bearing on Economic Performance'. *NIER*, 112: 53–76.

Pratten, C. F. 1976. *Labour Productivity Differentials within International Companies*. Cambridge: CUP.

Reader, W. J. 1975. *Imperial Chemical Industries, a History*, vol. 2, 1926–52. Oxford: OUP.

Reader, W. J. 1979. 'The Chemical Industry'. In *British Industry between the Wars: Instability and Industrial Development, 1919–39*, ed. N. K. Buxton and D. H. Aldcroft: 156–78. Scolar Press.

Roberts, R. 1984. 'The Administrative Origins of Industrial Diplomacy: An Aspect of Government–Industry Relations'. In *Businessmen and Politics: Studies of Business Activities in British Politics, 1900–1945*, ed. J. Turner: 93–104. Heinemann.

Roberts, R. 1992. 'Regulatory Responses to the Rise of the Market for Corporate Control in Britain in the 1950s'. *BH*, 34: 183–200.

Robinson, O. 1988. 'The Changing Labour Market: Growth of Part-time Employment and Labour Market Segmentation in Britain'. In *Gender Segregation at Work*, ed. S. Walby: 114–34. Milton Keynes: Open University Press.

Rollings, N. 1994. 'Poor Mr Butskell: A Short Life Wrecked by Schizophrenia?' *TCBH*, 5: 183–205.

Ross, D. 1990. 'The Clearing Banks and Industry: New Perspectives on the Interwar Years'. In *Capitalism in a Mature Economy: Financial Institutions, Capital Exports and British Industry, 1870–1939*, ed. J. J. van Helten and Y. Cassis: 52–70. Aldershot: Edward Elgar.

Rowntree, S. 1901. *Poverty: A Study of Town Life*. Longman.

Rowntree, S. 1941. *Poverty and Progress: A Second Survey of York*. Longman.

Rowthorn, R. E. and Wells, J. R. 1987. *De-industrialisation and Foreign Trade*. Cambridge: CUP.

Rubinstein, W. D. 1993. *Capitalism, Culture and Decline in Britain, 1750–1990*. Routledge.

Sandberg, L. 1970. 'American Rings and English Mules: The Role of Economic Rationality'. In *Technological Change: The United States and Britain in the Nineteenth Century*, ed. S. B. Saul: 120–40. Methuen.

Sanderson, M. 1988. 'Education and Economic Decline, 1890 to the 1990s'. *OREP*, 4: 38–50.

Sanderson, M. 1990. 'The Missing Stratum: The Problem of Technical School Education in England, 1900–1960s'. In *Education and Economic Growth since the Industrial Revolution*, ed. G. Tortella: 247–71. Valencia: Generalitat Valenciana.

Sanderson, M. 1994. *The Missing Stratum: Technical School Education in England, 1900–1990s*. Athlone.

Sayers, R.S. 1955. *Financial Policy, 1939–45*. Longman.

Sayers, R.S. 1976. *The Bank of England, 1891–1944*. Cambridge: CUP (3 vols).

Schenk, C. 1994. *Britain and the Sterling Area: From Devaluation to Convertibility in the 1950s*. Routledge.

Schulze, M-S. and Woodward, N. C. 1996. 'The Emergence of Rapid Inflation'. In *Britain in the 1970s: The Troubled Economy*, ed. R. Coopey and N. C. Woodward: 106–35. UCL Press.

Schumpeter, J. 1939. *Business Cycles: A Theoretical, Historical and Statistical Analysis of the Capitalist Process*. New York: McGraw Hill.

Schumpeter, J. 1954. *Capitalism, Socialism and Democracy*. Allen and Unwin, 4th edn.

Searle, G. R. 1971. *The Quest for National Efficiency: A Study in British Politics and Political Thought, 1899–1914*. Allen and Unwin.

Sefton, J. and Weale, M. 1995. *Reconciliation of National Income and Expenditure: Balanced Estimates of National Income for the UK, 1920–90*. Cambridge: CUP.

Smith, H. 1986. *War and Social Change: British Society in the Second World War*. Manchester: MUP.

Solomou, S. and Weale, M. 1991. 'Balanced Estimates of UK GDP, 1870–1913'. *EEH*, 28: 54–63.

Solomou, S. and Weale, M. 1996. 'UK National Income, 1920–38: The Implication of Balanced Estimates'. *EcHR*, 49: 101–15.

Solomou, S. and Weale, M. 1997. 'Personal Sector Wealth in the UK, 1920–56'. *Review of Income and Wealth*, 43: 297–318.

Stark, T. 1977. *The Distribution of Income in Eight Countries*. Royal Commission on the Distribution of Income and Wealth, Background Paper 4. HMSO.

Steedman, A. and Wagner, K. 1987. 'A Second Look at Productivity, Machinery and Skills in Britain and Germany'. *NIER*, 122: 84–95.

Stewart, M. 1990. 'Union Wage Differentials, Product Market Influences and the Division of Rents'. *EJ*, 100: 1122–37.

Stewart, M. 1991. 'Union Wage Differentials in the Face of Changes in the Economic and Legal Environment'. *Economica*, 58: 155–72.

Stout, D. 1976. *International Price Competitiveness, Non-price Factors in International Trade*. NEDO.

Strange, S. 1986. *Casino Capitalism*. Oxford: Blackwell.

Streeck, W. 1992. *Social Institutions and Economic Performance: Studies of Industrial Relations in Advanced Capitalist Economies*. Sage.

Supple, B. 1994a. 'Fear of Failing: Economic History and the Decline of Britain'. *EcHR*, 47: 441–58.

Supple, B. 1994b. 'British Economic Decline since 1945'. In *The Economic History of Britain since 1700*, vol. 3, ed. R. C. Floud and D. N. McCloskey: 318–46. Cambridge: CUP, 2nd edn.

Taylor, R. 1993. *The Trade Union Question in British Politics: Government and Unions since 1945*. Oxford: Blackwell.

Thom, D. 1986. 'The 1944 Education Act: "The Art of the Possible?"' In *War and Social Change: British Society in the Second World War*, ed. H. Smith: 101–28. Manchester: MUP.

Thomas, M. 1994. 'The Macroeconomics of the Interwar Years'. In *The Economic History of Britain since 1700*, vol. 2, ed. R. C. Floud and D. N. McCloskey: 320–58. Cambridge: CUP, 2nd edn.

Thompson, P. 1989. *The Nature of Work: An Introduction to Debates on the Labour Process*. Macmillan – now Palgrave, 2nd edn.

Thoms, D. 1990. 'Technical Education and the Transformation of Coventry's Industrial Economy, 1900–39'. In *Technical Education and the State since 1850: Historical and Contemporary Perspectives*, ed. P. Summerfield and E. J. Evans: 37–54. Manchester: MUP.

Tiratsoo, N. and Tomlinson, J. 1997. 'Exporting the "Gospel of Productivity": US Technical Assistance and British Industry, 1945–60'. *BHR*, 71: 41–81.

Tiratsoo, N. and Tomlinson, J. 1998a. 'Americanisation beyond the Mass Production Paradigm: The Case of British Industry'. In *The Amer-*

icanisation of European Business: The Marshall Plan and the Transfer of US Management Models, ed. M. Kipping and O. Bjarnar: 115–32. Routledge.

Tiratsoo, N. and Tomlinson, J. 1998b. *The Conservatives and Industrial Efficiency: Thirteen Wasted Years?* Routledge.

Titmuss, R. 1958. *Essays on the Welfare State*. Unwin.

Tolliday, S. 1987. *Business, Banking and Politics: The Case of British Steel, 1918–1939*. Cambridge, Mass.: Harvard UP.

Tomlinson, J. 1990. *Public Policy and the Economy since 1900*. Oxford: OUP.

Tomlinson, J. 1994. *Government and the Enterprise since 1900*. Oxford: Clarendon Press.

Tomlinson, J. 1995. 'An Unfortunate Alliance: Keynesianism and the Conservatives, 1945–64,' *History of Political Economy*, annual supplement, 27: 61–85.

Tomlinson, J. 1996. 'Inventing "Decline": The Falling Behind of the British Economy in the Postwar Years'. *EcHR*, 49: 731–57.

Tomlinson, J. 1997. *Democratic Socialism and Economic Policy: The Attlee Years, 1945–51*. Cambridge: CUP.

Tomlinson, J. and Tiratsoo, N. 1998. 'An Old Story Freshly Told? A Comment on Broadberry and Crafts' Approach to Britain's Early Postwar Economic Performance'. *BH*, 40: 62–72.

Townsend, P. 1979. *Poverty in the UK*. Harmondsworth: Penguin.

Townsend, P. and Davidson, N. 1982. *Inequalities in Health: The Black Report*. Harmondsworth: Penguin.

Turner, H. A., Clack, G. and Roberts, G. 1967. *Labour Relations in the Motor Industry*. Allen and Unwin.

Vlaeminke, M. 1990. 'The Subordination of Technical Education in Secondary Schooling, 1870–1914'. In *Technical Education and the State since 1850: Historical and Comparative Perspectives*, ed. P. Summerfield and E. J. Evans: 55–76. Manchester: MUP.

Webster, C. 1982. 'Healthy or Hungry Thirties?' *History Workshop Journal*, 10: 110–29.

Wells, J. R. 1989. 'Uneven Development and De-industrialisation in the UK since 1979'. In *The Restructuring of the UK Economy*, ed. F. Green: 25–64. Hemel Hempstead: Harvester.

Westall, O. 1994. 'The Competitive Environment for British Business, 1850–1914'. In *Business Enterprise in Modern Britain from the Eighteenth to the Twentieth Century*, ed. M. W. Kirby and M. Rose: 207–35. Manchester: MUP.

Westergaard, J. and Resler, H. 1976. *Class in a Capitalist Society: A Study of Contemporary Britain*. Harmondsworth: Penguin.

Whiteside, N. 1979. 'Welfare Insurance and Casual Labour: A Study of Administrative Intervention in Industrial Employment, 1906–26'. *EcHR*, 32: 507–22.

Whiteside, N. 1987. 'The Social Consequences of Interwar Unemployment'. In *The Road to Full Employment*, ed. S. Glynn and A. Booth: 17–30. Allen and Unwin.

Whiteside, N. and Gillespie, J. 1991. 'Deconstructing Unemployment: Developments in Britain in the Interwar Years'. *EcHR*, 44: 665–82.

Whiting, A. 1976. 'An International Comparison of the Instability of Economic Growth'. *Three Banks Review*, 109: 26–46.

Wiener, M. J. 1981. *English Culture and the Decline of the Industrial Spirit, 1850–1980*. Cambridge: CUP.

Wigham, E. 1973. *The Power to Manage: A History of the Engineering Employers' Federation*. Macmillan – now Palgrave.

Williams, K., Haslam, C., Johal, S. and Williams, J. 1994. *Cars: Analysis, History, Cases*. Oxford: Berghahn.

Williams, K., Williams, J. and Haslam, C. 1987. *The Breakdown of Austin Rover: A Case Study in the Failure of Business Strategy and Industrial Policy*. Leamington Spa: Berg.

Williams, K., Williams, J. and Thomas, D. 1983. *Why Are the British Bad at Manufacturing?* Routledge.

Wilson, C. 1965. 'Economy and Society in Late Victorian Britain'. *EcHR*, 18: 183–98.

Woodward, N. C. 1991. 'Inflation'. In *The British Economy since 1945*, ed. N. F. R. Crafts and N. C. Woodward: 180–211. Oxford: Clarendon Press.

Woodward, N. C. 1996. 'The Retreat from Full Employment'. In *Britain in the 1970s: The Troubled Economy*, ed. R. Coopey and N. C. Woodward: 136–62. UCL Press.

Wrigley, C. 1982. 'The Ministry of Munitions: An Innovatory Department'. In *War and the State: The Transformation of British Government, 1914–19*, ed. K. Burk: 32–56. Allen and Unwin.

Wrigley, C. 1987a. 'The First World War and State Intervention in Industrial Relations, 1914–18'. In *A History of British Industrial Relations*, vol. 2, 1914–1939, ed. C. Wrigley: 23–70. Brighton: Harvester.

Wrigley, C. 1987b. 'Trade Unions between the Wars'. In *A History of British Industrial Relations*, vol. 2, 1914–1939, ed. C. Wrigley: 71–128. Brighton: Harvester.

Wurm, C. 1993. *Business, Politics and International Relations: Steel, Cotton and International Cartels in British Politics, 1924–39*. Cambridge: CUP.

Zeitlin, J. 1995. 'Americanisation and its Limits: Theory and Practice in the Reconstruction of Britain's Engineering Industries, 1945–55'. *Business and Economic History*, 24: 277–86.

Index